S0-BRB-333

AMERICAN ACTIVITIES

in the

Central Pacific

1790–1870

Chief Poulaho, Tonga, From Cook's *Voyages*.

AMERICAN ACTIVITIES

in the

Central Pacific

1790–1870

*A history, geography and ethnography
pertaining to American involvement
and Americans in the Pacific
taken from contemporary
newspapers, etc.*

Volume 7

EDITED BY
R. GERARD WARD
*Department of Geography
University College, London*

INTRODUCTION BY
ERNEST S. DODGE
*Director, Peabody Museum
Salem, Massachusetts*

THE GREGG PRESS / RIDGEWOOD, N. J.

Copyright © 1967 by THE GREGG PRESS, INC.
Library of Congress Catalog Card No. 66-28171
Printed by
McQUIDDY PRINTING CO., NASHVILLE, TENNESSEE
represented by RAY FREIMAN & COMPANY, New York

TABLE OF CONTENTS

LIST OF ILLUSTRATIONS

*All illustrations courtesy of the Peabody Museum of Salem,
unless otherwise indicated.*

ISLANDS
Featured in This Volume

TAHITI
TAHUATA
TAIWAN
TAMANA
TAONGI
TARAWA
TASMANIA
TAUMAKO GROUP
TAUU
TEMATANGI
TIKEI
TINIAN
TONGA
TONGATABU
TONUMEIA
TORI SHIMA
TORRES STRAIT
TUTUILA
UA HUKA
UA POU
UJELANG
ULITHI
UNITED STATES OF AMERICA
UPOLU
UVEA (WALLIS)
VANAVANA
VANUA LEVU
VATOA
VAVAU
VITI LEVU

VOSTOCK
WAKE
WASHINGTON
WILLIS
WINSLOW REEF
WRECK REEF
ZEPHYR SHOAL

KEY TO HEADING INFORMATION

EXAMPLE

[a]   STARBUCK 35
[b]   *Daily Atlas,* [c] Boston, Mass.
[d]   Apr. 10, 1837: [e] 5, [f] 4, [g] 3
[h]   MHi

[a]   Island name and serial number of report.
[b]   Name of newspaper or periodical.
[c]   Place of publication. Not printed if given in name of newspaper.
[d]   Date of publication.
[e]   Volume of newspaper.
[f]   Page of newspaper.
[g]   Column(s) in which report appears.
[h]   National Union Catalog symbol of library holding newspaper.

THE REPORTS

TAHITI 1

The Recorder, Boston, Mass.
Oct. 28, 1817: 2, 184, 5
MBC

OTAHEITE

In a paper published at Sydney, New South Wales, Aug. 8, 1816, it is said that the attack made upon the prayer people, of Taheite, was reserved for the Sabbath-day, when their opponents considered they would be employed in the duties of devotion; and so sudden was the attack, that the latter immediately gave way, until, by the presence of mind and bravery of an Englishman, who resided among them, the ardor of the assailants received a check, and the pursuers were in turn pursued with a considerable loss.

Capt. Burnet of the Trial (who sailed from Port Jackson May 27, 1815, and shared in the conflict at New Zealand Aug. 20, and who touched at Taheite) reports, that the attack taking place close to the seaside, the Englishman fixed a swivel on the stern of one of their canoes, which he plied with such wonderful effect, that, after a few discharges, the assailants commenced a precipitate retreat, leaving upwards of 40 dead on the beach.

Capt. Burnet proceeded then to the Marquesas, and on his return to Eimeo, which occupied an internal of three months, had the pleasure to learn that the engagement above alluded to, had been decisive; first, in placing Pomarre in the full sovereignty of the islands; and next, in thoroughly subduing the spirit of revolt among his rebellious subjects.

It had formerly been the plan of warfare to hunt the defeated party up into the mountains, and upon both sides kill all within their power; but from an excellence of policy, for which this venerable chief is undoubtedly indebted to the wise and benevolent council of his Christian friends, the Missionaries, he adopted the more conciliatory course of extending an amnesty to the revolters, from whom a solemn promise of allegiance was exacted upon their return to good order.

C.P.I. Ed. Note: The text of this report is one item in a news column headed "OTAHEITE," the rest of which is irrelevant. Complete text is used. . . .

Moorea (Eimeo) Island is (Lat. 17° 30′ S., Lon. 149° 50′ W. H.O. Chart No. 2065 *(H.O. Pub.* No. 166, Vol. II, 4th Ed., 1933 P. 102.)

The southeastern group [*of the Marquesas*] was discovered in 1595 and named The Isles de Marquesas de Mendoca; . . . The northwestern group was not discovered until 1791, when the islands were sighted by the American ship Hope of Boston. *(H.O. Pub.* No. 166, Vol. II, Ed., 1933, P.167.). H.O. Chart No. 1797-1.

TAHITI 2

Columbian Centinel, Boston, Mass.
Sept. 11, 1819: No. 3693, 2, 3
MHi

SOUTH SEA ISLANDS

A letter from the Rev. W. P. Cook, a Missionary, dated Wilk's Harbor, Otaheite, says, "The whole of this group of islands is now professedly sic Christain; and if we are to judge of their conduct by that of nominal Christians, in general, they have vastly the advantage. Theft is unknown among them. Family prayer is set up in every house. The Missionaries (16 in number) have held their aniversary meeting; A Mission Society has been established of which the King is President.—3000 copies of Luke have been published, and 10 gallons of cocoanut oil is given as the price of each."

C.P.I. Ed. Note: The text of this report is an item in a newspaper column headed "SOUTH SEA ISLANDS," . . .

Otaheite mentioned in the text is now known as Tahiti.

Otaheite (Tahiti) Island is situated in lat. 17° 38′S., lon. 149° 33′W., H.O. Chart No. 2065, *(H.O. Pub.* No. 166, Vol. II, 4th ed., 1933, P. 72.)

Papeete Harbor, Tahiti. From Dumont D'Urville, *Voyage au Pole Sud,* 2nd expedition, 1837-1840, plate 62.

TAHITI 3

Salem Gazette
Dec. 17, 1819: 33, 1, 4
MHi

LATEST FROM OTAHEITE. EXTRACT OF A LETTER FROM MR. CHARLES E. BOWERS, DATED OTAHEITE, NOV. 1818.

We arrived on the 3d of this month; immediately on coming to anchor, Mr. Wilson, one of the English Missionaries who has resided here since the year 1801, came on board: he informed me that the King and all his subjects in this and the neighboring islands were become, he believed, hopeful Christians, and their whole study and pleasure was to serve the Lord. In the afternoon, agreeable to the invitation (sic) of Mr. Wilson, the Captain and myself went on shore; as we entered the house of worship, in which he had been catechizing the people (probably two hundred in number) they were singing a hymn, and I was struck with astonishment to see these untaught savages, in such a serious solemn manner as I never witnessed before, go through the hymn; after Mr. Wilson arose, when they all kneeled down, while he made a prayer of some length, which closed the services, and they all retired with their books to their respective dwellings.

C.P.I. Ed. Note: The text of this report is one item in a newspaper column headed "LATEST FROM OTAHEITE. EXTRACT OF A LETTER FROM MR. CHARLES E. BOWERS, DATED OTAHEITE, NOV. 1818," the rest of which is irrelevant.

Tahiti, the largest of the Society Islands, was formerly called Otaheite, is Lat. 17° 38′ S., Lon. 149° 33′ W. H.O. Chart No. 2065. (*H.O. Pub.* No. 166, Vol. II, 4th Ed., 1933, P. 72.)

TAHITI 4

Christian Watchman, Boston, Mass.
June 12, 1824: 5, 1, 5
MH

OTAHEITE

In no part of the heathen world, perhaps, has the power of the Gospel been more signally displayed than in the South Sea Islands; and no where have Missionaries encountered greater difficulties and dangers in their first attempts to plant the cross in the strong holds of Pagan idolatry.

A letter, dated Otaheite, the 13th of May last contains the following statement.

—"The Isle of Otaheite is now so different from what it was in the time of Capt. Cook, in 1767, that it is impossible for me to give you a complete idea in so short a letter, written in all haste. The Missionaries have totally changed the direction of the morals and customs of the inhabitants. Idolatry exists no longer; Christianity is generally adopted. The women now behave with extraordinary reserve; they no longer go on board the ships; and even on land it is impossible to form with them the least connexion, the least attachment. Marriages are contracted as in Europe—even the king at present can have but one wife. The practice of destroying children and human sacrifices, no longer takes place. Almost all the inhabitants can write and read; they all have religious books written in their language, and printed in the Island.

Sixty-six magnificent churches have been built, and twice a week, the people go in great devotion to hear the preacher. Individuals are often seen taking notes with their pencil and paper, of the most interesting passages of the sermon.

The Missionaries yearly convoke at Paparo the whole of the

population, which amounts to 7000 souls. This assembly is at present holden. There is now a discussion going on respecting a new code or laws, and the principal Chiefs of the nation ascend the Tribune, and speak for whole hours with a vehemence truly extraordinary.

About two months ago the Isle of Otaheite declared itself independent of England; it only recognizes its Missionaries. A red flag, with a white star in the upper corner, is now mounted on the point which Bougainville named Point Venus."

Geo. Missionary.

[*The text has been taken from original newspaper as C.P.I. worker copied only the last two sentences and the date of the letter.*]

A human sacrifice on a morai, Tahiti. From Cook's *Voyages*.

A dance in Tahiti. From Cook's *Voyages.*

TAHITI 5

Niles' Weekly Register, Baltimore, Md.
Sept. 24, 1825: 29, 55, 1
MNBedf

Printing-presses are established at Otaheite and in Van Dei-man's land, and books are published in those distant and late barbarous places.

TAHITI 6

Niles' Weekly Register, Baltimore, Md.
Oct. 1, 1825: 29, 74, 2
MNBedf

OTAHEITE

The Nantucket Inquirer states, that about fifty of the natives of Otaheite are employed in the whale-ships belonging to that port, some of whom are in Nantucket. They are tractable and ingenuous.

TAHITI 7

Boston Patriot & Daily Mercantile Advertiser
June 11, 1828: 22, 2, 6
MHi

Office of the Mercury, Newport, June 9

Ar. ship Alliance, Otaheita, 140, with 2300 bbls. sperm oil. . . .

C.P.I. Ed. Note: The text of this report is one item in a newspaper column.

[*For additional C.P.I. Ed. Note see TAHITI 2.*]

TAHITI 8

Christian Watchman, Boston, Mass.
Feb. 6, 1829: 10, 3, 1
MH

The South Seas

We have before us, says the N.Y. Observer, a letter just received by a gentleman of this city, from the Rev. Thomas Kendall, dated at Sydney, New South Wales in which an account is given of the writer's passage from Valparaiso to that place. The first land made was the island of Tahiti (Otaheite) where Mr. K. met the Rev. Charles Wilson, (who has been employed by the London Missionary Society more than twenty-seven years,) and two young New Zealanders, formerly his pupils who came over the hills nearly thirty miles, to see him. After leaving Tahiti they passed Eimeo, and the towns and mission stations of Huahine, Raiatea, and Taha, with their "large churches and long ranges of neat white cottages," and in light days come in sight of Waitutake (Aitutake) an island which has been civilized solely through the instrumentality of native missionaries from Tahiti. As the Captain wished to trade with the natives, Mr. Kendall had an opportunity to visit the native missionaries and attend public worship.

C.P.I. Ed. Note: The text of this report is one item in a newspaper column headed "The South Seas," the rest of which is irrelevant.

[*For additional C.P.I. Ed. Note see TAHITI* 2.]

TAHITI 9

Columbian Centinel, Boston, Mass.
July 20, 1831: No. 4932, 1, 6
M

NEW BEDFORD, July 17—Arrived ship Maria Theresa, Wilcox, 109 days from Otaheite, with a full cargo of oil. Reports Feb 1st, lat 1 S lon 141 W ship Anne, of Nantucket, with 225 bbls. The Anne had spoken Jan 20, ship Pacific, of New Bedford, with 1100 bbls; 7th, ship Minerva, of Edgartown, 453 bls; 20th, ship Braganza, of New Bedford, with 300 bbls.—Ship Fabius, of Nantucket, with 800 bbls sailed from Otaheite March 21st, all for Japan. Spoke, July 13, lat 37 40, N lon 71 19, brig Pilgrim, Rice, from Boston for New Orleans.

At Holmes' Hole, 16th, ship President, Robbins, of Nantucket, for the Pacific Ocean, with a full cargo of oil.

At Falmouth, 15th, ship Uncas, Bunker, 110 days from South Pacific Ocean, with 3500 bbls oil. Reports March 13, ship Zone, Russell, 300-20th, Euphrates, 300-27th, Susan & Sarah, Halifax, 400.

C.P.I. Ed. Note: The text of this report is one item in a newspaper column headed "CLEARED," the rest of which is irrelevant.

[*The C.P.I. worker omitted several lines of this report. Whole text has been taken from original newspaper. For additional C.P.I. Ed. Note see TAHITI 2.*]

TAHITI 10

Am. & Com. Daily Adv., Baltimore, Md.
Feb. 6, 1833: —, 2, 7
MB

U. S. Ship Potomac.—Extract from a Letter Dated Valpariso, October 29th

This beautiful ship, bearing the broad pennant of Commodore John Downs, anchored in our harbour on the morning of the 23rd inst. after having performed her cruise in the China Seas, and last from the Otaheite Islands. Commodore D,, officers and crew all well. I was one of our many countrymen who visited her, and her appearance was truly gratifying to all of us, and reflected the highest credit upon her Commander and Officers.

—The Commodore decidedly popular on board, and pleasingly remembered by most persons here.

C.P.I. Ed. Note: The text of this report is one item in a newspaper column headed "U.S.S. Potomac," the rest of which is irrelevant.

[*For additional C.P.I. Ed. Note see TAHITI 2.*]

TAHITI 11

Boston Evening Transcript
May 11, 1833: 3, 2, 3
M; MB

THE OTAHEITE PHENOMENON

Kotzebue, who visited the island of Otaheite only a few years ago, was the first to communicate to the world the singular law by which the tides at this island are regulated, namely, that the time of high water is precisely at noon and midnight all of the year around. The island of Otaheite was first discovered by Capt. Wallis: in 1767 it was visited by the celebrated Capt. Cook, accompanied by Dr. Solander and Joseph Bankes. An accurate survey of the whole island was made by them. It has since been visited by hundreds of navigators from all quarters of the old and new world, yet none of them (except Kotzebue) has condescended to notice this wonderful phenomenon, though it is of a nature to attract of the most careless observer.

C.P.I. Ed. Note: The text of this report is an item in a newspaper column headed "THE OTAHEITE PHENOMENON," . . . .

[For additional C.P.I. Ed. Note see TAHITI 2.]

TAHITI 12

Lynn Record
June 25, 1834: 5, 3, 2
MLy

Distressing—We learn from Capt. Mayhew, of the ship Warren of Warren, recently arrived at that port, that Capt. Charles Spooner, of the ship Erie, of Newport, whose extraordinary marriage to Miss Kingatarn Oruruth, a native of Otaheite Island, has been lately noticed in most of the papers of this country, was deprived of his bride soon after his marriage, under the following painful circumstances: She had gone into the water to amuse her husband with an exhibition of her extraordinary feats of swimming, when she was attacked by a large shark. The shark first seized her by a limb, but releasing his hold he made another attack and with one effort of his powerful jaws, severed her body in two. The unhappy husband was a spectator of this awful scene, but could render no assistance.

C.P.I. Ed. Note: The text of this report is an item in a newspaper column headed "DISTRESSING," the rest of which is irrelevant.

[*For additional C.P.I. Ed. Note see TAHITI 3.*]

TAHITI 13

Daily Evening Transcript, Boston, Mass.
June 27, 1834: 4, 2, 2
MH

ARRIVAL OF MISSIONARIES

The ship Telegraph, Sayre, from the Pacific Ocean, last from Taheite, arrived at Sag Harbor on the 19th inst., having on board the following passengers: Mr. Samuel Ruggles, wife, son, and daughter, Miss Lucy Bingham and Miss Emily Whitney, from the Sandwich Islands, and Mr. David D. Hammond, from Society Islands.

C.P.I. Ed. Note: The text of this report is one item in a newspaper column headed "ARRIVAL OF MISSIONARIES."
Complete text is used. . . .

[For additional C.P.I. Ed. Note see TAHITI 2.]

TAHITI 14

Salem Gazette
Mar. 24, 1835: 13, 3, 2
MHi

Arrived at New Bedford, 19, ship Brighton, Tuckerman, from Tahiti. Society Islands, 11th Nov. with 2400 bbls. sperm oil. (Passenger Mr. John B. Williams, of Salem, late supercargo of brig Malta, of Boston.)

C.P.I. Ed. Note: The text of this report is one item in a newspaper column. . . .

[*For additional C.P.I. Ed. Note see TAHITI 2.*]

TAHITI 15

Daily Centinel & Gazette, Boston, Mass.
Mar. 17, 1837: 1, 2, 5
MHi

WHALERS

At Otaheite, Nov. 2, barque Palestine, Cartwright, of Salem with 550 bbls. sperm oil—had lost John F. Jerrels, of Lynn, taken from the boat by line.

C.P.I. Ed. Note: The text of this report is one item in a newspaper column headed "WHALERS."

[*For additional C.P.I. Ed. Note see TAHITI 2.*]

TAHITI 16

New Bedford Mercury
Oct. 13, 1837: 31, 1, 4
MNBedf

LOSS OF THE SHIP OREGON

The ship Oregon, Capt. Harding, of Fairhaven, was wrecked in working out of the harbor at Tahita on the 4th of May last. She had on board at the time 2200 barrels of sperm oil, 1450 of which were saved—together with officers and crew.

The bark Ospray, Hoyer, was condemned at Tahita on the 9th of May, and her oil (800 bbls.) sold.

TAHITI 17

Columbian Centinel, Boston, Mass.
Nov. 24, 1838: No. 5699, 4, 5
M

WHALERS

Nantucket, Nov. 20. Arr. ship Congress, Upham, Pacific Ocean, last from Society Island, with 1900 bbls. sperm oil. Capt. U. reports that ship Victory, Cotton, of N. Bedford, was condemned at Otaheite in July, at which time she had 1600 bbls. oil, 200 bbls. of which have arrived in the Congress, and 300 was shipped on board the Atlantic for Nantucket. Vessel sold for $750. Mr. Macy, first officer of the Victory, became a passenger in the Congress.

C.P.I. Ed. Note: The text of this report is one item in a newspaper column headed "WHALERS," the rest of which is irrelevant. Complete text is used. . . .

[*For additional C.P.I. Ed. Note see TAHITI 2.*]

TAHITI 18

Columbian Centinel, Boston, Mass.
Nov. 28, 1838: No. 5700, 1, 5
M

WHALERS

Ship Congress, of Nantucket, at Edgertown, 140 days from Tahita has 2100 bbls. oil, exclusive of 200 bbls. on freight.—Left at
Tahiti, Aug. 1st. ships Magnet. Warren 1400, Helvetia Cottie,
Hudson, 350, Atlantic, Russell, Nantucket 1600, for home in 4
or 5 days.

C.P.I. Ed. Note: The text of this report is one item in a newspaper column headed "WHALERS," complete text is used. . . .

[*For additional C.P.I. Ed. Note see TAHITI 2.*]

TAHITI 19

Columbian Centinel, Boston, Mass.
May 8, 1839: No. 5746, 2, 5
M

WHALERS

Letters received from Capt. Richmond, of ship Ann, of Bristol, R.I. reports her at Otaheite, Dec. 21st, 12 months out, had stowed down 1040 bbls. sperm oil—officers and crew all well. Had spoken on off shore ground, ships Omega, 30 mos. out, 1900 bbls., Frances, N. Bedford, 29 mos. out, 1950 bbls.—Heard from, ship Matecom, Grinnell, of Bristol, at Woahoo, 350 bbls. The ship Victory, Cotton of N.Bedford, had been condemned at Otaheite, as unseaworthy—Capt.C. had procured a brig and shipped his oil to the Spanish Main, intending to sell it.

C.P.I. Ed. Note: The text of this report is one item in a newspaper column headed "WHALERS," the rest of which is irrelevant. Complete text is used. . . .

[*For additional C.P.I. Ed. Note see TAHITI 2.*]

TAHITI 20

Columbian Centinel, Boston, Mass.
Feb. 5, 1840: No. 5825, 1, 6
M

WHALER

At Tahita, Sept. 21st ship Mechanic, Pratt of Newport, 13½ months out, with 900 bbls. sperm oil, all well—had discharged 2d mate, got a new mainmast, and was to sail on a cruise in a few days.

C.P.I. Ed. Note: The text of this report is one item in a newspaper column headed "WHALER."

[*For additional C.P.I. Ed. Note see TAHITI 2.*]

TAHITI 21

The Atlas, Boston, Mass.
May 15, 1841: 9, 2, 1
MBr

Naval. (Per Hatch's New Bedford Express)

The U. S. Brig Porpoise, Capt. Ringgold, was at Tahiti Jan. 26, to sail on a cruise next day, intending to visit the Society Islands. P. has now been from home about two years and a half, has discovered some new islands, and visited many of the Fejee and other islands never before explored. The officers and crew were all well at the above date, and wished to be reported.

C.P.I. Ed. Note: The text of this report is one item in a news column headed "NAVAL," the rest of which is irrelevant. Complete text is used. . . .

Fejee Island mentioned is probably meant for Fiji Island. The Fiji Islands are 15° to 21'S., 176°W. to 176° E., H.O. Chart No. 2850 *(H.O. Pub.* No. 166, vol. II, 4th ed. 1933 P. 283.)

[*For additional C.P.I. Ed. Note see TAHITI 3.*]

TAHITI 22

Mercantile Journal, Boston, Mass.
Jan. 11, 1842: 7, 4, 4
MB

SMALL POX AT TAHITI

The following is an extract of a letter received here from Tahiti, (Society Islands) Sept. 20, 1841. It gives a fearful picture of the ravages of the Small Pox:

"Found this place in a shocking state, owing to that dreadful scourge, the Small Pox—which is spreading to a fearful extent, though many precautionary measures are taken to prevent the spreading among the natives—there is no business doing. I have not been on shore—no one lands from the ship, and we take nothing on board except water. The people are completely paralyzed. Almost every native who takes the disease dies. No whites have taken the disease as yet. The Don Quixotte left here for Oahu unaware that they had left the fatal disease at this island.—She may introduce the disease at the Sandwich Islands. Traders here are afraid to buy goods, not knowing what will be the effect on future business.

C.P.I. Ed. Note: The text of this report is an item in a newspaper column headed "SMALL POX AT TAHITI," the rest of which is irrelevant.

[*For additional C.P.I. Ed. Note see TAHITI 3.*]

TAHITI 23

Boston Semi-Weekly Advertiser
Apr. 9, 1842: 79, 3, 1
MH

At Tahiti, July 1, Geo. Washington of Wareham, 250. The English whale ship Sir Andrew Hammond, Hewley, was lost (no date, supposed near Society Islands) in lat. 3 N., on a reef about three miles from land, crew saved, and abt. 400 bbls. oil.

C.P.I. Ed. Note: The text of this report is one item in a news column headed "WHALERS," the rest of which is irrelevant.

Possibly the *Sir Andrew Hammond,* was wrecked near the Christmas Island instead of the Society group as mentioned in text. The Society Islands are south of the equator and latitude 3 N. mentioned in text places the wreck in the vicinity of Christmas Island.

Christmas Island is 1° 55′ N., 157° 20′ W., H.O.Chart No. 1839. *(H.O. Pub.* No. 165, Vol. I, 4th ed. 1938, p. 491.)

TAHITI 24

Boston Post
July 19, 1842: 16, 2, 5
M

WHALERS

A letter from Captain Wyer, of ship Enterprise of Nantucket, reports her at Talcahuana April 16, with 1400 bbls. sp. The ship had been hove out at Tahiti, and a leak which caused some trouble and much pumping during the voyage stopped. She was in good order at the date of the letter, and would sail on a cruise in a few days.

C.P.I. Ed. Note: The text of the above report is one item in a newspaper column headed "WHALERS," the rest of which is irrelevant.

[*For additional C.P.I. Ed. Note see TAHITI 2.*]

TAHITI 25

The Bay State Democrat, Boston, Mass.
Feb. 14, 1843: 4, 2, 4
MH

TAHITI

The French it appears, have taken possession of this Island, in default of $10,000 black mail, levied by the authorities of that nation. The Daily Advertiser says, in relation to this matter, "we have seen letters from the American Consul at that place. Mr. Blackler, to Sept. 11, from which we learn that the French Admiral, Dupetit Thouars, arrived there on the 8th, and made a demand on the Tahitians, of the sum of $10,000 in reparation for abuses, and as a guaranty for their future adherence to treaties. It seems, they immediately entered into negotiations for the surrender of the Sovereignty of the Island. Four of the Chiefs on the 9th signed a paper to that effect, but the Queen had then refused to sign it. At the last date, the question of acknowledgment of the sovereignty of France was supposed to be settled, as all demonstrations of hostility had ceased, but the French flag was not yet hoisted. The La Reine Blanche was at Tahiti.

C.P.I. Ed. Note: The text of the above report is a copy of an article in a newspaper column headed "TAHITI," taken for a single report on the island and the vessel mentioned.

[For additional C.P.I. Ed. Note see TAHITI 2.]

TAHITI 26

New England Puritan, Boston, Mass.
Feb. 17, 1843: 4, 3, 4 & 16
MH

[Report in *Christian Watchman,* Boston, Feb. 17, 1843 (MH) is identical to first paragraph.]

THE SOCIETY ISLANDS

The New Bedford Mercury states on the authority of Capt. Adams, of the ship Brandt, which has arrived at that port, having left Tahiti Sept. 10, that the French have taken possession of The Society Islands. Admiral Dupetit Thouars, the Commandant of the French forces in the Pacific, by whom the Marquesas Islands were lately taken possession of, was at Tahiti Sept.10, in the flag ship La Reine Blanche.—[adv.]

From Tahiti—Since writing the notice relative to the occupation of Tahiti by the French, we have seen letters from the American Consul at that place, Mr. Blackler, to Sept.11, from which we learn that the French Admiral Dupetit Thouars, arrived there on the 8th, and made a demand on the Tahitians, of the sum of $10,000, in reparation for abuses, and as a guaranty for their future adherence to treaties. It seems they immediatley entered into negotiations for the surrender of the sovereignty of the island. Four of the Chiefs, on the 9th, signed a paper to that effect, but the Queen had then refused to sign it.

At the last date, the question of acknowledgement of the sovereignty of France was supposed to be settled, as all demonstrations of hostility had ceased, but the French flag was not yet hoisted. The La Reine Blanche was at Tahiti.—[ib]

C.P.I. Ed. Note: The text of the above report is one item in a newspaper column headed "THE SOCIETY ISLANDS," the rest of which is irrelevant. Society Islands are approximately between 16°17′S and 17°53′S., and between 148°05′W and 154°43′W. H.O.Chart No. 2023,2065. *(H.O. Pub.* No. 166, Vol. II, 4th ed., 1933, pp 69 to 122.)

[For additional C.P.I. Ed. Notes see TAHITI 1 & 2.]

TAHITI 27

Boston Daily Advertiser
Aug. 5, 1843: 62, 2, 6
MB

CRUISE OF THE BOSTON

The N.E. exit from the China Seas not being practicable, on account of the early setting in of the monsoon with strong gales, the Boston ran down the China Seas, through the Straits of Sunda, around New Holland, and after touching at Sidney a few days, resumed her way to the Society Islands. Remaining only five days at Tahiti, she next sailed for Oahu, and arrived there at a critical period for American interests.

It is a fortunate circumstance that we were represented by a naval force at the Sandwich Islands, during the difficulties between them and the English. The opportunity of finding an asylum on board one of our ships of war, in the event of hostilities, was certainly a great relief to the American residents, as well as gratifying to those offering the protection; indeed, for some time the state of things was unsettled, that it was apprehended that some intervention might become necessary for the affectual protection of the lives and property of our citizens, who are nearly five hundred in number, not including the crews of the whale ships and.whose interest covers some millions of dollars. As soon as it was expedient to leave Oahu, the Boston proceeded to the southward, and being unable to fetch the Marquesas, touched again at Tahiti. The unsettled state of this Island, as well as frequent difficulties with the crews of whalers, made her visits highly desirable.

The engagements of most of her crew being now on the eve of expiring precluded a further stay in the Pacific, and leaving the west coast unvisited, she took her departure from Tahiti for Cape Horn, on her homeward bound passage. Notwithstanding adverse gales, she arrived in Rio in 69 days. She remained in that port 10 days, and thence sailed for the United States. Out of the last eleven months she has been at sea, the whole amount of her sailing is upwards of 50,000 miles.

C.P.I. Ed. Note: The text of the above report is a copy of an article in a newspaper column headed "Cruise of the Boston," . . .

[*For additional C.P.I. Ed. Note see TAHITI 2.*]

TAHITI 28

The Daily Atlas, Boston, Mass.
Aug. 8, 1843: 12, 2, 6
MHi

WHALERS

At Tahiti, Apr. 13th ship Good Return, of New Bedford, with 2000 bbls oil, had lost in a squall, main-mast head, lore, main, and mizzen topmasts, main and maintopgallant yards, mizzen topgallant mast and yards, would be ready for N.W. Coast in 10 or 15 days.

C.P.I. Ed. Note: The text of the above report is a copy of an item in a newspaper column headed "WHALERS," the rest of which is irrelevant.

[*For additional C.P.I. Ed. Note see TAHITI 2.*]

TAHITI 29

The Daily Atlas, Boston, Mass.
Sept. 9, 1843: 12, 2, 6
MHi

WHALERS

. . . .The whale ship Good Return, of New Bedford, (since reported at later dates) put into Tahiti, April 18th, dismasted, having been struck by a squall in the night, in lat. 25° S. She repaired and sailed in about 20 days.

C.P.I. Ed. Note: The text of the above report is a copy of an item in a newspaper column headed "WHALERS," . . . the rest of which is irrelevant.

[For additional C.P.I. Ed. Note see TAHITI 2.]

TAHITI 30

New England Puritan, Boston, Mass.
Oct. 12, 1843: —, —, —
MH

MISSIONS IN POLYNESIA

The Rev. Thomas Heath, for several years a Missionary at the Navigators' Islands, South Pacific, and successor of the Rev. John Williams in the missionary brig, Camden, proposes shortly to publish in England, by subscription, a volume on the progress and present state of the Protestant Missions, in Polynesia. The work will contain a history of the important mission at the Navigators' Islands; the voyages of the brig, Camden; the commencement of operations at the New Hebrides, Loyalty, and New Caledonia groups, with an account of the natural history, manners, customs and superstitions of the natives; a review of the older missions; the proceedings of the French in the Pacific; and an extensive comparison of the Malay with the Polynesian languages, and of several of the Polynesian and Papuan dialects, both as to their grammatical structure and vocabularies. The work may be considered as a continuation of Williams' "Missionary Enterprises". The price to the subscriber will not exceed 10s 6d.

We learn by the London Patriot, that on Thursday evening, August 24th, a special meeting of the Directors and friends of the London Missionary Society was held at Finsburg Chapel, to welcome the Rev. Thomas Heath, Missionary from the South Seas, on his return to that country, and to receive from him interesting and important communications relative to the state and prospects of the Society's Missions in the Navigators' Islands, Tahiti, the Hervey group, and other Islands in the South Pacific. Mr. Heath was accompanied by a Christian Chief and a native Evangelist from Samoa. Rev. J. Arundel, Rev. A. F. Lacroix, Rev. J. J. Freeman, Rev. G. Collisson, and the two Tahitians, took part in the exercises. Rev. Mr. Heath said, that the missions of the Society include the Marquesas, Georgian and Society Islands, with many of the smaller islands attached to them —that is, the Austral and Paumotu and others. The Hervey group, the Samoans, the Island of Rotumah, the five islands of the New Hebrides, two of the Loyalty group, and two of the New Caledonian group; and that the Camden which is owned by the Society, which is employed in visiting the different islands, and which has been found to be too small for their increasing labours, has sailed more than 80,000 miles since she left England in 1838, or more than 12,000 miles per year. In the Navigators' Islands, about 3000 have been baptized on their profession of Christianity; there were nearly 2000 in christian communion when he left, in whose piety the missionaries cherish a pleasing confidence, and numbers of Candidates.

About 27,000 (nearly one half of the population) of Samoa have learned to read. Many of them read portions of the Scriptures which the Missionaries have translated and others elementary books. Some thousands can write upon slates; for we have neither copy-books, pen nor ink.

At the Marquesas, our missions are suspended. The Romish priests and the French frigates are there, and they are resolved to make those islands subject to France, and the centre of their operations in the South Seas. Death has likewise occurred there—twenty Frenchmen have been cut off for their ill usage of the people; and what the retaliation will be we do not know, but such is the commencement of French proceedings in the Marquesas.

The Hervey group is all we could wish with regard to missions. There is however, a lamentable decrease of the population by a kind of consumption.

I now come especially to Tahiti and the Tahitian islands.

You have heard much respecting the desertion of christian converts there, and the little dependence, it has been presumed, which is to be placed on the accounts of the success of the Gospel and of Missionary labour. I have visited those islands four times, and have spent some months there; during which time I have made it my business to institute close inquiries from the missionaries, from the people themselves, from the old chiefs, from the French and American Consuls, and other white residents. After examining all these parties and comparing notes, and looking at the whole matter, I have come to the conclusion that the accounts of desertion there have been much exaggerated.—Two or three Romish priests went to Tahiti about the year 1836. In the first instance the Queen and the Chiefs of Tahiti would not receive them, and required that the Captain should take them away again. I contend that they had a right to do so. At length however, poor Pomare and her people were obliged to repeal the law prohibiting the Catholics, so far as France was concerned. They could not do otherwise. Gradiloquent despatches were sent home to France, full of bombast, and papers were written to the Tahitian authorities, about the wrongs done to Frenchmen. The Captain then demanded that $10,000. should be placed on his vessel till those alleged grievances were redressed; and if that were not done, he stated that he should take possession of the island—at the same time, if within twenty four hours the Tahitians authorities could suggest any plan by which severer measures could be prevented, well and good. He meant to say, that if Queen Pomare did not within the twenty-four hours sign a paper to the effect that France should become the protectorate of the island, he would seize it. The Queen delayed till the very last hour. She remonstrated; she wept; she looked for help, but she had no means of opposing the French frigate. At the last moment she was compelled to sign the paper, and then the French protectorate was formed; after

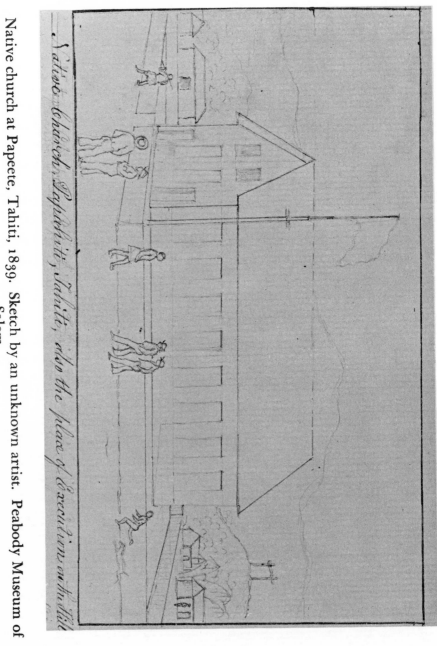

Native church at Papeete, Tahiti, 1839. Sketch by an unknown artist. Peabody Museum of Salem.

which there came forth a declaration, asserting liberty of worship to all parties.

C.P.I. Ed. Note: The text of the above report is an item in a news column headed "MISSIONS IN POLYNESIA," the rest of which is irrelevant.

Samoa (Navigators) Islands are 13° 30' S., to 14° 30' S., 166° 00' W., to 173°00' W. H.O. Chart No. 87, (*H.O. Pub.* No. 166, Vol. II, 4th Ed. 1933, P. 253.)

Hervey Islands are 19° 21' S., 158° 57' W. H. O. Chart No. 2000, and consists of two low islands, Manuae and Auotu. (*H.O. Pub.* No. 166, Vol. II, 4th. Ed., 1933, P. 65.) [*In this case the name probably refers to the Southern Cook Islands in General.*]

Austral Islands, lying about 350 miles southward from Tahiti, form a group of five islands of but little importance and are French protection.

Tabuai (Austral) island is situated in Lat. 23° 21½' S., Lon. 149° 28' W.

Rotumah Island is 12° 30' S., 177° 05' E. (*H.O. Pub.* No. 166, Vol. II, 4th. ed., 1933, P. 431.)

[*For additional C.P.I. Ed. Notes see TAHITI 2 & 26.*]

English church at Papeete, Tahiti, 1839. Sketch by an unknown artist. Peabody Museum of Salem.

(44)

TAHITI 31

The Bay State Democrat, Boston, Mass.
Oct. 24, 1843: 1, 2, 2
MH

FROM THE SOCIETY ISLANDS

Late advice from Tahiti, under date 25th of June last, state that Commodore Nicolas, of Her Britannic Majesty's ship, Vindictive, issued a proclamation of the British subjects in the Society Islands, in which he refuses to recognize the French Government established there, and states that he has instructions to cause the British subjects not to recognize said government. He says that England seeks not to obtain a Paramount influence in the islands; her object is to maintain the native sovereignty independent and free.

C.P.I. Ed. Note: The text of the above report is a copy of an article in a newspaper column headed "FROM THE SOCIETY ISLANDS," . . .

[*For additional C.P.I. Ed. Notes see TAHITI 2 & 26.*]

TAHITI 32

New England Puritan, Boston, Mass.
Oct. 27, 1843: 4, 3, 3
MH

[Identical report in *Boston Mercantile Journal*, Oct. 20, 1843 (MB). Report in *New York Observer*, Oct. 28, 1843 (MBC) omits information before 'Tahiti, June 26', but thereafter is identical.]

GENERAL INTELLIGENCE

Important from the Society Islands: A letter has been received in this city by J.M.Holden, from a friend, by an arrival at New Bedford, dated Tahiti, June 26, containing the information that the French held possession of the Island, but that the commander of the British Ship-of-war Vindictive, then in port, had ordered the French flag on shore to be hauled down, which had not been done. On the 20th inst., the following Manifesto or Proclamation was issued by the British Commodore:

To the principal British residents, and all other British subjects, in the Islands of Tahiti, and Moorea:

Her Britannic Majesty's Ship Vindinctive,
in Papeete Harbor, Tahiti,
June 20, '43.

Gentlemen:—It has become my duty to acquaint the subjects of her Britannic Majesty, now residing in the dominions of the Queen of Tahiti, that I have received instructions to cause them to seek for whatever justice they may require, from the officers of their own Sovereign, in this island, or through the established Court of Laws of the Queen Pomare; and that they are not to attend to any summons as jurors, nor to hold themselves subject to any regulations or jurisdictions of any sort, from the French authorities temporarily established here, under the style of a Provisional Government; nor to any officer of France, be his rank or station whatever it maybe, until the decision of the Queen of England, regarding Tahiti, is known.   Although determined to enforce this regulation, should it unhappily become necessary in the rigid fulfilment of the orders that I have received, yet I shall continue to do my best to preserve a good understanding with the officers of the French Navy stationed here; and I sincerely trust that nothing will arise to disturb the harmony which has hitherto subsisted between the subjects of our respective nations.

I deem it proper that I should here observe to you, that I feel quite assured that England seeks not, desires not, to maintain a paramount influence in these islands.   But, while she repudiates such an intention, and declares as she has so repeatedly done, in reply to the several solicitations of the successive sovereigns of Tahiti, to become its permanent protector, that she will not assume any preponderating power over its government; yet Great Britain is, I am equally assured, determined that no other Nation shall possess a greater influence or authority in these states, than that which, from her long and intimate connexion with them, she claims as her natural right to exercise.   More than all do I believe myself authorized to state, that it is the determination of the Queen of England to preserve the sovereignty of Tahiti independent and free.

I have the honor to be, gentlemen, yours, with every consideration,

J. Toup Nicolas, Commodore
(Mercantile Journal)

C.P.I. Ed. Note: The text of the above report is a copy of an article in a newspaper column headed "General Intelligence," . . .

[*For additional C.P.I. Ed. Notes see TAHITI 1 & 2.*]

TAHITI ₃₃

Mercantile Journal, [Boston, Mass.]
Jan. 19, 1844: 10, 2, 1
MB

[Report in *The Atlas,* Boston, Jan. 19, 1844 (MBr) ends at "detain her about a month' but is otherwise similar.]

FROM TAHITI

We learn from the Society Islands, that George Brown, United States Commissioner to the Sandwich Islands, who left Panama on the 11th of June last, in the Tender of H.B.M. Ship Vindictive, arrived at Tahiti on the 28th of August after a passage of 78 days. On the 14th of July, the tender at Cocos Island, lat.5°33′N., lon.87°02′W., fell in with the whaling ship Charles W. Morgan, Capt. Norton, of New Bedford, who kindly supplied them with provisions. Mr. Brown expected to sail from Tahiti on the 15th of September for Honolulu in the ship Catherine, which arrived a few days previously from Sidney.

On the 14th of September, there were in the harbor the American whale ship Enterprise of Nantucket, Capt. Cannon, with 1800 barrels of oil on board—and the Euphrates, Capt. Upham, of New Bedford, with about 450 barrels. The Euphrates had been ashore on a reef near one of the Gallaoagos Islands, through the carelessness of the pilot, and put into Tahiti for repairs. Her false keel was gone, and she would require about eighty feet of her garboard streak, and the next plank above taken out. Her forefoot is injured, as well as her main keel, and it will cost about $2,500 to repair her, and detain her about a month. On the 8th of September, the ship Eliza L.B.Jenney, of Fairhaven, arrived from a cruise, nine months out, with 450 barrels sperm oil. On the 10th the Jeanette, of New Bedford, arrived from a cruise of 16 months, with 800 barrels of sperm oil.

C.P.I. Ed. Note: The text of the above report is an article in a newspaper column headed "FROM TAHITI," . . .

Cocos Island mentioned in text is in lat.5°32'57"N, lon.87°02'10"W. Findlay, *Directory of the North Pacific Ocean.* Third Edition, 1886, p.924.

The Gallapagos Islands, mentioned in the text are a group of islands lying on the equator, $1\frac{1}{2}$° each side, about 87° lon., 600 miles off the coast of Ecuador to which they belong. (Findlay, *Directory of the South Pacific Ocean,* Fifth Edition, 1884, p.790.)

[*For additional C.P.I. Ed. Note see TAHITI 2.*]

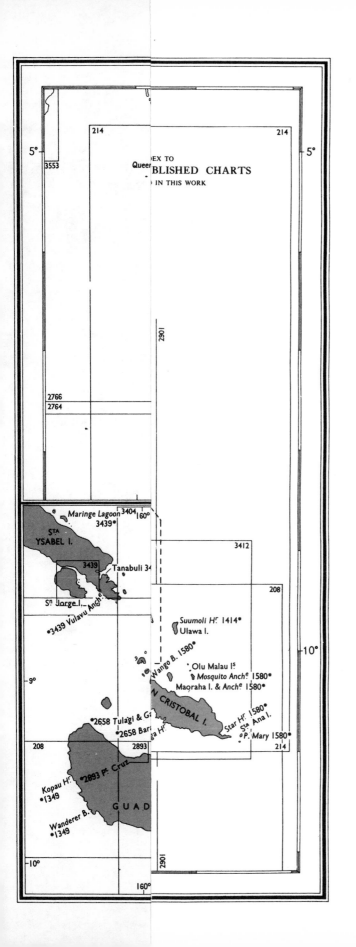

TAHITI 34

The Daily Mercury, New Bedford, Mass.
Jan. 20, 1844: 12, 2, 4
MNBedf

MARINE JOURNAL—PORT OF NEW BEDFORD

Ship Euphrates of New Bedford, before reported at Tahiti in Sept. repairing damages, had been ashore on a reef near one of the Gallipagos (not Chatham) Islands. Her false keel was gone, and she would require about 80 feet of her garboard streak, and the next plank above, to be taken out. Her fore foot was injured as well as her main keel.

TAHITI 35

Bay State Democrat, Boston, Mass.
Mar. 4, 1844: 1, 2, 7
MH

DISASTERS

Bark Lark (of New York) Tibbets, 95 days from Canton for Valparaizo, was at Tahiti Oct. 17, having put in to repair damages sustained on the 6th, 7th, and 8th of August, in a hurricane off the Island of Formosa; lost all her boats, bulwarks and main yard with other damage. Also sprung a leak.

C.P.I. Ed. Note: The text of the above report is a copy of an item in a newspaper column. . . the rest of which is irrelevant.

[*For additional C.P.I. Ed. Note see TAHITI 2.*]

TAHITI 36

New England Puritan, Boston, Mass.
Mar. 22, 1844: 5, 3, 3
MH

GENERAL INTELLIGENCE

From the Sandwich Islands.—We learn from "The Friend", a paper printed at Honolulu, under date of Jan. 1, that Admiral Du Petit Thours arrived at Tahiti on the 2d. Nov., with the "Reine Blanche" and "Danne" of 50 guns each, and the "Tranie" of 64 guns. Mons. Bruat, the director in the government of the protectorate, accompanied the Admiral. On the 6th, the Admiral dethroned the Queen and formally took possession of the Society Islands, for the Throne of France,—giving, as a reason for so doing, that the Queen had refused to haul down her flag, which had been presented to her by Commodore Nichols, of the English Zazee Vindictive. Mons. Bruat has changed his functions to that of "Governor of the French possessions in the Pacific." Mr. Pitchard, the English Consul, had struck his flag. The Admiral had landed about 300 troops, who with about 100 operatives and artisans were at work erecting fortifications,&c.—N.Y.Com.

C.P.I. Ed. Note: The text of this report is one item in a newspaper column headed "GENERAL INTELLIGENCE," the rest of which is irrelevant. Complete text is used. . . .

[*For additional C.P.I. Ed. Note see TAHITI 2.*]

TAHITI 37

Christian Register, Boston, Mass.
Mar. 30, 1844: 23, 3, 4
MH

SOCIETY ISLANDS

The news that the French had taken possession of Tahiti, and compelled Queen Pomane to place herself under their protection—the installation of a new Governor—the hoisting of the French and the lowering of the English flag, and other doings, had reached England, and excited considerable surprise as well as indignation. The subject was alluded to in the House of Commons, when Sir Robert Peel expressed his hope and belief that the proceedings had been done without the consent, or, even the knowledge of the French Government; and indeed the whole proceedings have been formally repudiated by Louis Phillippe and his cabinet.

C.P.I. Ed. Note: The text of this report is an item in a newspaper column headed "SOCIETY ISLANDS," the rest of which is irrelevant.

[*For additional C.P.I. Ed. Note see TAHITI 3.*]

TAHITI 38

New York Observer
Sept. 7, 1844: 22, 3, 2
MBC

Tahiti

Skirmish between the French and Natives

The Favourite, South-Sea whaler, lately arrived, bringing 14 days later from Tahiti. A skirmish had taken place between the French and the natives. By means of a telegraphic communication which the French have already established in the island, orders were conveyed a day or two before the Favourite left, to one of the French steam-frigates then lying in the Bay of Papeete, to embark troops and proceed to Tairapu, 40 miles distant, and situated at the other side of the island of Tahiti. At the time of starting she had 150 soldiers on board. This order is supposed to have been caused by an outbreak, the particulars of which, as far as could be gained, as follows:

A number of the natives, who now live in encampments up the mountains since they have been expelled the town, were seated taking a quiet meal, when some Frenchmen came upon one party, consisting of two chiefs and their wives, and seized hold of women, whom they attempted to drag on board their boat, then lying moored on the beach a short distance off. The chief resisted this aggression, and were immediately shot. A third chief then rose up, and exclaimed, "What are we dogs, that we are treated thus?" We are a quiet people, and wish for peace; but you will not let us have it." Whereupon the French fired at him, but missing their aim, he gave the signal to the natives for an onset. At the first charge 15 Frenchmen were either

killed or wounded, and a second attack almost immediately taking place, between 20 and 40 more of their number were killed
or disabled by the Tahitians.   Soon after this transaction had
taken place, it was reported that many of the French had deserted, saying they had only been brought out to be shot at.

The men generally do not seem at all contented, for they
appear half-starved and badly clothed.   The regulation that no
one is to be allowed out after 8 o'clock at night is strictly enforced against the natives and foreigners, but the French themselves seem to pay little or no attention to this order.

C.P.I. Ed. Note: The text of this report is one item in a newspaper column headed "Skirmish between the French and
Natives," the rest of which is irrelevant.

[*For additional C.P.I. Ed. Note see TAHITI 2.*]

TAHITI 39

Boston Courier
Nov. 1, 1844: 20, 2, 5
MB

FROM THE SOCIETY ISLANDS

The L. C. Richmond, Captain Luce, arrived at New Bedford yesterday having left Tahiti July 18th, and bringing nearly a month later intelligence from the Islands. She reports, said the Bulletin, that a few days previous to sailing, an action took place between the French troops and the natives, in which a large number of lives were lost, principally on the part of the natives. The French were strongly fortifying the islands.—The English missionaries were leaving, and confusion reigned among the inhabitants. There were at Tahiti one English steamer, one French steamer, and one French frigate.

C.P.I. Ed. Note: The text of this report is one item in a news column headed "FROM THE SOCIETY ISLANDS," the rest of which is irrelevant.

[*For additional C.P.I. Ed. Note see TAHITI 2.*]

TAHITI 40

Boston Daily Evening Transcript
Nov. 1, 1844: 15, 2, 4
MBAt

[Similar report in *Mercantile Evening Journal,* Boston, Nov. 1, 1844 (MB).]

FROM THE SOCIETY ISLANDS

The ship L. C. Richmond, arrived at New Bedford yesterday morning, having left Tahiti July 15 and bringing nearly a month's later intelligence from the Islands. She reports that a few days previous to sailing, an action took place between the French troops and natives, in which a large number of lives were lost, principally on the part of the natives. The French were strongly fortifying the Island—the English Missionaries were leaving—and confusion reigned among the inhabitants. There were at Tahiti one English steamer, one French do and one French frigate. The English frigate "Fishgood," touched at Tahiti on the 14th, and took on board the Queen and royal family for Bolabola.

C.P.I. Ed. Note: The text of the above report is a copy of an item in a newspaper column headed "FROM THE SOCIETY IS-LANDS," . . . Bolabola Island cannot be identified in any available reference material at our disposal.

[*It is Borabora 16°30'S., 151°45'W.). For additional C.P.I. Ed. Note see TAHITI 2.*]

TAHITI 41

New York Observer
Feb. 15, 1845: 23, 3, 4
MBC

Bloody Battle in the Society Islands

Accounts have been received from Tahiti of the battle between the French and the natives, more sanguinary than precious battle, which terminated in favor of the French. The natives had two hundred killed, and the French one hundred.

The battle took place at Matavai Bay, Point Venus, on the west coast of Tahiti, early in September, Queen Pomare had gone to Bulobulo, an island about 60 miles south of Tahiti. The French had banished from the islands a good many foreigners who had taken up arms on the side of the natives, or otherwise assisted them in their warfare with the French.

C.P.I. Ed. Note: The text of this report is an item in a newspaper column headed "Bloody Battle in the Society Islands," the rest of which is irrelevant.

[*For additional C.P.I. Ed. Note see TAHITI 3.*]

TAHITI 42

The Friend, Honolulu
Mar. 15, 1845: 3, 45, 3
MSaP

The American Consul at Tahiti, has sent home the American ship Timoleon, under the command of Mr. Brown, Sailing Master of the U. S. Brig Perry, on account of the drunkenness of the master of said ship.

C.P.I. Ed Note: The above is one item in a column headed "SHIPPING NEWS" the rest of which is irrelevant.

TAHITI 43

Boston Daily Journal
Apr. 30, 1845: 13, 1, 7
MB

FROM SOCIETY ISLANDS

We learn from Capt. Doane, of the brig Globe, which left Tahiti, Dec. 20, that the islands still remained in possession of the
French Authorities. Gen. Miller, the British Consul General
had arrived several weeks previously. The arrival of a French
Frigate from Valparaiso was daily expected with dispatches from
the French Government. Although the accounts of the arrangement between the British and French Governments had reached
Tahiti, it was not the general belief that the French intended to
restore Queen Pomare to her rightful authority:—Advertiser.

C.P.I. Ed. Note: The text of the above report is an item in a
newspaper column headed "FROM SOCIETY ISLANDS," the rest
of which is irrelevant.

[*For additional C.P.I. Ed. Note see TAHITI 3.*]

TAHITI 44

Boston Daily Journal
July 14, 1845: 13, 2, 1
MB

FROM THE PACIFIC

The whale ship Timoleon arrived at New Bedford on Saturday, in charge of Passed Mid. J. Hagan Brown, late sailing Master of U. S. Brig Perry, the above ship having been abandoned by the officers and crew at Tahiti, Sandwich Islands. Mr. Brown, a highly accomplished and intelligent officer, belonging to Alabama, has furnished Col. Hatch, with the following list of officers of the Perry, at Tahiti, February 7, 1845:

J. S. Paine, Commander.
H. N. Harrison, T. M. Crossan, John C. Howell, Lieutenants.
John Tilton, Purser.
J. D. Miller, Surgeon.
E. D. Denny, Walter W. Queen, E. F. Stone, Midshipmen.
Henry R. Wrightman, Captain's Clerk.
William Burgen, Boatswain.
William Collins, Gunner.
James Storer, Carpenter.
James Lown, Master's Mate.

The Perry sailed from Tahiti on the 7th of February for the Sandwich Islands, to meet the Brandy wine and St. Louis, thence to proceed to the coast of South America.

We extract the following paragraphs from the New Bedford Mercury. Midshipman Brown reports the loss of the ship Averick, Capt. Reynard, of this port, on the island of Ulitea, Feb. 15, having been blown on shore in a violent gale from N.W. and sunk in 2½ hours after striking the shore. The wreck was sold for eighteen hundred dollars, and her crew landed at Tahiti, Feb. 20th. The Averick had on board 600 bbls. oil, (70 sperm).

H. B. Majesty's frigate Talbot, arrived at Tahiti Feb. 10th, and in consequence of her commander refusing to salute the French Protectorate flag, Gov. Bruat ordered at boat from the French frigate Uranian to row a guard around her and allow no communication with the shore, which was strictly enforced.

The Talbot, with Hon. Gen. Miller on board, was towed to sea on the 15th, by H. B. Majesty's war steamer Salamander, intending to touch at Riatier, another of the Society Islands, and thence at Honolulu.

C.P.I. Ed. Note: Text of this report is one item in a newspaper column referring to Tahiti, the rest of which is irrelevant.

[*For additional C.P.I. Ed. Note see TAHITI* 2.]

U.S.S. *Brandywine*.

TAHITI 45

The Atlas, Boston, Mass.
July 15, 1845: 14, 2, 4
MBr

DISASTERS OF WHALESHIPS—LOSS OF THE AVERICK

The whaleship Timoleon, late Plaskett, of this port arrived here one Saturday in charge of Midshipman J. Hagan Brown, late sailing master of the W. S. brig Perry, having been abandoned by her officers and crew at Tahiti, Society Islands. The Timoleon sailed from this port Oct 9, 1843, and when about six months out, Capt. Plaskett fell from aloft and injured his head, probably deranging his faculties. The T. had been at Tahiti and its vicinity during nearly the whole period of his absence, and has taken only about 100 bbls. of oil; when taken charge of by the U. S. brig Perry, we understand that but one individual of her crew remained on board.

New Bedford Mercury.

C.P.I. Ed. Note: The text of this report is one item in a news column headed "DISASTERS OF WHALESHIPS," the rest of which is irrelevant. Complete text is used. . . .

[*For additional C.P.I. Ed. Note see TAHITI 2.*]

TAHITI 46

Boston Post
July 15, 1845: 27, 2, 6
M

WHALERS

Ar at New Bedford, 12th, ship Timoleon, from Tahiti Feb 21st via Pernambuco, in charge of passed Midshipman J. Hogan Brown, late sailing master of the U. S. brig Perry, with 100 bbls sp oil. Capt Plasket, late of the Timoleon, remained at Tahiti sick. Reports that ship Averick, Reynard, of N. B. was lost on the Island of Ulitea (one of the Society Is) on the 15th Feb last; she was blown on shore in an NNW gale and sunk in 2½ hours after striking. She had taken 600 bbls oil, about 75 of which was sp and was trying out a sp wh when she went on shore. The vessel and cargo was sold for $1800; crew all saved and landed at Tahiti on the 20th Feb.

C.P.I. Ed. Note: The text of the above report is a copy of an item in a newspaper column headed "WHALERS," . . .

Ulitea in text is another spelling for Ulietea.

Ulietea mentioned in text is identified as Raiatea (Findlay, *Directory of the South Pacific Ocean*, Fifth Edition, 1884, p. 645.)

Raiatea, one of the Society Islands is in lat. 16°50'S., lon. 151°25'W. H. O. Chart No. 2023. (*H. O. Pub.* No. 166, Vol. II, 4th ed. 1933, p. 110.)

[*For additional C.P.I. Ed. Note see TAHITI 2.*]

TAHITI 47

Salem Gazette
Sept. 2, 1845: 64, 2, 2
MSaE

American brig Elizabeth, Capt. King of Salem, with arms and ammunition for the Feejees, was at Tahiti last of March. The French soldiers were kept constantly on board, to prevent her landing arms, and the French steamer was to see her clear of the islands.

TAHITI 48

Evening Daily Traveller, Boston, Mass.
Sept. 8, 1845: 1, 2, 4
MH

AFFAIRS IN THE SOCIETY ISLANDS

We make the following extract from a letter lately received from the whale ship Venice, of New London, dated Otahite, Society Islands, March 15, 1845.

There is a war going on here between the French and Natives. There was an engagement between them a few days since, in which the French lost 400 men and the Natives about 80.

There is now an army of natives, 8000 strong, in sight. They are waiting for some movements of the English and Americans, when they will attack the towns now in possession of the French.—It is thought that the French, who are much to be blamed for coming here and starving the peaceful natives, driving them from their towns, will get the worst of it. I was on shore yesterday, and saw a great many of the French soldiers who were wounded in the last battle.

Queen Pomare has left the Isle and gone to another. She restrains the natives of the other Isles for the sake of peace, but they will soon rebel against her orders; they are strong, and will assist their brethren to rid the Islands of the French usurped authority.

Two English frigates are daily expected. The French have a frigate and steamer here; and the English have one steamer, but the Frenchman will not let her depart, because she will not salute their flag. They have threatened to fire into her if she does not. Some music is expected between the English and French when an additional English force arrives.—Hartford Times.

C.P.I. Ed. Note: The text of the above report is a copy of an article in a newspaper column headed "AFFAIRS IN THE SOCIETY ISLANDS," ...

[*For additional C.P.I. Ed. Note see TAHITI 2.*]

TAHITI 49

Daily Evening Traveller, Boston, Mass.
Oct. 11, 1845: 1, 2, 1
MH

FROM THE PACIFIC

Tahiti:—The American brig Elizabeth, Captain King, of Salem, laden with arms and ammunition for the Fejee Islands, sailed from Tahiti in April, having been closely watched and guarded by the French while at the latter.

Queen Pomare still remained at Raiatea, blockaded by French forces, and one of her chiefs who aided in the assassination of some Frenchmen, had been shot by the French authorities.

C.P.I. Ed. Note: The text of this report is one item in a news column headed "FROM THE PACIFIC," the rest of which is irrelevant. Complete text is used. . . .

[*For additional C.P.I. Ed. Notes see TAHITI 2 & 21.*]

TAHITI 50

Boston Post
Feb. 5, 1846: 28, 2, 7
M

WHALERS

Ship Hy Clay, of Nantucket, at Tahiti, Aug 26, was ashore at Chatham Islands in July last, and received some damage, which compelled her to put into Tahiti where she would be obliged to heave out for repairs.

C.P.I. Ed. Note: The text of this report is an item in a newspaper column headed "WHALERS," . . . the rest of which is irrelevant.

[*For additional C.P.I. Ed. Note see TAHITI 2.*]

TAHITI 51

The Liberator, Boston, Mass.
July 31, 1846: 16, 3, 4
MLy

FROM TAHITI

Capt. Baker, of ship Desdemonia, arrived at this port yesterday, reports left at that place Feb 27th, H.B.M. war steamer Salamander, one French war steamer and three corveltes. The trouble between the natives and the French remain in an unsettled state. The natives had retired to the mountains and were still in arms, and embraced every opportunity to annoy the outposts of the French. They had made descent on their deserted town and reduced it to ashes.

——At Bolabolo, which island the French had taken a short time previous there had been a battle between the French and natives, in which the French had been obliged to retire from the island. The French frigate Urania had taken Huaheina, and were fortifying the place. The natives remained unsubdued, and the white population were compelled to seek refuge on board the frigate.

Mr. Harris. formerly of Nantucket who was acting as pilot to the French had been killed.—New Bedford Mercury, 21st.

C.P.I. Ed. Note: The text of this report is one item in a newspaper column headed "FROM TAHITI," the rest of which is irrelevant.

Bola Bola, or Bora-Bora is about 8 miles N.W. of Tahaa described in Findlay's *Directory of the South Pacific Ocean,* Fifth Ed. 1884, p. 646.

Huaheina is probably another spelling for Huahine. Huahine one of the Society Islands is 16° 45′ S, 151° 00′ W., H. O. Chart No. 2023. (*H. O. Pub.* No. 166, Vol. II, 4th ed. 1933. p. 107.)

[*For additional C.P.I. Ed. Note see TAHITI 2.*]

TAHITI 52

New York Observer
Aug. 12, 1846: 24, 3, 4
MBC

FROM THE SOCIETY ISLANDS

By a recent arrival at New Bedford, advices have been received from Tahiti to April 15. The natives had made a vigorous assault upon the French garrison, and had driven them from the land. The European residents had been compelled to flee with their effects on board the French vessels of war. After the evacuation of the town, the French vessels had opened a fire upon it. IB.

C.P.I. Ed. Note: The text of the above report is an item in a newspaper column headed "FROM THE SOCIETY ISLANDS," . . . the rest of which is irrelevant.

[For additional C.P.I. Ed. Note see TAHITI 2.]

TAHITI 53

Daily Evening Traveller, Boston, Mass.
Sept. 22, 1846: 2, 2, 6
MH

FROM THE SOCIETY ISLANDS

The Friend publishes some interesting documents, on the subject of the difficulties between the French and Queen Pomare.

More fighting had taken place between the French and the natives, and on one occasion, while the American whale ship Peruvian, Capt. Brown, was lying at Papeite, a company of the natives rushed into the barracks of the French, killed several soldiers, and for a few moments held possession, but were soon driven out; and near the beach there was an engagement between several hundred of the French soldiers and about 150 natives securely fortified; but numbers were killed in each side.

The natives had driven the French from their position at Point Venus. Among the natives is an Italian, who inspired them with great courage, so that they are represented as by no means wanting in bravery. On several occassions the foreign population had fled on board the ships in the harbor for security. The country is in the hands of the natives, and of course all the provisions, and the French, it was said, would be starved or die of scarcity, if no relief was afforded them.

C.P.I. Ed. Note: The text of this report is an item in a newspaper column headed "FROM THE SOCIETY ISLANDS, . . .

Point Venus is identified as Venus Point.

Venus Point, the northern point of Tahiti is situated in lat.

17° 29′ S. lon. 149° 29′ W. H. O. Chart No. 2025. (*H. O. Pub.* No. 166, Vol. II.)

[*For additional C.P.I. Ed. Note see TAHITI 2.*]

Papeete Harbor, Tahiti, circa 1880. From a painting by C. F. Gordon Cumming.

TAHITI 54

Boston Daily Advertiser
Sept. 23, 1846: 68, 2, 4
MB

SOCIETY ISLANDS

Difficulties still exist there between the natives and the French. While the American whale ship Peruvian, Capt. Brown, was lying at Papiete, a company of the natives rushed into the barracks of the French, killed several soldiers and for a few moments held possession, but was soon driven out; and near the beach there was an engagement between several hundred of the French soldiers and about 150 natives securely fortified; numbers were killed on each side. The natives had driven the French from their position at Point Venus. Among the natives there is an Italian, who inspired them with great courage, so that they are represented as by no means wanting in bravery. The Polynesian of April 4th gives an account of a battle between the French and the natives or Tahiti early in January. About twenty fell in this action and forty were wounded. The action took place on the northern side of the island, but the steamer returned to Tahiti, with the wounded. The town had been almost wholly destroyed by fire, and attack on Papiete was hourly expected. A reinforcement of 280 troops had arrived from France. The Friend (of Honolulu) of June 1st publishes a letter from Tahiti, dated 4th of April. Three corvettes had arrived with 200 troops—the Fortune, Heroine and Seine. The Tahitians had declared the purpose of attacking Papiete and the Governor in council decided to attack the encampment of the natives unless they lay down their arms. He despatched the steamer with an offer to Pomare to return and receive her king-

dom, etc. The steamer returned and reported that Queen Pomare had accepted the offer and would soon be up, and in the
meantime wishes her people of Tahiti *not to fight!* All were
now quiet for a few days, the Seine sailed for New Zealand, and
the next day the steamer sailed for Hiahine. The natives having no confidence in the French, at once supposed that both
steamer and the frigate had gone to carry on hostilities at Huahine. The excitement was very great, when a worthless youth,
installed as Governor at Point Venus, applied the spark and all
is now in a blaze. The natives soon attacked the town, and before an alarm was given they had passed the battery, killed the
native judge under the French, and burned the house of Major
Fergus, French Judge. The troops were turned out, and continued volleys of musketry and firing of artillery closed the day.
The frigate fired through several houses, and Mr. Moor's house
was burned to the ground, most probably of the fire of the
steamer. Occasional firing is still kept up, and has been for this
fortnight past. The struggle will be decisive, and the French
will maintain their position if possible until the Virginie arrive,
then they will attack. The natives will never submit without
their Queen. When attacked they have the best of it. The
French are confined to their military past. They cannot go for
musket shot from the town. All French houses out of town have
been destroyed. The country is in the hands of the natives, and
of course all provisions except salted stores in the French Magazines. The natives will kill the cattle and pigs, poultry, etc.
The poor French men will be starved or die of scurvy if this continues. All is confusion. The arrival of H.B.M. steamer Cor-
morant had excited great interest among the people of Honolulu. We learn farther that news had reached Honolulu from
Tahiti bearing date up to the 20th of April, and that the fighting continued with much loss of life. Particulars not given.

Extract of a letter, dated

Honolulu June 3, 1846

"The opportunity by which is a chance French Ship from Tahiti (La Jeune,) on route from Mazatlan, with news of great doings at the former place, between the French and natives. She is to be off immediately, so that I have not time to say more."

(The above letter is from a well informed source, but we are not able to ascertain whether the events it refers to have been already reported or not. At that date the French Ship left Tahiti. Her arrival is not reported in the Honolulu papers of June 1.).

F.S.J. of A.

C.P.I. Ed. Note: The text of the above report is an item from a newspaper column headed "Society Islands" the rest of which is irrelevant.

[*For additional C.P.I. Ed. Note see TAHITI 2.*]

TAHITI 55

Daily Evening Traveller, Boston, Mass.
Nov. 12, 1846: 2, 2, 1
MH

AFFAIRS AT TAHITI

The papers received by the last steamer give an account of some late movements of the French at Tahiti, which are worthy of a passing notice.

In May last, Governor Bruat was able to muster about one thousand men at Papeete and he resolved to march against the natives at Papenoo.—The missionaries offered to mediate; but the Governor wished them to presuade the people to accept the French protectorate, and this they could not do. He had previously sent to Queen Pomare to return. She replied, "No, never."

The natives at first attempted to defend Papenoo; but seeing that the force brought against them was too powerful, they abandoned the place and retired to a strong position in the interior, carrying with them their families and valuable effects. The French followed them but were repulsed with severe loss. After this defeat, the Governor returned to the beach, plundered and destroyed the village, cut down the bread-fruit trees, cocoa nut trees, orange trees etc. and left a desert, where he had found a district of unparalleled fertility, comfort and beauty. The troops destroyed all the churches through which they passed except the one at Point Venus, and the materials of the church at Papenoo were taken to Papeete for the use of the French Government. The dwellings of the late Rev. T. S. McKean and Rev. C. Wilson have been burned to the ground.

Governor Bruat next led his troops up the valley of Han-

tana. The people retired at their approach, and took possession
of their mountain fortresses. The French followed, and, after a
brisk fire, which kept up for sometime, they were again repulsed
with loss. As at Papenoo, the wrath of the discomforted army
was wrecked upon houses, plantations and especially the church
of the valley. The loss of the bread-fruit trees will be severely
felt by the afflicted and oppressed people. If they grow again,
six or seven years must elapse before they can bear. But lest
they should, even then, yield something for the support of the
Tahitians, Governor Bruat has burned the roots with fire.

The next expedition of the French was at Bunaania. The
natives retreated; their invaders followed and attacked them on
the Sabbath; but with the same result as before. The commandant of the French troops, M. De Brea, received a severe wound,
of which he died the next day. Failing of success in their con-
test with the natives, they made another onset upon the bread-
fruit trees, etc., thousands of which were destroyed, the very
roots in many cases being burned as before to prevent their
future growth.

The loss of the natives in these different battles appear to
have been very trifling; while that of the French must have been
very severe. The official account of Governor Bruat does not
report a very large number among the killed and wounded; but
the English letter-writers tell a very different story. According
to the correspondent of the London Patriot, the first repulse was
attended by a loss of eighty-seven killed and wounded. At any
rate, the despatch of the Governor is said to have occasioned
some discussion at a council of the French Ministry; and it was
thought necessary to take measures to save the honor of "the
grand nation."

Why will not Louis Philippe and N. Guizot see, that the
only honorable course for them to take, is to restore Pomare to

her throne and her people, and abandon Tahiti forever?   There is no glory to be won in that field.

C.P.I. Ed. Note: The text of the above report is a long article in a newspaper column headed "AFFAIRS OF TAHITI," . . .

[*For additional C.P.I. Ed. Note see TAHITI 2.*]

TAHITI 56

Boston Daily Advertiser
Jan. 21, 1847: 69, 3, 2
M

[Report in *Boston Post,* Jan 23, 1847 (M) omits reference to 'N. Y. Ship List' and has ' . . . New Bedford Mercury of the 18th inst. that . . .' but is otherwise similar.]

DISASTERS

Whale ship Sarah of New York, was the vessel which put in Tahiti, was condemned, hull sold for $1050 etc. The N. Y. Ship List states that the S. has a very severe gale near the Sandwich Islands, in July and was obliged to put into Tahiti. Her cargo abt 3000 bbls oil, would be shipped home by the first vessel; vessel and cargo insured in N. York for abt $50,000. The account in the New Bedford Mercury that Capt. Myrick had shipped part of his oil to Bremen, and part to Valparaiso, and would send the balance to the United States first opportunity, was probably of a later date than that received in New York, which does not mention the sale of the vessel.

C.P.I. Ed. Note: The text of this report is one item in a news column headed "DISASTERS," the rest of which is irrelevant.

[*For additional C.P.I. Ed. Note see TAHITI 2.*]

TAHITI 57

Boston Daily Advertiser
Jan. 24, 1847: 71, 3, 1
M

WHALERS

At Tahiti Feb. 26, '47 Autumn, Perry, Stonington 200 Sp; had been on reef near Tahiti, and was hove out for repairs.

C.P.I. Ed. Note: The text of the above report is a copy of an item in a newspaper column headed "WHALERS," . . . the rest of which is irrelevant.

[*For additional C.P.I. Ed. Note see TAHITI 2.*]

TAHITI 58

Boston Post
Oct. 28, 1847: 31, 2, 6
M

WHALERS

Ship Factor, Hawes, N. B. was condemned at Tahiti on the 8th July last. Had 2200 wh and 500 sp. which would be shipped to Valparaiso. There is insurance on vessel and catchings for $26000 at two offices in that town, $6000 at the Warren office, Boston, and $5000 at the same office, New York. The F. sailed from Sydney, Feb. 18, for NW Coast, and may have encountered the typhoon which was experienced on the 17th March, in lat. 16°, lon. 171° W. in which several ships suffered damage, as before reported.

C.P.I. Ed. Note: The text of this report is one item in a newspaper column headed "WHALERS," the rest of which is irrelevant.

[*For additional C.P.I. Ed. Note see TAHITI 2.*]

TAHITI 59

Boston Daily Advertiser
Oct. 28, 1847: 70, 2, 8
M

DISASTERS

Ship Factor, Hawes of New Bedford, was condemned at Tahiti, July 8. Had on board 2200 bbls wh and 500 do sp oil, which would be shipped to Valparaiso. No further particulars. The New Bedford Mercury states that there is insurance on vessel and catching for $26,000 at two offices in New Bedford, $6,000 at the Warren Office, Boston and $5,000 at the Sun Office, New York. The Factor sailed from Sydney Feb. 13, for the North West Coast, and may have encountered the typhoon which was experienced March 16, in lat. 16°S, lon. 171° W, in which several ships suffered damage as before reported.

C.P.I. Ed. Note: The text of this report is an item in a newspaper column headed "DISASTERS," the rest of which is irrelevant.

[*For additional C.P.I. Ed. Note see TAHITI 2.*]

TAHITI 60

Boston Post
Oct. 30, 1847: 31, 2, 6
M

WHALERS

The report of the condemnation of ship Factor, of New Bedford was received in New York in a letter from Alsop & Co., dated Valparaiso, Aug. 27, which says—"We will mention here in case it should interest any of you insurers, that information had been received here of the condemnation of whaleship Factor, of New Bedford, at Tahiti, on the 8th of July last. She had a cargo of 2200 bbls. wh and 500 sp oil, which it was intended to ship to this place, our informant could not say whether to be forwarded to the U.S. or for sale—we should suppose the former.

C.P.I. Ed. Note: The text of this report is one item in a newspaper column headed "MARINE JOURNAL," the rest of which is irrelevant.

[*For additional C.P.I. Ed. Note see TAHITI 3.*]

TAHITI 61

Boston Daily Advertiser
Oct. 31, 1847: 70, 2, 8
M

DISASTERS

The report of the condemnation of ship Factor, of New Bedford, at Tahiti, comes through a letter from Messrs Alsop & Co.
Valaparaiso dated Aug 27. Her cargo was to be shipped to V.
but whether to be forwarded to the United States, or for sale was
not known, although Messrs A & Co., supposed to be forwarded.

C.P.I. Ed. Note: The text of this report is an item in a newspaper column headed "DISASTERS," the rest of which is irrelevant.

Tahiti Island (formally called Otaheite) is 33 miles in
length, in 17°38'S., lon.149°33'W., H. O. Chart No. 2065. (*H.
O. Pub.* No. 166, Vol. II, 4th ed. 1933, p. 72.)

TAHITI 62

Boston Daily Advertiser
Apr. 25, 1849: 73, 2, 6
M

WHALERS

Ar at New Bedford 23, barque Mt. Wallaston, Bowen, Honolulu Nov. 31, Tahiti Dec 29, with 191 casks oil and 3685 bdls whalebone, on freight for many different whale ships in New Bedford, Providence, New London etc. and $20,000 in gold dust.

C.P.I. Ed. Note: The text of the above report is one item in a newspaper column headed "WHALERS," the rest of which is irrelevant.

[For additional C.P.I. Ed. Note see TAHITI 2.]

TAHITI 63

Boston Daily Advertiser
Aug. 16, 1849: 74, 3, 1
M

WHALERS

At Tahiti, Feb. 21, Wm. Hamilton, Shockly, N. B., 125 sp., 525 Wh. (reported Jan. 28, 150 sp 550 wh. . . . At Honolulu, Feb. 26, New England, Wilcox, N. L. 23 sp. (rep. Feb. 28, at Maui clean).

C.P.I. Ed. Note: The text of this report is an item in a newspaper column headed "WHALERS," . . . the rest of which is irrelevant.

[For additional C.P.I. Ed. Note see TAHITI 2.]

TAHITI 64

Boston Daily Advertiser
Dec. 25, 1849: 150, 2, 6
M

WHALERS

At Tahiti June 23, Arnolda, Wood, N B. 500 sp., Capt. W. had purchased 890 gals. sp. oil, landed at T. by sch. Alfred, of New Bedford, and had shipped it by the Barclay, which he supposed would arrive home in November. He does not state whether it was the Barclay of N B, or Nan.

C.P.I. Ed. Note: The text of the above report is one item in a newspaper column headed "WHALERS," the rest of which is irrelevant.

[*Two copies of this report are incorrect in that one has 'June 23, Barclay, Wood, N. B. . . .' and the other 'June 23, Alfred, Wood, N B. . . .' The text has been checked against the original newspaper and the correct version of the report is printed here. For additional C.P.I. Ed. Note see TAHITI 2.*]

TAHITI 65

Daily Traveller, Boston, Mass.
Jan. 17, 1850: 5, 3, 2
MBAt

WHALERS

A letter from Capt. Wright of ship George & Susan of New Bedford, reports her at Tahiti Sept. 18th, with 350 bbls sperm oil, touched to land, Mr. White, 2nd mate, who had been injured by a whale. The George & Susan it will be recollected, lost her mate and boat's crew a short time previous, while in pursuit of whales, who landed at Tahiti. Capt. Wright found that upon his arrival at Tahiti that the mate had left for California. One man only of the boat's crew, Joseph Francis, returned to the ship. Capt. Wright states that upon losing sight of the boat he commenced cruising for her, and beat to the windward all the succeeding night with lights set. In the morning he fell in with boat which the whale had cut. The George and Susan was bound upon the line to cruise 2 mos. (with only one officer, the 3d mate, on board) and to return to Tahiti for Mr. White.

C.P.I. Ed. Note: The text of this report is an item in a newspaper column headed "WHALERS," the rest of which is irrelevant.

[*For additional C.P.I. Ed. Note see TAHITI 2.*]

TAHITI 66

The Friend, Honolulu
Apr. 1, 1850: 8, 29, 1
MSaP

December 30th, the French vessel, L'Albert was wrecked at Tahiti.   The pilot and crew narrowly escaped.

C.P.I. Ed. Note: The text of this report is one item in a news
column headed "MARINE INTELLIGENCE," the rest of which is
irrelevant.

[For additional C.P.I. Ed. Note see TAHITI 2.]

TAHITI 67

Boston Daily Advertiser
Apr. 9, 1850: 75, 2, —
M

WHALERS

Also arrived ship Champion, Parker, North Pacific, Tahiti Dec. 10, 325 bbls sp, 2500 do wh oil, 23,000 bone. Spoke Nov. 21, on the line, lon. 156 W, ship Gen. Scott, FH 650 sp.

C.P.I. Ed. Note: The text of the above report is a copy of an item in a newspaper column headed "WHALERS," . . . the rest of which is irrelevant.

[*For additional C.P.I. Ed. Note see TAHITI 2.*]

TAHITI 68

Boston Daily Evening Transcript
May 23, 1850: 22, 2, 4
MBAt

[Similar reports in *Boston Evening Transcript,* May 23, 1850(M) and *Boston Post,* May 24, 1850 (M) both have 'Edmund Allen'.]

MORE GOLD AND A SUCCESSFUL VOYAGE

The whale ship Sylph, Captain Francis Gardner, arrived at this port yesterday, last from Otaheite, Society Islands, Feb 6, with $25,000 in gold dust to her owner, Edmond Allen, Esq, Fairhaven, and $6,000 to the master. She brings half a million lbs of whale bone and 400 bbls whale oil shipped by whalers at the Sandwich Islands. The Sylph sailed hence in July, 1847 on a whaling voyage, and sent home 500 bbls sperm oil from the Western Islands. She proceeded to the Pacific, and arrived at Panama at the commencement of the California gold fever, took a freight of passengers from Panama to San Francisco, at the highest rates and thence proceeded to the Sandwich Islands, where she took on board a full freight for Home. New Bedford Mercury, May 23d.

C.P.I. Ed. Note: The text of the above report is one item in a newspaper column headed "MORE GOLD AND A SUCCESSFUL VOYAGE," the rest of which is irrelevant.

[*For additional C.P.I. Ed. Note see TAHITI 61.*]

TAHITI 69

Boston Daily Advertiser
May 24, 1850: 75, 2, 7
M

WHALERS

Arrived at New Bedford 22 d, ship Sylph, of Fairhaven Gardner, Honolulu, Nov. 14, Tahiti Feb. 6. Left at Tahiti Cossac, Barker, of and for Sippican, 40 sp since leaving Oahu.

C.P.I. Ed. Note: The text of the above report is a copy of an item in a newspaper column headed "WHALERS," . . . the rest of which is irrelevant.

[*For additional C.P.I. Ed. Note see TAHITI 2.*]

TAHITI 70

Boston Daily Advertiser
July 26, 1850: 76, 2, 8
M

WHALERS

At Tahiti Mar. 6, Roscoe, McCleave N.B. oil not stated.—

C.P.I. Ed. Note: The text of the above report is an excerpt from a copy of an item in a newspaper column headed "WHALERS," . . . the rest of which is irrelevant.

[*For additional C.P.I. Ed. Note see TAHITI 2.*]

TAHITI 71

Boston Post
Aug. 12, 1850: 36, 2, 5
M

WHALERS

A letter from Capt. White, of ship George and Susan of New Bedford, reports her at Tahiti March 14, with 600 bbls, sp oil—had shipped Mr. John R. Lawrence (late mate of the Minerva Smyth of N.B.) as mate for the voyage. Mr. White the former 2d mate of Geo. & Susan, who was left sick at Tahiti in Sept. last had recovered and sailed for California.

C.P.I. Ed. Note: The text of this report is an item in a newspaper column headed "WHALERS," . . . the rest of which is irrelevant.

[*For additional C.P.I. Ed. Note see TAHITI 2.*]

TAHITI 72

Boston Daily Adv[ertiser]
Sept. 4, 1850: 76, 2, 7
M

WHALERS

At Tahiti, May 7, Jeanette, West, N. B., 200 sp., 3100 wh. oil, (of which 1730 from the wreck of ship Margaret, of Newport, before reported); would sail home, next day.

C.P.I. Ed. Note: The text of the above report is one item in a newspaper column headed "WHALERS," the rest of which is irrelevant.

[*For additional C.P.I. Ed. Note see TAHITI 2.*]

TAHITI 73

Boston Daily Advertiser
Oct. 5, 1850: 76, 2, 7
M

[Report in *Boston Post,* Oct. 5, 1850 (M) has same information but different word order.]

WHALERS

At Tahiti about May 5, Nile, Hamlin, N B. 400 sp. 700 wh. fitting for a cruise of 3 or 4 mos. and then home. Had discharged her mate. Seamen were scarce at Tahiti, and Capt. H. expected to proceed to Roratonga to complete his crew.

C.P.I. Ed. Note: The text of the above report is one item in a newspaper column headed "MARINE JOURNAL," the rest of which is irrelevant.

[*For additional C.P.I. Ed. Note see TAHITI 2.*]

TAHITI 74

Daily Evening Traveler, Boston, Mass.
Nov. 12, 1850: 30, 3, 4
MBAt

WHALERS

A letter from Capt. Marshall, of ship President, of Nantucket, reports her at Tahiti, July 24, with 1200 bbls. sp. oil on board. Reports on off shore ground June 15, Barque Pantheon, Worth, N. Bedford, 300 sp. at Tahiti, July 24, Corinthian, Armington, do 1000 sp., Lalla Rookh, Gardiner, 600 sp., and nearly all hands had deserted both ships.

C.P.I. Ed. Note: The text of this report is one item in a newspaper column headed "WHALERS," the rest of which is irrelevant. Complete text is used. . . .

[*For additional C.P.I. Ed. Note see TAHITI 2.*]

TAHITI 75

Boston Post
Dec. 9, 1850: 37, 2, 7
M

DISASTERS &C.

Capt. Reed, of bring Emma at San Francisco from Tahiti, reports, Oct 8th in lat. 37 24 N., long.137 27 W. discovered two rocks, not laid down in the chart, running N.E. and S.W., one 150 fathoms long, 66 wide, the other about 100 fathoms long and 38 wide; on sounding 5 fathoms, were got on one port, and 3 fathoms alongside the rock. Capt. R. is of opinion that in heavy weather the sea would break over it.

C.P.I. Ed. Note: The text of this report is one item in a newspaper column headed "DISASTERS &C.," the rest of which is irrelevant.

[*For additional C.P.I. Ed. Note see TAHITI 2.*]

TAHITI 76

Boston Daily Adv[ertiser]
Dec. 12, 1850: 76, 2, 8
M

[Report in *Boston Post,* Dec. 12, 1850 (M) omits first sentence, but is otherwise similar.]

WHALERS

Ar. at Edgartown, 10th ship President, Marshall, Pacific Ocean, last from Tahiti, of and for Nantucket, 1350 bbls. sp. oil. Left T. Aug. 5.

At Tahiti Aug. 28, Lalla Rookh, Gardner, N.B. 600 sp. Mr. McNulty, first officer, in attempting to swim from the shore to the ship Aug. 23, was drowned. Capt. G. was bound to Hobart Town for a crew, the ship having been deserted by all but the third mate and three green hands.

C.P.I. Ed. Note: The above reports are excerpts taken from a newspaper column headed "WHALERS," the rest of which is irrelevant. Complete text is used. . . .

[For additional C.P.I. Ed. Note see TAHITI 2.]

TAHITI 77

Daily Evening Traveller, Boston, Mass.
Mar. 5, 1851: 6, 3, 2
M

WHALERS

A letter from Wm. & Eliza, Allen of New Bedford, reports her in lat. 16° S. lon. 77° W. Dec. 15, with 900 bbls sp oil, had taken 100 bbls since leaving Tahiti Oct. 23.

C.P.I. Ed. Note: The text of the above report is an item in a newspaper column headed "WHALERS," . . . the rest of which is irrelevant.

[*For additional C.P.I. Ed. Note see TAHITI 2.*]

TAHITI 78

Boston Post
Apr. 24, 1851: 38, 2, 5
M

[Report in *Daily Evening Traveler,* Boston, Apr. 23, 1851 (M) starts 'At Tahiti Feb. 2 . . .' but thereafter is similar.]

WHALERS

A letter from Mr. F. C. Sanford, reports at Tahiti Feb. 2 ship Rambler, Houghton, of Nant, with 1850 blls sp oil She had been hove out, and her leak stopped; was reloading, and would sail soon on a cruise.

C.P.I. Ed. Note: The text of this report is one item in a newspaper column headed "WHALERS," the rest of which is irrelevant.

[For additional C.P.I. Ed. Note see TAHITI 2.]

TAHITI 79

Boston Daily Advertiser
May 3, 1851: 77, 2, 7
M

WHALERS

At Tahiti Dec.28, Lion, Nichols, of Providence, 220 sp, on board for New Zealand; incorrectly reported Dec.27, 180 sp.

C.P.I. Ed. Note: The text of the above report is a copy of an item in a newspaper column headed "WHALERS," the rest of which is irrelevant.

[*For additional C.P.I. Ed. Note see TAHITI 2.*]

TAHITI 80

Daily Evening Traveler, Boston, Mass.
May 7, 1851: 7, 2, 7
M

WHALERS

At Tahiti Feb. 1, Phoenix, Winslow, Nantucket, 600 sp; Rambler, Horton, do 1550 sp. had been hove out to stop a leak, which was discovered to be in the garboard, owing to oakum having worked out.

C.P.I. Ed. Note: The text of this report is an item in a newspaper column headed "WHALERS," the rest of which is irrelevant.

[*For additional C.P.I. Ed. Note see TAHITI 61.*]

TAHITI 81

Boston Daily Advertiser
June 8, 1851: 78, 2, 8
M

WHALERS

The Montreal, N.B. before reported, sailed from Tahiti, March 15, 300 sp. had sent home prev. to 4th., 115 sp. had still on board 110 sp. and 135 wh.

C.P.I. Ed. Note: The text of the above report is an excerpt from an item in a newspaper column headed "WHALERS," . . . the rest of which is irrelevant.

[*For additional C.P.I. Ed. Note see TAHITI 2.*]

TAHITI 8₂

Boston Daily Advertiser
July 4, 1851: 78, 2, 7
M

[Report in *Boston Post,* July 4, 1851(M) gives Captain's name as 'Shocley', omits '(before reported 400 wh)' and has different word order.]

WHALERS

At Tahiti Jan 24, (by letter from Capt. Shockley) Wm. Hamilton, N.B. 450 bbls. sp oil, (before reported 400 wh) to sail next day for Arctic Seas via Guam. Had discharged J. Smith, boat steerer, (sick) and Thos. Coleman, seaman.

C.P.I. Ed. Note: The text of the above report is a copy of an item in a newspaper column headed "WHALERS," . . . the rest of which is irrelevant.

[For additional C.P.I. Ed. Note see TAHITI 2.]

TAHITI 8₃

Boston Daily Adv[ertiser]
Aug. 8, 1851: No. 33, 2, 8
M

WHALERS

At Lahaina, May 29, Vineyard, Coffin, of Edgartown, 6 mos. out, 400 sp.

At Tahiti, May 2, Oliver Crocker, Cash, N. B., to cruise; Janet, Crowell, of Wesport, for Honolulu.

C.P.I. Ed. Note: The text of the above report is an excerpt from an item in a newspaper column headed "WHALERS," . . . the rest of which is irrelevant.

[*For additional C.P.I. Ed. Note see TAHITI 2.*]

TAHITI 84

Boston Post
Aug. 12, 1851: 36, 2, 6
M

[Similar report in *Daily Morning Commonwealth*, Boston, Aug. 14, 1851 (MH).]

WHALERS

Ship Mowhawk, Swain, of Nantucket, at Tahiti, April 19th, had 30 bbls. sp. oil. A plan to set fire to the ship or murder the captain and officers had been discovered in season to put a stop to it. The second mate, carpenter and two or three others were engaged in the scheme. The two men were in prison at Tahiti, and the second mate, Mr. Clark, had been discharged, but was at large. The ship would sail shortly on a cruise.

C.P.I. Ed. Note: The text of this report is one item in a newspaper column headed "WHALERS," the rest of which is irrelevant.

[*For additional C.P.I. Ed. Note see TAHITI 2.*]

TAHITI 85

Boston Daily Advertiser
Aug. 15, 1851: 78, 2, 7
M

WHALERS

Sailed from Tahiti, May 25, ship Oliver Crocker, Cash, N. B., to cruise. . . . Arrived at Lahaian June 5, Anadis, Swift, N. B., 5 months out clean.

C.P.I. Ed. Note: The text of the above report is an excerpt from an item in a newspaper column headed "WHALERS," . . . the rest of which is irrelevant.

[*For additional C.P.I. Ed. Note see TAHITI 2.*]

TAHITI 86

Daily Evening Traveler, Boston, Mass.
Aug. 25, 1851: 7, 2, 6
M

FROM TAHITI

The U.S. Ship St. Mary's was at Tahiti on the 23d of May, Callao on the 10th of March, and arrived at Nukahiva on the 27th, and having settled all the existing difficulties, left that Island on the 3d of May. Experiencing light and variable winds, she arrived at Papaeta, island of Tahiti, on the 12th. List of her officers, who, with crew, are all well:—

The St. Mary's would leave Papaeta on the 10th of June for Navigator's and Tiger Islands.

Mr. Kelley, U.S. Consul, and family, had arrived at Papaeta, in 144 days from Boston, by ship Colchis.

C.P.I. Ed. Note: The text of this report is one item in a newspaper column headed "FROM TAHITI," the rest of which is irrelevant. Complete text is used. . . . Nuka Hiva Island is 8° 52' S., 140° 08' W., H. O. Chart No. 1806. *(H.O. Pub.* No. 166, Vol. II, 4th ed., 1933, P. 182.)

Nuka is identified as the Federal Island of Ingraham, the Adams Island of Roberts, and the Sir Henry Martin Island of Lieut. Hergest. *(Directory of the South Pacific Ocean,* Findlay, 5th ed. 1884, p. 812.)

[*For additional C.P.I. Ed. Note see TAHITI 2.*]

Fort in the Harbour, opposite the Town of Papeahiti, the Island of Eimio in the Distance. July 13, 1839

Fort in Harbor of Papeete, 1839. Sketch by an unknown artist. Peabody Museum of Salem.

TAHITI 87

Boston Daily Advertiser
Apr. 29, 1852: 79, 2, 7
M

WHALERS

Arrived at New Bedford, 28th, Alfred, Davenport, Pacific Ocean, Tahiti, Dec. 28, Pernambuco 30 days, with 50 bbls. sp. oil on board. Sent home and sold on voyage, 2150 bbls. sp. oil. Also freight, 208 bbls. cocoanut oil, and 7000 lbs. arrowroot, to H. A. Pierce, of Boston. The yellow fever had nearly disappeared at Pernambuco.

C.P.I. Ed. Note: The text of this report is one item in a newspaper column headed "WHALERS," the rest of which is irrelevant.

[*For additional C.P.I. Ed. Note see TAHITI 2.*]

TAHITI 88

Daily Evening Traveler, Boston,Mass.
May 8, 1852: 8, 3, 1
M

WHALERS

A letter received in Edgartown from Capt. Norton, of ship
Abrm Barker, of N.B., reports her at Otaheite, Feb. 15, with 50
bbls. sp.oil and 2 sp. whales for boiling-bd. to Sandwich Islands.
Had heard from, no date etc., Ship Vineyard, Coffin, of Edgartown, with 600 bbls. sp. (rep. Oct 26, 42 sp. 800 Wh.) The Sch.
Pilgrim, Wm. Mayhew, was on the opposite side of Otaheite,
loading with passengers for San Francisco.

C.P.I. Ed. Note: The text of this report is one item in a newspaper column headed "WHALERS," the rest of which is irrelevant.

[*For additional C.P.I. Ed. Note see TAHITI 61.*]

TAHITI 89

Boston Daily Advertiser
May 10, 1852: 79, 2, 6
M

WHALERS

At Tahiti, Feb. 15, (by letter from Capt. Norton) Abm. Barker, N.B. 50 bbls. sp. oil and 2 sp whaler ready for boiling, bd to Sandwich Islands. Had heard from no date, &c. Vineyard, Coffin, of Edgartown, 600 sp (reported Oct. 25, 425 sp. 700 wh.

C.P.I. Ed. Note: The text of this report is one item in a news column headed "WHALERS," the rest of which is irrelevant. Complete text is used. . . .

[For additional C.P.I. Ed. Note see TAHITI 2.]

TAHITI 90

Daily Evening Traveler, Boston, Mass.
July 16, 1852: 8, 3, 1
M

WHALERS

At Tahiti; April 20, Ontario, Slocum, N.B. 600 bbls. oil, recruiting: Mariner Coffin, Nantucket, 600 do; and others before reported.

C.P.I. Ed. Note: The text of the above report is one item in a newspaper column headed "MARINE JOURNAL," the rest of which is irrelevant. Complete text is used. . . .

[*For additional C.P.I. Ed. Note see TAHITI 2.*]

TAHITI 91

New York Observer
July 22, 1852: 30, 2, 6
MBC

TAHITI

SUCCESS OF THE REPUBLICANS AND FLIGHT OF QUEEN POMARE

The Panama Star of July 6th, has news from Tahiti to the 16th June, that the half breed native who was elected by the Natives as President, some time since, had been overpowered by the adherents of Queen Pomare, and compelled to vacate his seat, But the triumph of the royalists was only a brief one, as the republicans obtained a reinforcement, ousted the royalists and again installed the half-breed in the executive chair. The Queen on learning the discomfiture of her party, started for the scene of action, to attempt the subjugation of her rebellious subjects; but such was their force that she was compelled to flee, and barely escape for her life. She took refuge on board a French frigate, which sailed for the Sandwich Islands and arrived at Lahaima, on the day Capt. Wilson sailed. All was quiet at Riatea, at last accounts, under the new republican President. The Falmouth brings no papers.

C.P.I. Ed. Note: The text of the above report is one item from a newspaper column headed "SUCCESS OF THE REPUBLICAN AND FLIGHT OF QUEEN POMARE," the rest of which is irrelevant.

[For additional C.P.I. Ed. Note see TAHITI 2.]

TAHITI 92

Boston Daily Adv[ertiser]
Aug. 11, 1852: 80, 2, 7
M

WHALERS

Ar at New Bedford 9th, ship Hector, Smith, Pacific Ocean, Tahiti, Apl 20, with 2200 bbls sp oil. Left at Tahiti Apl 20, Nauticon, Veder Nant. 900 sp 300 wh; Concordia, French, SH, 32 mos out, clean. Capt. Smith, spoke the sch Supply, of Sydney, who reported the total loss of the Ontario, Slocum, of New Bedford, on Pitt's Island, King's Mill Group, about the middle of January last. The Supply had on board about 300 bbls of oil belonging to the Ontario, and also had on board part of the crew bound to Sydney.

Also spoke in Feb. Phocion, Nichols, NB. 1300 sp. The Palso had on board 300 bbls wh. saved from the wreck of the Ontario, (200 purchased and 100 picked up.) Capt. Slocum and the remainder of the crew, were on board of the P, bound home. There was insurance on the Ontario and cargo, at several offices in New Bedford, to the amount of about $35,000.

C.P.I. Ed. Note: The text of this report is one item in a newspaper column headed "WHALERS," the rest of which is irrelevant. Complete text is used. . . .

[*For additional C.P.I. Ed. Note see TAHITI 2.*]

TAHITI 93

Boston Daily Advertiser
Aug. 18, 1852: 80, 2, 7
M

WHALERS

The Wm. & Eliza, Allen, for New Bedford, and Ontario, Cathcart, Nan, remained at Tahiti, May 23. The O was refitting for a cruise.

C.P.I. Ed. Note: The text of this report is one item in a newspaper column headed "WHALERS," the rest of which is irrelevant. Complete text is used. . . .

[*For additional C.P.I. Ed. Note see TAHITI 2.*]

TAHITI 94

Boston Post
Oct. 5, 1852: 41, 2, 4
M

[One copy of typescript of this report gives 'Jerry Eaton'. Report in *Boston Daily Advertiser,* Oct. 5, 1852 (M) is similar to first sentence.]

WHALERS

Ar. at New Bedford 4th inst. ship Wm. & Eliza, Allen Pacific Ocean, Tahiti, May 28 with 1400 bbls. sp. oil. Left at Tahiti, ship Ontario, Cathcart, Nan., 600 sp., to sail on a cruise in 8 days. Died on board the Mary & Eliza Aug. 2d, of consumption, Ira Williams, aged about 22, Aug. 30, Jersy Eaton, about 24, seamen.

C.P.I. Ed. Note: The text of this report is one item in a newspaper column headed "WHALERS," the rest of which is irrelevant. Complete text is used. . . .

[*For additional C.P.I. Ed. Note see TAHITI 2.*]

TAHITI 95

Boston Daily Adv[ertiser]
Dec. 20, 1852: 80, 2, 6
M

WHALERS

At Tahiti Sept. 13, by letter from Capt. Winepenny, J. A. Robb, FH, 550 sp. having taken 50 on last cruise.

C.P.I. Ed. Note: The text of this report is one item in a news column headed "WHALERS," the rest of which is irrelevant.

[*For additional C.P.I. Ed. Note see TAHITI 2.*]

TAHITI 96

Daily Evening Traveler, Boston, Mass.
Dec. 21, 1852: 7, 2, 5
MBAt

SOCIETY'S ISLANDS

We copy from the San Francisco Times, the following Summary of commercial and police regulations of these islands, transmitted by the American Consul at Tahiti to the collector at San Francisco: no stranger is at liberty to establish his domicil (sic) at Tahiti, or to reside there for any length of time, without having first obtained permission to do so, and made known his domicils (sic). Every infringement will be punished by a fine of from twenty to fifty francs. Sea Captains can save themselves much annoyance, by taking no firearms into port with their vessels; whatever weapons they may have however, should be manifested at once. Captains are required to report the number of their crews and passengers and from whence they came. They must neither embark any person without a permit from the European police; a failure to comply with this regulation being punishable by a five of from 200 to 500 frances. The sale of wines is not allowed on board ships. All goods admitted to entry may be sold by wholesale on shipboard, provided a license is first obtained. The sale of munitions of war, gun powder, or arms of any kind is prohibited under penalties of from one to ten thousand francs, except by special permission from the commissioner of the French Government. Within twenty four hours after arrival at Tahiti, every captain must present his manifest to the director of customs, giving a detailed statement of the spiritual liquors, ammunitions and arms of every kind on board his vessel. Any captain making a false declaration respecting prohibited goods or for the sale of which is restricted will be fined from one to five thousand francs. It is important that sea captains should thoroughly understand the above regulations, as by a late decision rendered at Tahiti, that government is not required to put on board of ships the port regulations.

C.P.I. Ed. Note: The text of this report is one item in a newspaper column headed "Society Islands," the rest of which is irrelevant.

[*For additional C.P.I. Ed. Note see TAHITI* 2.]

TAHITI 97

Daily Evening Traveller, Boston, Mass.
Jan. 28, 1853: 8, 2, 5
MBAt

FROM SOCIETY ISLANDS

In the Society Islands the French are reported as extending their power and influence rapidly. The French Governor has despatched an expedition against Navigator Islands to punish the natives for insulting missionaries and French traders.

C.P.I. Ed. Note: The text of this report is one item in a newspaper column headed "FROM SOCIETY ISLANDS," the rest of which is irrelevant. Complete text is used. . . .

"Society Islands (H.O. Charts Nos. 2023, 2005)—. . .

"The Windward Group consists of the islands Mehetia, Tahiti, Tetiaroa, and Tapuaemanu (Tabai Manua.) "The Leeward Group consists of Raiatea, Huahine, Tahaa, Bora-Bora, Maupiti, and the islets. Motu Iti or Tubai, Mopeha, Fenua Ura, and Motu One. *(H.O. Pub.* No. 166, Vol. II, 4th ed., 1933, P. 69.)

"The Society Islands lie approximately between Motu Iti (Tubai) Island, Lat. 16°, 17′ S., and Mehetia Island, Lat. 17°, 53′ S. and between Mehetia Island Long. 148°, 05′ W., and Fenua Ura (Scilly) Islands, Lon. 154°, 43′W., *(Ibid.* PP. 120, 72, 121, respectively).

Navigator Islands (Samoa) are Lat. 13°, 30′ S., to 14°, 30′S., Lon. 168°, 00′W. to 173°, 00′W. H.O. Chart No. 87. *(H.O. Pub.* No. 166, Vol. II, 4th ed., 1933, P. 253.)

Mt. Orohena, Tahiti. From a painting by C. F. Gordon Cumming.

TAHITI 98

Daily Evening Traveller, Boston, Mass.
Jan. 29, 1853: 8, 2, 1
MBAt

FROM THE SOCIETY ISLANDS

The last accounts from the Society Islands reports that the French are gradually strengthening their position and consolidating their power in that quarter, with the evident intention of building up a permanent colony and establishing a military force in garrison; have established a regular interior and foreign trade; constructed a marine railway for the repair of vessels, and are fast making a civilized country of Tahiti. Among other things they were about to despatch an expedition to the Navigators Islands; to chastise the inhabitants for alleged insults to the French missionaries and traders at those islands.

C.P.I. Ed. Note: The text of this report is an item in a newspaper column headed "FROM THE SOCIETY ISLANDS."

[*For additional C.P.I. Ed. Note see TAHITI 2.*]

TAHITI 99

Daily Evening Traveler, Boston, Mass.
Feb. 15, 1853: 8, 1, 8
MBAt

FROM TAHITI

Advices from Tahiti to the 15th of November had been received at San Francisco. The report of a revolt by the natives against the French authorities, brought by a previous arrival is contradicted, Not only was there no trouble, but the entire population were eager to respond to the call of the French Governor, to aid the completion of the new docks and railway, which were expected to render the island of Tahiti, and especially the port of Papetec, one of the centres of commerce of the Pacific.

The report that the French forces on the island amounted to only two or three hundred, is also contradicted. The force there is said to be more than sufficient to maintain order and the French authority in the Archipelago.

The American Barque, Asa Parker, Capt. Tessiers arrived at Papetec on the 4th of November, in 37 days from San Francisco, and the schooner China, Capt. Frost, on the 12th in 64 days from San Juan del Sud. The Ship, Callao and the schooner Emma Parker, were in port.—N.Y. Evening Post.

C.P.I. Ed. Note: The text of this report is one item in a newspaper column headed "FROM TAHITI," the rest of which is irrelevant. Complete text is used. . . .

Port of Papetec is probably meant for Papeete Harbor. Tahiti Island, Papeete Harbor is Lat. 17° 32′ S., Lon. 149° 34′ W. H.O. Chart, No. 1514. (*H.O. Pub.* No. 166, Vol. II, 4th Ed. 1933, P. 77.)

TAHITI 100

Boston Daily Advertiser
Feb. 16, 1853: 81, 2, 6
M

LEFT ETC.

At Tahiti, Nov. 26, schooner Fides, Carleton, 29 ds. from San Francisco, arrived 24th, China, Frost, (not Nash as misprinted), unc. sailed previously, barque Asa Parker, (from San Francisco, late Crothers, who died 6 ds. before the A. P. arrived at Tahiti) Sydney, N.S.W.

C.P.I. Ed. Note: The text of this report is one item in a newspaper column headed "LEFT, ETC.," the rest of which is irrelevant.

[*For additional C.P.I. Ed. Note see TAHITI 2.*]

TAHITI 101

Daily Evening Traveller, Boston, Mass.
Mar. 5, 1853: 8, 3, 1
MBAt

[Report in *Boston Post,* Mar. 7, 1853 (M) has 'Capt. Wine-penny' but is otherwise similar to first paragraph. Note differences in dates given on TAHITI 102.]

WHALERS

A letter from Capt. Wimpenny, of barque John A. Robb of Fair Haven, reports her at Tahiti, Sept.16th (so stated probable Jan.16th) sailed from Tahiti, Sept.16th, but returned on the 16th on account of the sickness of Capt. Wimpenny; and left on same day for a cruise of one week. Capt.Wimpenny says he shall take the season on Callao ground, and then leave for home.

A letter from Mr. Courtney, 2nd officer of barque J.E. Donnell of New Bedford, dated Honolulu Dec.21, states that all the oil had been saved from the ship A.H.Howland, of New Bedford, and that hopes were entertained of saving the ship also, but Mr. Courtney thinks she will not be got off. The J.E. Donnell was to leave for home in 2 or 3 days.

C.P.I. Ed. Note: The text of this report is one item in a newspaper column headed "WHALERS."

[*For additional C.P.I. Ed. Note see TAHITI 2.*]

TAHITI 102

Boston Daily Adv[ertiser]
Mar. 7, 1853: 81, 2, 5 & 6
M

WHALERS

At Tahiti Sept. 16, by letter from Capt. Wimpenny, John A. Robb, F. H. to leave same day for a cruise of a few weeks; had sld 14th, but returning 16th, on account of sickness of Capt. W., will take the season on Callao Ground, and then leave for home.

C.P.I. Ed. Note: The text of this report is one item in a newspaper column headed "WHALERS," the rest of which is irrelevant.

[For additional C.P.I. Ed. Note see TAHITI 2.]

TAHITI 103

Boston Daily Advertiser
May 1, 1853: 81, 2, 6
M

DISASTERS

A letter from Capt. Green, of brig. Emeline, of Boston, from Honolulu for New Bedford, dated Tahiti Jan. 26, states, that she was struck by a heavy easterly squall night of Jan. 21, lat. 13° 18′ S., long. 151° 59′, near Flint Island while under double reefs, and on soundings the pumps, twelve inches of water was found in the hold. After pumping three hours, could not keep her free by constant pumping. She put into Papetite, Tahiti, Jan. 25. A government pilot was on board, and run against the point of the weather reef while going at the rate of 6 knots. She struck forward of the main rigging, but did not stip. It injured her bottom badly, as the leak had increased very much. Would be hauled to the Gov't yard and discharged; and if necessary, go upon the railway.

C.P.I. Ed. Note: The text of this report is one item in a newspaper column headed "DISASTERS," the rest of which is irrelevant.

Papetite mentioned in text is probably meant for Papeete Harbor Tahiti.

Papeete Harbor Tahiti (17° 32′ S., 149° 34′ W. H.O. Chart No. 1514) is the most important and affords the best shelter of any harbor in the island of Tahiti. (*H.O. Pub.* No. 166, Vol. II, 4th ed., 1933, p. 77.)

TAHITI 104

Boston Daily Atlas
May 11, 1853: 21, 2, 6 & 7
MBr

Brig Emeline (of Boston), Green, from Sandwich Islands for New Bedford, was at Tahiti Jan. 26th, having put into that port leaky. The Captain reports on night of Jan. 21 lat. 18S, lon. 151 59W., was struck by a heavy squall, and on sounding the pumps found 12 inches of water in the wall and as the vessel could only be kept free with one pump constantly going, it was thought prudent to put into port. While going into Papeite, Tahiti, in charge of a pilot, she was run on a reef, which increased the leak very badly, but was got off, and would discharge for repairs. It was supposed her bottom was badly injured.

C.P.I. Ed. Note: The text of this report is one item in a newspaper column, the rest of which is irrelevant.

[*For additional C.P.I. Ed. Note see TAHITI 2.*]

Tahitian mourner. From Cook's *Voyages*.

TAHITI 105

New England Farmer, Boston, Mass.
May 14, 1853: 8, 2, 7
MH

DISASTERS AT SEA

Brig Emeline, (of Boston) Green, from Sandwich Islands for New Bedford, with a cargo of oil and bone, at Papeiti, Tahiti, on the 26th Jan., lat. 12°, 18′ S., 151°, 59′ W., was struck by a heavy squall, and on sounding the pumps soon after, found 12 inches of water in the well, and as the vessel could only be kept free with one pump constantly going, Capt. G. thought it advisable to bear up for the above port. While going in in charge of a pilot, she was run on a reef, but got off again, leaking considerably, and it was supposed that her bottom was much damaged. She would have to discharge for repairs.

C.P.I. Ed. Note: The text of this report is one item in a newspaper column headed "DISASTERS AT SEA," the rest of which is irrelevant.

[*For additional C.P.I. Ed. Note see TAHITI 103.*]

TAHITI 106

Boston Post
May 26, 1853: 42, 2, 5
M

DISASTER

Brigadier Emeline (of Boston) Green from Honolulu for New Bedford, which put into Tahiti in a leaky condition for repairs, had been abandoned to the French Authorities prior to the 14th of February. The following is Captain Green's reason for pursuing this course. I put into this port to stop a leak. I discharged my cargo, and stored it safe, and in good order, in the government yard, and hauled to the railway. While hauling up by the government officials she fell off the cradle, and there she has laid ever since a wreck, and bogged six inches. They can get her neither up or down, and I have today (14th February) abandoned her to the French government in a formal manner, and claim for vessel freight and consequented expenses $15000.

C.P.I. Ed. Note: The text of this report is an item in a newspaper column headed "DISASTER," . . . the rest of which is irrelevant.

[For additional C.P.I. Ed. Note see TAHITI 2.]

TAHITI 107

Boston Daily Advertiser
May 26, 1853: 81, 2, 5
M

DISASTERS

Brig Emeline, Green, from Honolulu, for New Bedford, before reported at Tahiti in distress, remained. Feb. 14. Her cargo had been discharged and stored in good order, in the government yard. While the government officials were hauling her upon the railway she fell off the cradle, and remained a wreck, hogged six inches. They could neither get her up or down, and Capt. G. had formally abandoned her to the French government, claiming for vessel, freight and incidental expenses $16,000.

C.P.I. Ed. Note: The text of this report is an item in a newspaper column headed "DISASTERS," the rest of which is irrelevant.

[*For additional C.P.I. Ed. Note see TAHITI 3.*]

TAHITI 108

Boston Post
May 26, 1853: 42, 2, 5
M

WHALERS

Ship James Edward, Luce, of New Bedford, was ashore at Tahiti February 14th. The captain writes: "On the 9th of February the ship James Edward took her anchor to proceed to sea with the land breeze. In the first place the pilot saw me on the outer buoy, and took off some of my copper. The ship then stood on the wind but fell off at the mouth of the passage. We let go both anchors, with 45 fathoms of chain on one side, and 30 fathoms on the other; the the ship struck her stern on the reef, dragged to about midship, and then rolled and struck heavily, where she lay about 25 minutes. With the assistance of boats, and whale ships, and men of war, we hauled her off, but could not keep her clear with five pumps; we got her into the wharf where she now lies full of water. I am making every exertion of roll her to save the ship and cargo."

C.P.I. Ed. Note: The text of this report is an item in a newspaper column headed "WHALERS," . . . the rest of which is irrelevant.

[*For additional C.P.I. Ed. Note see TAHITI 2.*]

TAHITI 109

Boston Daily Atlas
May 27, 1853: 26, 2, 6
MBr

A letter from Capt. Luce of ship James Edward, of New Bedford, published in the Honolulu Polynesian, dated Tahiti Feb.14, says—On the 9th the ship James Edward, under my command, took her anchor at 6 AM to proceed to sea with the land breeze in the first place the pilot ran me on the outer buoy, and took off some of my copper. The ship then stood on the wind, but fell off at the mouth of the passage. We let go both anchors, with 45 fathoms to chain on one, and 30 fathoms on the other, but the ship struck her stern on the reef, dragged to about amidships, and then rolled and struck heavily where she lay about 25 minutes.

With the assistance of boats of the whaleships and Men-of-War, who hauled her off, but we could not keep her clear with 5 pumps. We got her into the wharf, where she now lies full of water. I am making every exersion (sic) to roll her, to save the whip and cargo. The James Edward was last reported spoken Jan. 10th, with 170 bbls. sp. 900 do. wh. oil.

C.P.I. Ed. Note: The text of this report is one item in a news column, the rest of which is irrelevant.

[*For additional C.P.I. Ed. Note see TAHITI 2.*]

TAHITI 110

Boston Post
June 15, 1853: 42, 2, 4
M

DISASTERS &C.

A letter from Captain Davis, of ship Ellen Brooks, at Tahiti March 20th. reports his arrival at that port on the 10th. in a very leaky condition, having sprung a leak in a gale from S.E., on the 9th., in lat. 17° 38′ S., lon. 149° 33′ W. Capt. Davis says —immediately had a survey on the ship which ordered her to be hauled into school water, and her cargo be discharged. The pumps have been going constantly since the ship sprung a leak without freeing her; and I expect she will be condemned as the expense of repairing will amount to more than her value.

C.P.I. Ed. Note: The text of this report is an item in a newspaper column headed "DISASTERS," . . . the rest of which is irrelevant.

[*For additional C.P.I. Ed. Note see TAHITI 2.*]

TAHITI 111

Daily Evening Traveler, Boston, Mass.
June 24, 1853: 8, 1, 7
MBAt

SOCIETY ISLANDS

The Placer Times publishes a letter from E. Wakemen, Captain of the Steamship New Orleans, at Tahiti, Society Islands, bound to Sydney, N.S.W. from San Francisco, in which he speaks in very strong terms of the inconveniences of stopping at the Society Islands. He says, "I should recommend all sail craft to go straight to Sydney, west of the Feejees; touch at Honolulu, where everything can be had cheap and in one day; and if necessary touch at the Feejees or Navigators where two days is sufficient to get all that was wanted. Here nothing can be had but water. Anchorage is charged by the French Governor at the rate of ten dollars a vessel. Water can be had, but it is attended with much difficulty, and it would take a long time to water a steamer. Nothing can be got in the way of the ship's supplies. Pork is from 10 to 20 cents per pound on the foot. The destitute condition of the Island is owing to the French monopolizing everything. The King was about to be baptized in the Catholic faith. We are here all well. The Monumental City sailed a week ago. There are about one thousand tons of English coal here—it has been exposed to the sun for ten years and is good for nothing. But we like the Monumental City, will have to take it, and pay about thirty dollars a ton, put on board. Labor here is $1.00 per day. The railway, which it was said could take up a ship of nine hundred tons, cannot take up a brig of two hundred."

C.P.I. Ed. Note: The text of this report is one item in a newspaper column headed "SOCIETY ISLANDS," the rest of which is irrelevant. Complete text is used. . . .

[For additional C.P.I. Ed. Note see TAHITI 2.]

TAHITI 112

Boston Daily Atlas
July 13, 1853: 22, 2, 8
MBr

Sch. Emma Packer, Ashby, at San Francisco, from Tahiti fell in with a Chinese or Japanese junk May 30, 1853, lat. 28 50 n., lon. 158 46 W., boarded her and found she was waterlogged, dismasted, rudder gone, etc., found one man with signs of life, and three others dead in the hold; took him on board, and after careful attention he came to and recovered. Capt. A. was unable to learn anything from him, as he could not speak one word of English.

C.P.I. Ed. Note: The text of this report is one item in a newspaper column headed "TAHITI."

[*For additional C.P.I. Ed. Note see TAHITI 3.*]

TAHITI 113

Boston Daily Advertiser
July 27, 1853: 82, 2, 7
M

DISASTERS

Ships Ellen Brooks, Davis, from Honolulu, and Emily Taylor, Riddle, from do, both for New Bedford, before reported, put into Tahiti, leaky, had been sold prior to May 2. Their cargoes would be forwarded to the United States. The Brig. Emeline from do for do, before reported, put into Tahiti, and condemned, had been got on the lock, and found to be in good condition.

C.P.I. Ed. Note: The text of this report is an item in a newspaper column headed "DISASTERS," . . . the rest of which is irrelevant.

[For additional C.P.I. Ed. Note see TAHITI 2.]

TAHITI 114

Boston Post
Aug. 2, 1853: 43, 2, 4
M

WHALERS

A letter from Capt. Luce of ship James Edward of New Bedford dated Tahiti April 28th, reports touched at that port April 23d, ship Elizabeth Barker, New Bedford, from New Zealand with 700 bbls, bound on the line. Sld from do April 8th, ship Rodman allyn N.B. for Actic Ocean. All well. Capt. Luce states that the James Edward would complete her repairs about the 1st May, and take freight of oil and bone for New Bedford.

C.P.I. Ed. Note: The text of this report is an item in a newspaper column headed "WHALERS," . . . the rest of which is irrelevant.

[*For additional C.P.I. Ed. Note see TAHITI 2.*]

TAHITI 115

Boston Post
Aug. 2, 1853: 43, 2, 4
M

DISASTERS &C.

Ship Ellen Brooks, before reported at Tahiti in distress had discharged her cargo on the 28th April, and would hove out for examination. It was doubtful whether she would be repaired. The Emily Taylor, (before reported) was discharging preparatory to heaving out for examination. (The report that these two ships had been sold at Tahiti is therefore incorrect.)

C.P.I. Ed. Note: The text of this report is one item in a news column headed "DISASTERS," the rest of which is irrelevant. Complete text is used. . . .

[*For additional C.P.I. Ed. Note see TAHITI 2.*]

TAHITI 116

Boston Daily Adv[ertiser]
Nov. 12, 1853: 82, 2, 8
M

WHALERS

Ar. at New Bedford, 11th, James Edward, Luce, Tahiti, July 6, with the cargo of bone from brig Emeline, (condemned at Tahiti); 40,000 lbs. do from ship Eilen Brooks, The J.E. has no oil on board, having sent home 170 bbls. sp. 530 do. wh. and 15,000 lbs. bone, and sold 350 bbls. wh. Sept. 25, signalized Cortez, Stetson, N.B. bound S.

C.P.I. Ed. Note: The text of this report is one item in a newspaper column headed "WHALERS," the rest of which is irrelevant. Complete text is used. . . .

[*For additional C.P.I. Ed. Note see TAHITI 2.*]

TAHITI 117

Boston Daily Adv[ertiser]
Nov. 14, 1853: 82, 2, 6
M

[Similar report in *Boston Post,* Nov. 14, 1853 (M).]

DISASTERS

A letter from Tahiti Aug. 10 reports that ship Orpheus, West, from Honolulu for New Bedford, with oil and bone, had finally been condemned. Capt. West had sent to San Francisco for a ship to take the cargo forward.

C.P.I. Ed. Note: The text of this report is one item in a newspaper column headed "DISASTERS," the rest of which is irrelevant.

[For additional C.P.I. Ed. Note see TAHITI 2.]

TAHITI 118

Boston Post
Feb. 14, 1854: 44, 2, 6
M

WHALERS

A letter from ship Euphrates of N.B. reports her at Tahiti, Nov 18, put into land Capt. Peakes who was hurt by a line while fast to a whale. The Euprates had taken 3 sp. whs. since leaving the Sandwich Islands. Another letter from Capt. Peakes states that he had recovered and joined the ship Nov 29. Would cruise among the islands till Feb.

C.P.I. Ed. Note: The text of this report is an item in a newspaper column headed "WHALERS," . . . the rest of which is irrelevant.

[*For additional C.P.I. Ed. Note see TAHITI 2.*]

TAHITI 119

Boston Post
Apr. 3, 1854: 41, 2, 6
M

WHALERS

A letter from Capt. Cleone of New Bedford, dated Tahiti Jan. 18, states that he had put in 3 weeks previous, for a new mainmast, having sprung the old one in a gale of wind, was ready for sea 18th bound to Ochotas sea via Guam. Had taken 82 bbls since leaving Sandwich Islands.

C.P.I. Ed. Note: The text of this report is an item in a newspaper column headed "WHALERS," . . .

[*For additional C.P.I. Ed. Note see TAHITI 2.*]

TAHITI 120

Boston Post
Apr. 3, 1854: 41, 2, 6
M

WHALERS

A letter from Capt. Kempton of ship Waverly of N. Bedford dated Tahiti Jan 26, states that she was taking 1000 bbls of oil and would sail for home in a few days.

C.P.I. Ed. Note: The text of this report is one item in a newspaper column headed "WHALERS," the rest of which is irrelevant.

[For additional C.P.I. Ed. Note see TAHITI 2.]

TAHITI 121

Salem Gazette
June 13, 1854: No. 47, 1, 3
MSaE

TAHITI

News from Tahiti is to the 2d of April:—
On the nights of the 27th and 28th, a portion of the crew and passengers of the American ship Auckland, mutined and began to pillage and try to get at the liquors. The captain sent for the police, who after some difficulty, took all the mutineers, imprisoned them, and gave the captain peaceable possession of his vessel. He afterwards took the mutineers on board.

TAHITI 122

Lynn News
July 14, 1854: 2, 2, 5
MLy

The American barque Gay Head for Boston was at Tahiti where the Golden Age called for coal.

C.P.I. Ed. Note: The text of this report is an item in a newspaper column, . . . the rest of which is irrelevant.

[*For additional C.P.I. Ed. Note see TAHITI 51.*]

TAHITI 123

Daily Evening Traveller, Boston, Mass.
Dec. 6, 1854: 10, 2, 1
MB

FROM THE SOCIETY ISLANDS

Advices from Tahiti to the 13th of August have been received at San Francisco. The frightful epidemic which had been raging amongst the native population appeared to be drawing to a drawing to a close. Whilst it had entirely spared the white race, the deaths had been double amongst the natives in one district, that of Papara, one-seventh of the population having been carried off. The schools were deserted.—Trade was suspended; provisions became scarce, and the inhabitants were forced to depend on supplies from the government.

The proportions of victims at the Windward Islands is greater even than at Tahiti, were affairs, bad as they have been, were beginning to wear an improved aspect.

C.P.I. Ed. Note: The text of this report is one item in a news column headed "FROM THE SOCIETY ISLANDS," the rest of which is irrelevant.

[*For additional C.P.I. Ed. Note see TAHITI 2.*]

Tahitian young men, circa 1880.

Tahitian women, circa 1880.

TAHITI 124

The Friend, Honolulu
Feb. 1, 1855: 12, 16, 3
MSaP

[Report in *Daily Evening Traveller,* Boston, Mar. 14, 1855 (MB) is similar but gives 'lon. 102° W', ends at '. . . hear more of this matter', gives 'San Francisco Herald, Feb. 16' as source, and begins with following additional introduction: 'We have received intelligence by the St. Mary of the safety of the clipper-ship John Land, Capt. Howes, from Boston, via Valparaiso, for this port, for whose safety fears have been entertained some time since. The whaleship George Howland arrived at Honolulu Jan. 27, and reported her as having touched at Tahiti in distress, and the crew in a state of mutiny. Everything, however, was subsequently arranged, and she was to have sailed soon for this port. . . .']

MEMORANDA

The following report is given by Capt. Bryant, of the whaleship George Howland, recently arrived from the Marquesas:—

"The whale ship D.M. Hall, of Fall River, Capt. Pratt, fell in with the ship John Land, Capt. Percival, in lat. 4N., long 02 W., with a signal of distress at her fore-topsail-yard-arm. Capt. Pratt went on board and found her leaking 7,000 or 8,000 strokes an hour. Capt. Percival asked for assistance, and offered $5,000 if the bark would lie by him 24 hours, which Capt. Pratt refused. Capt. Percival said money was hardly a consideration if Pratt would assist him in getting into port. Capt. Pratt refused to do any thing for the assistance of the John Land, unless she was abandoned to him. After some time taken to consider this proposition it was acceded to by Capt. Percival The crews were transferred.—Capt. Percival, officers and crew, going on board the bark. The bark's crew after 48 hours trial, found they could not keep her free alone, when Capt. Pratt made a new contract with Capt. Percival, to the effect that if he would give him a cargo for his bark, he would re-deliver up the ship, and the two crews would join in working her into port; on which they took out cargo to the amount, in their judgement, of $50,000. The weather coming on bad, they stopped. After this the crews mutinied, and those on the ship hailed the bark, and demanded her to heave-to, which was done. They came on board and demanded the papers which conveyed the ship back to Percival, and obtained them. This put the whole control again into the hands of Pratt, who proceeded against the wishes of Percival, to Nukuhiva, one of the Marquesas Islands, where no authorities existed to take cognisance of the matter.

On arrival, Capt. Percival asked assistance from the French, to take charge of his men, who were in a state of mutiny.—Some where put in irons and taken onshore before the governor, but were finally released by his order, (who had a consultation with Capt. Pratt,) for which he probably received a gratification.

The foregoing is the report received from both parties by Capt. Bryant. Capt. Percival applied to Capt. Bryant for assistance, which was offered to the extent of his power, by discharging his ship and lighting the John Land, for the purpose of finding the leak, which a diver reported as under her forefeet. Capt. Pratt threw impediments in the way, but would consent to it on condition that the crew agreed. They probably were tampered with, as they would allow it to be done.

Up to this time, Capt. Percival and officers were on the bark, but it became Capt. Pratt's policy for Capt. Percival to command, (nominally) his ship to Tahiti, and he went on board without his officers or passengers, or anyone who could sympathise or advise with him,—constrained to do so, as Pratt said, by the crew. The bark and the ship sailed for Tahiti previous to Capt. Bryant's leaving. Capt. Percival had been so harrassed and troubled by the conduct of the crews, in destroying cargo, damaging cabin, and other mischievous acts, that at the time his mind was almost gone."

The above is the report of Capt. Bryant; and we give it in his own language, without pretending to be cognizant of the facts of the case, of our own knowledge. If, however, the facts of the case are as stated, it seems to be a case of refusal to offer aid in circumstances of great peril, which we can hardly believe any captain and crew, of ordinary humanity, could have been guilty of. But if the story proves to be true, we have not the slightest doubt that the indignation of the world would be most justly exhibited towards the captain and crew of the bark, in such a manner as to drive them in disgrace from the profession. As the vessels had sailed for Tahiti, we shall probably hear more of this matter, and shall hold our columns open for Capt. Pratt to explain his conduct if he sees fit to do so.

The John Land was bound from Boston to San Francisco, with a full cargo of Merchandise.

[*Longitude given, '02W.' is a misprint for '102W'. For C.P.I. Ed. Note see TAHITI 86.*]

TAHITI 125

Boston Post
Mar. 15, 1855: 46, 2, 5
M

DISASTERS &C.

Clipper ship John Land, Percival, from Boston, via Valparaiso, for whose safety fears have been entertained arrived at Tahiti prev. to Jan. 29, in distress. The following report is given in the Honolulu Polynesian, furnished by Capt. Bryant of whaleship Gideon Howland, at that port from Marquesas, "The whaleship D.M. Hall of Fall River, Capt. Pratt, fell in with the ship John Land, Capt. Percival in lat. 4° N., lon. 102° W., with a signal of distress at her foretopsail yard arm. Capt. Pratt went on board and found her leaking 7000 or 8000 strokes an hour. Capt. Percival asked for assistance and offered $5000 if the bark would lie by him 24 hours which Capt. Pratt refused. Capt. Percival said money was hardly a consideration, if Pratt would assist him in getting into port. Capt. Pratt refused to do anything for the assistance of John Land, unless she was abandoned to him. After some time taken to consider this proposition, it was acceded to by Captain Percival. The crews were transferred —Capt. Percival, officers and crew going on board the bark. The bark's crew after 48 hours trial found they could not keep her free alone, when Capt. Pratt made a new contract with Capt. Percival to the effect that if he would give him a cargo for his bark, he would redeliver up the ship, and the two crews would join in working her into port; upon which they took out cargo to the amount in their judgement $50,000. The weather coming on bad they stopped, after this the crews mutinized (sic) and those on the ship hailed the bark and demanded her to heave to which was done. They came on board and demanded the papers which conveyed the ship back to Percival and obtained them. This put the whole control again in the hands of Pratt who proceeded against the wishes of Percival to Nukuhiva one of the Marquesas Islands, where no authorities existed to take cognizance of the matter. On arrival Capt. Percival asked assistance from the French to take charge of his men who were in a state of mutiny.

Some were put in irons and taken on shore before the governor, but were finally released by his order, (who had a consultation with Capt. Pratt) for which he probably received a consideration. The foregoing is the report received from both parties by Capt. Bryant. Capt. Percival applied to Capt. Bryant for assistance, which was offered to the extent of his power, by discharging his ship and lightening the John Land for the purpose of finding the leak, which a diver reported as under her forefoot. Capt. Pratt threw impediments in the way, but would consent to it on condition that the crew agreed. They were probably tampered with, as they would not allow it to be done. Up to this time Capt. Percival and officers were on the bark, but it became Capt. Pratt's policy for Capt. Percival to command (nominally) his ship to Tahiti and went on board without his officers or passengers. The bark and the ship sailed for Tahiti previous to Capt. Bryant's leaving. Capt. Percival had been so harrassed (sic) and troubled by the conduct of his crew, in destroying cargo, damaging cabin, and other mischievous acts at the time his mind was almost gone.

The U.S. Consul at Tahiti and Capt. Dorwin, of U.S. sloop Portsmouth, had interested themselves in saving cargo, &c. for waste. She was discharging at the last accounts, and Capt. Pratt had commenced selling the cargo against the protest of Capt. Percival.

C.P.I. Ed. Note: The text of this report is one item in a newspaper column headed "Disasters," the rest of which is irrelevant. Complete text is used. . . .

[*For additional C.P.I. Ed. Note see TAHITI 2.*]

TAHITI 126

Boston Post
Mar. 26, 1855: 46, 2, 5
M

DISASTER &c.

A gentleman who was a passenger in ship John Land and who had left the ship at Tahiti, and had arrived in San Francisco, states that Capt. Percival was discharging the ship and would heave her out. He had all the crew in irons in the fort. Capt. Pratt of the bark D.M.Hall, was still in port, and threatened to follow the ship John Land, when she sailed from Tahiti, to try and take possession of her for imaginary services rendered in getting her into port.

C.P.I. Ed. Note: The text of this report is one item in a news column headed "DISASTER," the rest of which is irrelevant. Complete text is used. . . .

[*For additional C.P.I. Ed. Note see TAHITI 2.*]

TAHITI 127

Boston Daily Advertiser
Apr. 2, 1855: 85, 1, 5
M

DISASTERS

Whaleship America, of Edgartown, at Tahiti Jan. 5, repairing, had struck upon a sunken rock, off Cape Maria, no date, &c.

C.P.I. Ed. Note: The text of this report is one item in a newspaper column headed "DISASTERS," the rest of which is irrelevant.

[*For additional C.P.I. Ed. Note see TAHITI 2.*]

TAHITI 128

Boston Post
Apr. 14, 1855: 46, 1, 3
M

WHALERS

A letter from Capt. Jernegan, of ship American, of Edgartown, reports her at Tahiti, Dec. 28th. repg. He had discharged his oil (1700 gals) and sent it home per ship Marengo, of New Bedford. He was caulking in order to heave out, having been on some sunken rocks off Cape Maria. Would sail on a sp whale cruise between seasons.

C.P.I. Ed. Note: The text of this report is an item in a newspaper column headed "WHALERS," . . . the rest of which is irrelevant.

[*For additional C.P.I. Ed. Note see TAHITI 2.*]

TAHITI 129

Essex County Mercury, Salem, Mass.
June 13, 1855: 16, 4, 6
MSaE

MARINE JOURNAL

The ship John Land had arrived from Tahiti, with a number of
her crew in irons for mutiny. She was immediately libelled (sic)
by the whaler "D.M.Hall". An examination of the charge of
mutiny was gone into the U.S. District Court, when the Judge
decided that as the captain of the vessel had virtually abandoned
her and lost all control, the crew had a right to select their own
captain as they did by vote. They were therefore discharged.
Advices from the Sandwich Islands report that the British frigates President and Alceste, sloop-of-war Dido, and steamer
Brisk, had all left that place for the north; their supposed desti-
nation being Petropolowski.

C.P.I. Ed. Note: The text of this report is an item in a newspaper column headed "MARINE JOURNAL," the rest of which is irrelevant. Complete text is used. . . .

[For additional C.P.I. Ed. Note see TAHITI 2.]

TAHITI 130

The Friend, Honolulu
Mar. 31, 1857: 14, 23, 2
MSaP

Arrived at Tahiti, Feb. 1st, the captain and crew of the three masted schooler *Archimedes,* of Sydney, lost on the 24th of Jan., about 600 miles S.E. of Tahiti, bound from Valparaiso to Sydney with a cargo of flour. The capt. and crew come to Tahiti in their boat.

C.P.I. Ed. Note: The text of this report is one item in a news column headed "MARINE JOURNAL," the rest of which is irrelevant.

The exact position of wreck is not given in text. About 600 miles S.E. of Tahiti, as it reads in text places it approximately at 25° oo′ S., 143° oo′ W.

TAHITI 131

Boston Daily Advertiser
May 1, 1857: 89, 1, 3
M

WHALERS

Touched at Tahiti Jan. 10, Maria Theresa, Davis, N.B. lay off and on to land Capt. Davis, (sick with billious (sic) fever). The ship sld. the same day in charge of the mate; Returned Feb. 2, and sld. 3d. for New Zealand, and home. Capt. Davis had recovered so as to go in the ship.

C.P.I. Ed. Note: The text of this report is one item in a newspaper column headed "WHALERS."

[For additional C.P.I. Ed. Note see TAHITI 2.]

TAHITI 132

Boston Daily Traveler
July 15, 1857: 50, 8, 5
M

WHALERS

A letter from Capt. Peakes, of barque Virginia, N.B. reports her at Otaheite, Society Islands, Apl 26, with 200 bbls sp oil all told, bound on a cruise and would be at the Paita in October.

C.P.I. Ed. Note: The text of this report is an item in a newspaper column headed "WHALERS," . . . the rest of which is irrelevant.

[*For additional C.P.I. Ed. Note see TAHITI 3.*]

TAHITI 133

Boston Daily Journal
Aug. 1, 1857: 25, 3, 2
MHi

[Similar report in *Boston Daily Traveler*, Aug. 3, 1857 (M).]

WHALERS

A letter from the second officer of ship Elizabeth, Pierce, of New Bedford, reports her at Tahiti April 30, with 550 bbls sp oil, bound to the Equator; had discharged the first officer.

C.P.I. Ed. Note: The text of this report is an item in a newspaper column headed "WHALERS," . . . the rest of which is irrelevant.

[*For additional C.P.I. Ed. Note see TAHITI 61.*]

TAHITI 134

Boston Daily Traveler
Oct. 6, 1857: 11, 4, 7
M

MARINE JOURNAL

Arrived at Pepeete, Tahiti, May 2, Elliot C. Cowden, Bailey, of Dartmouth, last from Sydney, whole voyage 330 sp, on board 275 sp; season's catch 90 sp; 24th, Matilda Sears, Wing, of Dartmouth, last from Bay of Islands, whole voyage, 400 sp. season's catch 250 sp; 28th, Monticello, Baker, of Nantucket, last from Strong's Island, whole voyage, 1200 sp; on board 1200 sp; season's catch 250 sp; 29th, Isaac Howland, Hobbs, of New Bedford, last from Strong's Islands, whole voyage 650 sp, on board, 300 sp, season's catch, 50 sp.

C.P.I. Ed. Note: The text of the above report is one item in a newspaper column headed "MARINE JOURNAL," the rest of which is irrelevant.

Complete text is used. . . .

Strong's (Kusie, Ualan) or Strong Island, one of the Caroline Islands, was discovered in 1804 by Capt. Crozer, commanding an American ship who gave it the name of Strong Island after the governor of Massachusetts (Ibid. [Findlay] p. 975). Strong Island is at northeast end is 5°, 22′N., 163°, 01′ E. H.O. Chart No. 5420. (*H.O. Pub.* No. 165, Vol. I, 4th ed., 1938, P. 522.)

[*For additional C.P.I. Ed. Note see TAHITI 3.*]

TAHITI 135

Daily Evening Traveller, Boston, Mass.
Mar. 18, 1858: 13, 4, 3
MBAt

WHALERS

A letter from the first officer of ship Caravan, Bragg, of New
Bedford, reports her at sea Dec. 27th, no lat. etc., bound to Tahiti to procure potatoes, and thence to the Sandwich Islands.
Had taken 450 bbls. wh. oil this season. (This sets at rest all
fears for the safety of the Caravan, which was supposed to have
been lost.)

C.P.I. Ed. Note: The text of this report is one item in a newspaper column headed "WHALERS."

[For additional C.P.I. Ed. Note see TAHITI 2.]

TAHITI 136

Boston Daily Journal
Oct. 29, 1858: 26, 2, 2
MHi

DISGRACEFUL CONDUCT OF THE U.S. CONSUL AT TAHITI
The San Francisco Bulletin says it has received repeated accounts of the disgraceful conduct of Henry Owner, U.S. Consul at Tahiti. He is drunk a large portion of the time, and has repeatedly been picked up in the streets intoxicated, even in his consular uniform, and carried home. Lately in one of his drunken sprees, he fell from a bridge into a gutter, and striking his face upon a stone, was picked up not only dripping with filth, but with a broken nose. On another occasion some sailors found him in a taropatch and carried him to the calaboose as a "drunk". He however was not confined as the French officer recognized in him the Consul of the United States.

Capt. Knowles, of the ship Wild Wave, lost in the South Seas, went to Owner for the purpose of having the usual protest in such cases noted and extended—a proceeding necessary to obtain the insurance. Owner kept the log-book six days, refusing to give it up, but also further annoying Capt. Knowles, returned it, demanding the modest price of $199.70 for the papers which he had made out, whereas the legal price for such documents ought not to have exceeded $10.

C.P.I. Ed. Note: The text of the above report is a copy of an article in a newspaper column headed "DISGRACEFUL CONDUCT OF THE U.S. CONSUL AT TAHITI." . . .

[*For additional C.P.I. Ed. Note see TAHITI 2.*]

TAHITI 137

Boston Daily Traveler
Jan. 24, 1859: 3, 3, 5
M

WHALERS

At Tahiti, Nov. 10th, Ship Caravan, Bragg, N. B., from Arctic Ocean, no report of oil; barque Harvest, Charry, F. H., last from Honolulu, both vessels were repairing and recoppering. Capt. Bragg of the Caravan, has been in poor health, and while at the North had been laboring under a species of insanity, during which he twice attempted suicide, but was prevented by his officers.

C.P.I. Ed. Note: The text of the above report is a copy of an item in a newspaper column headed "WHALERS," . . . the rest of which is irrelevant.

[*For additional C.P.I. Ed. Note see TAHITI 2.*]

TAHITI 138

Boston Daily Advertiser
Jan. 31, 1859: 93, 1, 5
M

WHALERS

A letter from Capt. Bragg, of ship Caravan, N.B. reports her at Tahiti, Nov. 10, repg. bows, &c., to sail in a few days for New Zealand.

C.P.I. Ed. Note: The text of this report is an item in a newspaper column headed "WHALERS." . . .

[*For additional C.P.I. Ed. Note see TAHITI 2.*]

TAHITI 139

Boston Daily Journal
Mar. 16, 1859: 27, 1, 8
MHi

WHALERS

A letter from Capt. Bragg, of ship Caravan, of New Bedford, dated Tahiti, Nov. 20, 1858, reports her ready for sea, having repaired, and would sail same day on a cruise.

C.P.I. Ed. Note: The text of the above report is a copy of an item in a newspaper column headed "WHALERS." . . .

[*For additional C.P.I. Ed. Note see TAHITI 2.*]

TAHITI 140

Boston Daily Traveler
Mar. 31, 1859: 3, 2, 8
M

WHALERS

A letter from Capt. Gifford, of ship Ocean, of N.B. reports her on and off at Tahiti Dec. 22nd, with 1600 bbls. sp. oil bound to New Zealand, reports, no date, barque Lafayette, Ray, N.B. 20 mos. out, 500 sp.

C.P.I. Ed. Note: The text of the above report is a copy of an item in a newspaper column headed "WHALERS." . . .

[*For additional C.P.I. Ed. Note see TAHITI 2.*]

TAHITI 141

Boston Daily Journal
May 28, 1859: 27, 1, 8
MHi

WHALERS

A letter from Capt. Gifford, of ship Hope, of New Bedford, dated Tahiti Feb 24, reports her put in for repairs, having been on a reef at Ascension. Was discharging cargo to heave out. Had shipped 165 spm by the Emily Morgan, Reports spoke Feb 1, on New Zealand, Norman, Ray, Nant. 150 bbls since leaving Sandwich Islands, Ocean, Gifford N.B. 1900 spm.

C.P.I. Ed. Note: The text of this report is one item in a news column headed "WHALERS," the rest of which is irrelevant.

[*For additional C.P.I. Ed. Note see TAHITI 2.*]

TAHITI 142

Boston Post
July 29, 1859: 55, 3, 4
M

WHALERS

Sailed from Tahiti, May 27, bark Alabama, Coffin, of Nantucket, with 1000 bbls. sp oil to cruise and home.

C.P.I. Ed. Note: The text of this report is one item in a newspaper column headed "WHALERS," the rest of which is irrelevant.

[*For additional C.P.I. Ed. Note see TAHITI 2.*]

TAHITI 143

Boston Daily Journal
Aug. 3, 1859: 27, 1, 8
MHi

WHALERS

A letter from Capt. Coffin, of barque Alabama of Nantucket, reports her at Tahiti, May 19, leaking—would stop leak and leave for home about May 28, with 1175 bbls spm oil on board.

C.P.I. Ed. Note: The text of this report is an item in a newspaper column headed "WHALERS." . . .

[*For additional C.P.I. Ed. Note see TAHITI 2.*]

TAHITI 144

Boston Daily Traveler
Nov. 19, 1859: 15, 3, 5
M

WHALERS

A letter from Capt. Bates, of barque Joshua Bragdon, of New Bedford, dated Tahiti, Aug. 30, reports her with 700 bbls. sp. oil, all well.

C.P.I. Ed. Note: The text of this report is one item in a newspaper column headed "WHALERS," the rest of which is irrelevant.

[*For additional C.P.I. Ed. Note see TAHITI 2.*]

TAHITI 145

Boston Daily Traveler
Apr. 7, 1860: 16, 3, 3
M

WHALERS

Ar. at New Bedford 6th, Ship Kutosoff, Wing, from Artic Ocean, Honolulu Nov. 15, Tahiti Dec. 15, with 1450 bbls. wh. oil and 13,000 lbs. bone on board. Sent home on the voyage 70 bbls. Sp., 1450 do wh. oil, and 21,400 lbs. bone. Reports spoke off Staten Land, Jan. 23rd, Ship Braganza, Turner, of New Bedford, clean.

C.P.I. Ed. Note: The text of this report is one item in a newspaper column headed "WHALERS," the rest of which is irrelevant.

[For additional C.P.I. Ed. Note see TAHITI 2.]

TAHITI 146

Boston Daily Traveler
Apr. 11, 1860: —, —, —
M

WHALERS

Ship Omega, Sanborn, at Honolu, last from Tahiti, reports that the Julian, Winegar, New Bedford, had arrived at Tahiti, leaking badly, discharged cargo, hove down and was repairing. Barque Warren, Miller, and Ship Splended, Pierson, had also arrived at Tahiti, both leaking, and would have to repair. The Omega left Tahiti Jan. 5, and put into Honolulu to repair, the ship leaking about 3000 strokes per day. Dec. 15, lon.160 W., lat. 21 S. Saw Ship Wm. Thompson, Childs, cutting into a large sperm whale. Dec. 28, lat. 15, lon.150. Spoke Barque Fanny, Boodry, bound home. The Omega has taken nothing since leaving Honolulu last Fall. Advices from Tahiti are, that whaler's bills were ruling at 25 per cent discount.

C.P.I. Ed. Note: The text of this report is one item in a newspaper column headed "WHALERS," the rest of which is irrelevant. Complete text is used. . . .

[*For additional C.P.I. Ed. Note see TAHITI 2.*]

TAHITI 147

Boston Daily Journal
Apr. 11, 1860: 28, 1, 8
MHi

DISASTERS, ETC.

Ship Modern Times, Overton, from McKean's Island Aug. 6 for Hampton Road, sailed from Tahiti Jan. 5. She had been detained at Tahiti over two months repairing, having sprung masts and lost spurs in a gale.

C.P.I. Ed. Note: The text of the above report is one item in a newspaper column "DISASTERS, ETC.," the rest of which is irrelevant. Complete text is used. . . . McKean's Island mentioned is probably meant for McKean Island. McKean Island is lat. 3°, 37′ S., lon. 174°, 07′ W. H.O. Chart No. 125. *(H.O. Pub.* 166, Vol. II, 4th ed., 1933, P. 472.)

[For additional C.P.I. Ed. Note see TAHITI 2.]

TAHITI 148

Boston Daily Traveler
Apr. 30, 1860: 16, 4, 4
M

[Report in *Boston Daily Journal,* Apr. 30, 1860 (MHi) is similar to second paragraph except for having '8000 strokes' for '800 strokes.'']

WHALERS

A letter from Capt. Luce of Barque Emily, N.B., reports her at Tahiti, Feb. 2, with 800 bbls. sp and 300 do wh oil all told—was bound on Off Shore Ground and the Line for a long cruise, and then to the Coast.

A letter from Capt. West of barque Frances Henrietta, N.B., reports her at Tahiti, Jan. 31, 1860—Ar. 18th. leaking 800 strokes per day—had recaulked and sheathed her upper works. The ship was then tight and ready for sea, waiting favorable wind. Expecting to be at home about the 1st. of June.

C.P.I. Ed. Note: The text of this report is one item in a newspaper column headed "WHALERS," the rest of which is irrelevant. Complete text is used. . . .

[For additional C.P.I. Ed. Note see TAHITI 2.]

TAHITI 149

Boston Daily Traveler
Nov. 9, 1860: 16, 4, 2
M

WHALERS

At Tahiti Aug. 25, barque Union, Hedges, Sag Harbor, to cruise home, oil not reported.

C.P.I. Ed. Note: The text of this report is one item in a newspaper column headed "WHALERS," the rest of which is irrelevant.

[For additional C.P.I. Ed. Note see TAHITI 2.]

TAHITI 150

Boston Post
Feb. 28, 1861: 58, 3, 4
MB

A letter from Capt. Winegar, of ship Julian, of New Bedford, reports her as having touched at Tahiti Nov. 9th, for men bound to New Zealand.

C.P.I. Ed. Note: The text of this report is one item in a news column headed "MARINE JOURNAL," the rest of which is irrelevant.

[*For additional C.P.I. Ed. Note see TAHITI 2.*]

TAHITI 151

Boston Daily Evening Transcript
Jan. 8, 1863: 35, 4, 2
MBAt

PYRAMIDS IN TAHITI

Our report over, the Tahitian invited me to follow him, and leading the way through an entangled glen amidst rocks and waterfalls he came upon an extensive pile of stone work in the form of a low pyramid, having a flight of steps on each side. My surprise was great at the sight of such a structure in an island where the best houses are built of bamboo. I found that on pacing the building it was about 260 ft. long by about 90 ft. broad, and from 40 ft. to 50 ft. high. The foundation of this remarkable structure consisted of rockstones, the steps being of coral, squared with considerable neatness, and laid with the utmost regularity, and the entire mass appeared as compact as if it had been erected by Europeans. The size of many of the blocks is remarkable but they bear no marks of the chisel, nor is it easy to understand how they were transported by savages unacquainted with mechanical science from the seashore to their present position. Who could have raised this imposing mass, was a question that involuntarily arose in the mind. It is scarcely possible that the present race of islanders, or even their ancestors could have performed such a task. They are unacquainted with mechanics or the use of iron tools to shape their stones with. From all that could be gleaned from the guide and from other natives afterwards, I felt convinced that they knew nothing of its history, for, as it was beyond their comprehension, they naturally said it was built by the gods and was as old as the world.

(Colburn's United Service Magazine.)

C.P.I. Ed. Note: The text of this report is one item in a news column headed "PYRAMIDS IN TAHITI," the rest of which is irrelevant.

[*For additional C.P.I. Ed. Note see TAHITI* 2.]

Making fire, Tahiti.

Tahitian sorcerer's lamp.

Double stone figure, Tahiti.   Peabody Museum of Salem.

TAHITI 152

Daily Evening Traveler, Boston, Mass.
Jun. 18, 1864: 20, 4, 3
M

WHALERS

A letter from Capt. Fisher, of barque John Wells, of N.B., reports her at Oteheite, Society Islands, March 31, clean, having taken nothing since leaving Sydney, N.S.W. Reports March 3, in lat. 28° S. lon. 170° W. experienced a typhoon, and ran under bar poles 17 hours; sprung a leak of 420 strokes per hour, lost starboard and waist boats, and sustained other damages.

C.P.I. Ed. Note: The text of this report is an item in a newspaper column headed "WHALERS," . . . the rest of which is irrelevant.

[*For additional C.P.I. Ed. Note see TAHITI 2.*]

TAHITI 153

Daily Evening Standard, New Bedford, Mass.
Oct. 31, 1864: 15, 3, 2
MNBedf

[Similar report in *Boston Daily Journal*, Nov. 1, 1864 (MH).
Report in *Daily Evening Traveler*, Boston, Nov. 1, 1864 (M)
ends '. . . at $36,000,' but is otherwise similar.]

LOSS OF SHIP PARACHUTE OF THIS PORT

A letter from Capt. Howard, of ship Parachute, of this port,
dated Tahiti June 25th, reports the loss of his ship June 10th,
on a reef a short distance to the windward of the Taunoa Passage, and about 3 miles from Papiete. The ship at the time was
in charge of the French government pilot. All hands were
saved. Had saved 880 bbls. sp. oil, and a portion of everything
in the ship. The ship had been sold at auction as she lay on the
reef. The oil would be shipped on the first opportunity.

The Parachute sailed hence Nov. 11th, 1859, and was last
reported at Sydney, NSW, Jan. 24th, 1864, with 1225 bbls. sp.
oil on board. She was owned by Edmund Maxfield and others,
and when she left port was valued, with outfits, at $36,000.—She
was 331 tons, and was rebuilt two voyages since. The ship and
catchings are insured at the offices in this city for $35,500.

C.P.I. Ed. Note: The text of this report is one item in a news
column headed "MARINE INTELLIGENCE," the rest of which is
irrelevant.

The reef on which the *Parachute* was lost is possibly
the reef mentioned in the following: "Taunoa Pass—Beacon—
Taunoa Pass is about 300 yards wide, with no dangerous bar,

and clearly marked by the edges of the reef awash on either side. On the eastern side, however, rocks with only 9 feet (2.7 m), on which the sea sometimes breaks, extend about 150 yards northwestward of the point of the reef awash. Another rock inside the pass near the western side, about 100 yards 166° from the eastern point of the western reef, is marked by a red beacon with conical topmark. . . ." (*H.O. Pub.* No. 166, Vol. II, 4th ed. 1933, p. 76.) Papeete Harbor is 17° 32′ S., 149° 34′ W., H.O. Chart No. 1514 (*Ibid.,* p. 77).

TAHITI 154

The Daily Mercury, New Bedford, Mass.
Nov. 1, 1864: 33, 3, 3
MNBedf

LOSS OF SHIP PARACHUTE

A letter from Capt. Howland, of ship Parachute, of this port, dated Tahiti June 25th, 1864, says:—"Ship Parachute was lost on the reef a short distance to the windward of the Taunoa Passage, and about three miles from Papeete. The accident happened on the 10th of June, the ship at the time being in charge of the French government pilot. No lives lost. Saved about 880 bbls. sperm oil, and a portion of everything in the ship. Had sold the wreck as she laid on the reef. Had not decided where to ship the oil as there was no vessel at Tahiti; but there were two or three expected soon from the Coast of California.

C.P.I. Ed. Note: The text of this report is one item in a news column headed "MERCURY MARINE JOURNAL," the rest of which is irrelevant.

[*For additional C.P.I. Ed. Note see TAHITI 153.*]

TAHITI 155

Daily Evening Traveler, Boston, Mass.
Nov. 9, 1864: 20, 3, 3
M

WHALERS

A letter from Captain Howland, late of ship Parachute, wrecked at Tahiti, dated Valparaiso, Oct. 1, states that being unable to procure a vessel to ship his oil to the United States or England he has stored the oil in the Custom House at Valpariso, and would wait instructions from home.

C.P.I. Ed. Note: The text of this report is one item in a newspaper column headed "WHALERS," used as a single report on the island and vessel mentioned.

[*For additional C.P.I. Ed. Note see TAHITI 2.*]

TAHITI 156

Boston Daily Transcript
Apr. 7, 1868: —, —, 2
MBAt

Tahiti advises to March 4 state that the Whaleship General Pike, with 900 bbls. of oil had arrived and was condemned and sold for $800.00

C.P.I. Ed. Note: The text of this report is one item in a newspaper column, the rest of which is irrelevant.

[For additional C.P.I. Ed. Note see TAHITI 2.]

TAHITI 157

New York Semi-Weekly Times
Apr. 26, 1870: 16, 3, 7
MBr

PACIFIC COAST

Lady Franklin sails for Victoria—the blasting of Blossom Rock—shipwreck at Tahiti—telegraph subsides in British Columbia—the gold mines.

The Ship Eli Whitney, from Sydney for San Francisco, put into Tahiti on the 17th of March in distress. She sold her cargo of coal for $8 per ton, and proceeded thence for the northeast side of the island to take on a cargo of oranges, and it is reported, was wrecked.

C.P.I. Ed. Note: The text of the above report is taken from a newspaper column headed "PACIFIC COAST," the rest of which is irrelevant. Complete text is used. . . .

[*For additional C.P.I. Ed. Note see TAHITI 3.*]

TAHITI 158

Boston Daily Advertiser
Apr. 26, 1870: 115, 4, 5
MBr

San Francisco, April 23, Barque Eli Wintney, Pleace, from New Castle, N S W, for San Francisco, put into Tahiti on the 17th of March, in distress. She sold her cargo of coal for S5. per ton, and proceeded thence for the northeast side of the island to take in a cargo of oranges; and it is reported was wrecked. The E.W. registered 532 tons, and was built at Medford, Mass., in 1834.

C.P.I. Ed. Note: The text of this report is one item in a news column headed "DISASTERS," the rest of which is irrelevant.

Barque *Eli Wintney,* mentioned in text is probably meant for barque *Eli Whitney.*

[For additional C.P.I. Ed. Note see TAHITI 2.]

TAHITI 159

Boston Daily Advertiser
Apr. 25, 1870: 115, 4, 7
MBr

The Clarissa was wrecked March 6 at Tahiti and became a total loss.

C.P.I. Ed. Note: The text of this report is one item in a news column headed "DISASTERS," the rest of which is irrelevant.

"Papeete Harbor (17°32′S., 149°34′W. H.O. Chart No. 1514) is the most important and affords the best shelter of any harbor in the island of Tahiti. *(H.O. Pub.* No. 166, Vol. II, 4th ed., 1933, p. 77.)

Papeete Pass—"The entrance into Papeete Harbor is a break about 550 yards wide in the barrier reef, but the channel is so narrowed by shallow water extending from the reefs, and especially from that on the western side, that the navigable breadth with depths of 4¼ fathoms (7.8m) is 70 yards." *(Ibid.* p. 77)

TAHITI 160

Boston Daily Advertiser
May 3, 1870: 115, 4, 4
MBr

Ship Clarissa, Dean, for San Francisco, before reported wrecked, went ashore on the South Reef in Papeie Passage, Tahiti, March 6, and became a total loss.

C.P.I. Ed. Note: The text of this report is one item in a news column headed "DISASTERS," the rest of which is irrelevant.

Papeie Passage mentioned in text is probably meant for Papeete Pass.

[*For additional C.P.I. Ed. Note see TAHITI 159.*]

TAHITI 161

The Friend, Honolulu
Nov. 1, 1873: 30, 93, 2
MSaP

REPORT OF SCHOONER DAUNTLESS, BERRILL, MASTER

Left Honolulu on the 28th of May, thence to the line in 9 days, which we crossed in long. 170°W., thence to within 200 miles off the coast of New South Wales, was detained for 12 days with a gale, accompanied with hail, lightning, rain and running sea. Sighted no land on the way down except Aneitan Island. Arrived in Sydney on the morning of July 12th. Found lying in Sydney an English man-of-war and the French iron-clad Atlantic. Several ship loads of the Communists had arrived in Sydney and were dispatched to New Caledonia. It seems that a lively trade had sprung up in supplying them with live stock. Several of them tried to escape, but were caught and delivered by the English authorities. Reports the Robert Cowan 40 days passage. Left Sydney Aug. 7th; afternoon same day saw a brig supposed to be the Onward, bound in to Sydney. Sighted Three Kings 14th Aug, and arrived at Tahiti Sept 4th. Heard of the loss of the William and Thomas, Capt. Ellis, of San Salvador, on Easter Island, March 17th. She was bound from Puget Sound to Callao, with lumber. Also the loss on the same island of the American ship Elizabeth Campbell, Capt. Kelly, bound to South America with lumber from Puget Sound. The crews of both vessels were saved and part of them had arrived at Tahiti in a vessel built on Easter Island. Left Tahiti Sept 8th. Sighted Hawaii on Sunday, the 28th, and made port on the morning of Sept. 30th. Had light winds and calms from Tahiti to port. Brig Wm H. Allen left Tahiti for Borabora Sept. 3d, to load firewood for Honolulu. Bark Ionia left Tahiti Sept. 4th for San

Francisco. In lat 12° N, long 150° W, passed an iron buoy. The only vessels at Tahiti were the French steamer Brilliante, which left on the 7th on a cruise—and the schooner Coronet, of Auckland. Bark Chavert was to leave soon for Easter Island, to pick up the wrecked crews of the vessels repeated above.

[For C.P.I. Ed. Note see TAHITI 2.]

TAHUATA 1

Sandwich Island Gazette and Journal of Commerce,
Honolulu
Nov. 5, 1836: 1, 2, 3
MH

Loss of the American Whale Ship Telegraph

During the month of May last the vessel was lying in Resolution Bay, Island of Sta. Christiana (Marquesas) when, one morning, the missionaries at the place were astonished to find the vessel gone, as the master had been at the house the preceding evening when he had no intention of leaving; a few moments elapsed when the natives gave intelligence of her being a wreck on the north part of the island which proved to be the case.

It appears they parted during the night (although there had been no wind) and the first the Captain knew of it was, that her jib-boom touched the shore, they then stood to the northward of the island, when they found themselves close in shore and before they could tack, the vessel touched the bottom and was wrecked. The crew were saved and a small portion of the stores; part of the crew left in a whaler, the rest remaining at Sta. Christiana.

C.P.I. Ed. Note: Tahuata (Santa Christina), one of the Marquesas is 9° 57' S., 139° 05' W., H.O. Chart No. 1599 *(H.O. Pub. No. 166, Vol. II, 4th ed. 1933, p. 170.)*

TAIWAN 1

Salem Gazette
Oct. 16, 1857: 83, 3, 2
MSaE

Ship Channing, (of New York) Jacobs, which was reported at Amoy July 8, is stated by telegraph to London to have been lost on Formosa. She was 600 tons, 3 years old.

C.P.I. Ed. Note: The above is one item in a column headed "MARINE JOURNAL," the rest of which is irrelevant.

[*Taiwan (Formosa) is 21° 55′ N., 120° 45′ E. at southern end.*]

TAMANA 1

The Friend, Honolulu
Jan. 1, 1856: 13, 6, 2
MSaP

PIRACY AND MURDER ON BOARD A NEW BEDFORD WHALER

The following account of the seizure of the ship John, of New Bedford, and the murder of the captain, first and second mates, and a number of the crew, is from the Empire, of Sydney, N.S.W. of July 11th:—

We are indebted to Capt. Bowles of the schooner Black Dog, which arrived from the Islands July 8th, for the following report of a daring and murderous piracy committed on board the ship John of New Bedford, by two South Sea Islanders. The particulars were supplied to Capt. Bowles by one Francis John, a white man stationed on Roche's Island, in lat. 2 degrees 32 minutes South, lon. 176 degrees 9 minutes East. It appears that on April 17, a vessel was seen standing towards the Island from the southeast, and the Black Dog being expected there several canoes put off to meet her. No sooner were they alongside, however, than two natives presented fire-arms and drove them away. Francis John, seeing the vessel in distress, then pulled to her, when he was hailed by the natives, who inquired to what country he belong, and if not to London. On answering in the affirmative, he was warned off, and told that "no white man was wanted alongside." Believing the vessel to have been forcibly taken by the two natives, he communicated a suspicion to two other natives who were in his canoe, and made an attempt to board her, but was repelled by loaded muskets. Finding it impossible to get on board, he returned to the shore. Subsequently another canoe, manned by natives, went alongside, and entered into conversation with the pirates, who divulged their horrid deed of which they were guilty, and the motives that led to its committal. The captain of the John having ill used them, they took advantage of the absence of two boats and the greater part of the crew, to indulge an insatiate desire for revenge. Besides the two natives, the captain, cook and cooper were left on board; these they killed.

After the capture of a whale, the mate's boat went alongside with it; he was killed with spades, and all his crew but one man, who pushed off from their reach and was left astern, the vessel having some way upon her. Soon after the second mate's boat was alongside, he and three men were killed, the remaining two pushed off from her, and joined the other boat.

In this predicament they were left on the wide sea without compass or food. This statement was voluntary on the part of the pirates, and from information gained from the natives of Roche's Island, is believed by Capt. Bowles to be correct. On being asked where the ship was bound, the pirates replied, "to Ocean Island," but if unable to make it, they would run her ashore where no white man lived. Francis John, the white man, read the ship's name,—"John, New Bedford," she had a jib, foresail, foretopsail, main and mizzen—topsail set. The main topgallant sail, and spanker, were also set. She was on the starboard tack, and seemed to have been so from the time of her seizure, as both fore and main tacks were well down, which could hardly be accomplished by two blacks. When last seen she was steering wild from north to west. Prior to leaving, the pirates offered tobacco and other inducements to the natives of Roche's Island to join them, but to no purpose. The Black Dog arrived at Roaches Island, April 29th, twelve days after the John's visit. Had the interval been shorter Capt. Bowles would have made an attempt to discover her whereabouts.

There seems to be no room for doubt that the officers and a portion of the crew were murdered, and that the remainder of

the crew were left to the mercy of the waves.   The captain of the
John was Otis Tilton of Edgartown, the first mate, Henry C.
Allen, son of Joseph Allen, Jr., of New Bedford, and the second
mate Isaac W. Gallop, of New London.   The ship was owned by
Frederick Parker, Esq, of New Bedford and was last reported at
Paita, Jan. 24, bound to the Sandwich Islands with 350 sperm,
and 350 whale oil.

C.P.I. Ed. Note: Tamana (Rotcher) Island is 2° 39′ S, 176° 53′
E., H.O. Chart No. 119 *(H.O. Pub.* No. 166, v. 2, 4th ed., 1933,
p. 449.)   Rotcher, given in the Sailing Directions is probably
the same as Roche's and Roaches, the latter two being spelling
variations in the text.

TAONGI 1

American Traveller, Boston, Mass.
Aug. 13, 1833: 9, 2, 2
MB

[Similar reports in *Boston Daily Advertiser and Patriot*, Aug. 14, 1833 (M;MB), *Boston Advertiser*, Aug. 14, 1833 (MB), *Salem Gazette*, Aug. 16, 1833 (MSaE), *The Evening Gazette*, Boston, Aug. 17, 1833 (MB), *The Sailor's Magazine and Naval Journal*, New York, Sept. 1833 (MNBedf) and *Am. & Comm. Daily Adv.*, Baltimore, Md. Sept. 23, 1833 (MB).]

NEW ISLAND IN THE PACIFIC

A small island was discovered by Capt. Underwood of the Am. brig Bolivar Liberator, in Lat. 14 46 N. Long. 169 18E. on the 9th Feb. on his passage from the Sandwich Islands. The Island, which has not been laid down in charts, is about 6 miles long, running W N W. and E S E, with a reef extending nearly ten miles from its W. extremity. It is visible at 4 to 5 miles distance from a ships deck. The name of Farnham's Island has been assigned to it.

C.P.I. Ed. Note: SMYTH ISLANDS, Gaspar Rico, or *Taongi* are considered as identical with Farnham Island seen by the American brig *Bolivar*. (Findlay's *Directory of the North Pacific Ocean*, Third Ed. 1886, pp. 1034, 1035.)

"Pokaakku (Taongi or Gaspar Rico) Atoll (south end, 14° 33′ N., 168° 56′ E., H.O. Chart 5427). . . ." *(H.O. Pub. No. 165, Vol. I, 4th ed. 1938, p. 506.)*

TAONGI 2

Daily Gazette, New Bedford, Mass.
Aug. 14, 1833: 1, 2, 3
MNBedf

NEW ISLAND IN THE PACIFIC

Capt. Underwood, of the brig Bolivar Liberator, at Canton, reports that on his passage to that port from the Sandwich Islands, on the 9th Feb. last, he discovered a small island in lat. 14 46 N. lon. 169 18 E. which is not laid down in any of the charts. It was about six miles long, running W N W. and E S E. with a reef extending nearly ten miles from its W. extremity. It is visible at 4 or 5 miles distance from a ships deck. He gave it the name of Farnham's Island.

[*For C.P.I. Ed. Note see TAONGI 1.*]

TAONGI 3

Essex Register, Salem, Mass.
Aug. 15, 1833: 33, 3, 1
MSaE

NEW ISLAND IN THE PACIFIC

A small island was discovered by Captain Underwood, of the brig Boliver Liberatore, or this port, in lat 14 46, N lon 169 18, E on the 9th Feb. on his passage from the Sandwich Island. This Island, which has not been laid down in the charts, is about 6 miles long, running W N W. and E.S E. with a reef extending nearly ten miles from its W. extremity. It is visible at 4 or 5 miles distance from a ship's deck. Capt. Underwood assigned to it the name of Farnham's Island, as a mark of respect for P.I. Farnham, of this town, his owner.

C.P.I. Ed. Note: The text of this report is one item in a news column headed "MARINE JOURNAL," the rest of which is irrelevant. Farnham's Island, mentioned in text, may possibly be Pokaakku (Taongi or Gaspar Rico) Atoll.
    The name of the vessel should be *Bolivar Liberator.*

[*For additional C.P.I. Ed. Note see TAONGI 1.*]

TAONGI 4

Salem Gazette
Aug. 16, 1833: 47, 2, 2
MSaE

On our first page will be found a notice of the discovery of a new island in the Pacific—The Bolivar Liberator, which made the discovery, is in the employ of P. I. Farnham & Co., and the island has been named after our enterprising and much re-spected townsman, P. I. Farnham, Esq.

[*For C.P.I. Ed. Note see* TAONGI *1. For report referred to in text see* TAONGI *1.*]

TAONGI 5

Daily Mercury, New Bedford, Mass.
Aug. 21, 1833: 3, 2, 4
MNBedf

[Identical report in *New Bedford Mercury*, Aug. 23, 1833 (MNBedf)]

FARNHAM'S ISLAND

By a reference to the last edition of Bowditch's Navigator, we find, says the Salem Register, that the island of Gaspar Rico is laid down in lat. 14 42 N. and lon. 169 03 E. A nautical friend informs us that this island is also laid down on a chart in his possession. The island discovered by Capt. Underwood, is stated to be in lat. 14 46 N and lon. 169 18 E. There can be no doubt that Gaspar Rico and Farnham's Island are one and the same. We like the new name, however, much the best, and hope the island will always hereafter bear the name of our worthy townsman, than whom no one is more enterprising and meritorious.

[*For C.P.I. Ed. Note see TAONGI 1.*]

TAONGI 6

Columbian Centinel, Boston, Mass.
Sept. 25, 1833: —, 2, 6
MH; MSaE

A correspondent of the New York Mercantile states that Gasper Island, (see Fanning's voyages page 235) is laid down on an old Spanish chart, in nearly the same latitude and longitude as the island lately discovered by Capt. Underwood of the Bolivar Liberator.

C.P.I. Ed. Note: The text of this report is a true copy of the article, and is one item in a news column headed "SHIPPING JOURNAL," the rest of which is irrelevant.

Gasper Island, mentioned in text, may possibly be Pokaakku (Taongi or Gasper Rico) Atoll.

[For additional C.P.I. Ed. Note see TAONGI 1.]

TAONGI 7

Boston Journal
Nov. 23, 1859: 27, 2, 7
MB

After leaving Honolulu the Cooper ran to the southward and westward as far as the position assigned to the northernmost island of the Radack group, and cruised about for a considerable time in search of sundry shoals and rocks which had been reported as occuring in that locality. None of these were found. Bad weather having at length set in, the course of the vessel was directed to the northward, calling at Johnston's Islands in Lat. 16° 23′ N, Long. 169° 31′ W. These islands are described as being surrounded with a reef about 10 miles long by 5 miles broad, on one side of which are a couple of low islets. It is somewhat difficult of approach, but susceptible of being made accessible with little labor.

The slopes of these islands are covered with guano, and were found to be in possession of parties from California. Some ten persons having with them a field piece, were residing on the larger island to look after the interest of the concern. They were living in houses made of gunny bags stretched on poles. Light and airy habitations for a warm climate, and a sparse population, says our writer, but rather too open in texture for denslly inhabited neighborhoods, abounding in inquisitive old ladies. These men seem to thrive well, despite the barrenness of the spot on which no tree occurred to break the monotony of the scene. The fishing at this island is spoken of as being quite extraordinary. Any desired number of the most varied and beautiful species of the finny tribe being readily captured.

After leaving Johnston's Island, the Cooper made, in the

beginning of April, the group known as Gaspar Rico, which consists of a reef surrounding some six or seven islands.

Several days were spent in surveying this and in vainly endeavoring to find some opening in the barrier reef through which the Ship might pass. The surf being so heavy upon the reef no landing could be effected. The writer dwells with enthusiasm upon the exquisite beauty of this clump of islands. It was the finest of the class which they had seen. The reef being well defined, and marking, as with a yellow band, the pale apple-green of the Shoal, Water within from the cold blue-black water of the Ocean without. Inside the barrier some of the islands are hilly and well wooded, while a number of high picturesque rocks are scattered here and there. Outside the barrier a tremendous surf was beating, and any number of Sharks were constantly playing about the vessel. A pleasant picture to recall, as the writer observes, but somewhat aggravating to men who after having been cramped upon board a Pilot Boat for weeks, were thinking more of having a run on shore than of merely feasting their eyes. The artist of the expedition, Mr. Kern, occupied himself, however, with his pencil with marked success. Lieut. Brooks obtained soundings at a thousand fathoms, close to the reef, and the whole party seemed to feel satisfied that survey of the island was well "worked up."

From Gaspar Rico they stood over to the Mariana group, spending a few days at Guam; thence they sailed to Hong Kong, going through Balington Passage. A succession of calms in this vicinity enabled them to obtain, to the eastward of the Passage, a number of capital soundings, in some cases bringing up mud and samples of water from depths of 3800 fathoms. After getting into the Chinese Sea bottom was reached at 900 fathoms, the mud brought up in this instance differed in character from that obtained in the Pacific.

The marked change for the better which had occurred in

the appearance of Hong Kong during the last three or four years is dwelt on at length. This improvement is due for the most part to the troubles at Canton, which have driven many persons from that place to seek protection under the British Flag.

After leaving Hong Kong, the Cooper would visit the Loo Choo Islands and cruise upon the Japanese Coast, so long as the weather permitted. She would probably pass a portion of the winter in some one of the Japanese Ports, in order to be ready for an early start in the Spring.

C.P.I. Ed. Note: The above text is . . . from a lengthy article in a newspaper column, . . . the rest of which is irrelevant. The Johnston Island, according to Findlay's *Directory of the North Pacific Ocean*, Third ed. 1886, page 1053 were discovered by Capt. Charles James Johnson on board H.M.S. Cornwallis, December 14, 1807 in lat. 16° 53′ 20″ N., long. 169° 31′ 30″ W.

The Marianas are identified as the Ladrone Islands *(H.O. Pub.* No. 165, vol. I, 4th ed., 1938, p. 565.) Guam Island, south end, in 13° 15′ N., 144° 43′ E., C.S. Chart 4202, is the largest and southernmost, of the Marianas. *(Ibid.* p. 856).

[*For additional C.P.I. Ed. Note see TAONGI 1.*]

TAONGI 8

The Friend, Honolulu
May 1, 1867: 18, 37, 3
MH

[Report in The *Pacific Commercial Advertiser,* Honolulu, Apr.
27, 1867 (MH) apparently similar but was shortened by C.P.I.
worker.]

CRUISE OF THE CAROLINE MILLS.—The American
schooner *Caroline Mills,* Capt. Nickols, returned to port on the
22d ult., having left here on a wrecking voyage to the westward
about three months ago. She was provided with all the appurtenances for recovering wrecked property, and her Captain and
crew were thoroughly experienced in those enterprises, and
equipped with the proper instruments for navigation. A complete modern diving apparatus was on board—commonly known
as a "submarine armor," with two men to operate it, one to don
the "armor," and the other to attend to the signals of his confederate while exploring the bottom of the ocean. The first island visited by the schooner, and the principal object of the expedition, was Wake or Halcyon Island, one of the Palmyra
group, lying in latitude 19° 11′ N. and longitude 166° 31′ E.
Here they obtained some flasks of quicksilver from the wreck of
the bark *Libelle,* which left here last year, having as passengers,
Madame Anne Bishop and others. On the voyage, Capt. Nickols
visited an island which is on some charts called Gasparico and
on others Cornwallis Island, in 14° 43′ north, and 169° 03′ east
longitude, where he found portions of a wreck that had evidently laid there for years. It was that of a teak-built ship, with
composition fastenings. By Lloyd's Register we find that a ship
called the *Canton,* left Bengal, and in 1832 was reported as miss-

ing, at Lloyds. From the fact of her having composition metal, which was only invented after 1840, it could not have been the *Canton* suggested by the *Gazette,* and besides, that vessel was not of the size by several hundred tons, as it is apparent was the ship, the remains of which were found by Capt. Nickols. Another circumstance which goes to prove that the wreck is a modern one, is that the masts, which are still to be seen, are what are called by seamen "made masts," that is, built in pieces and bound by iron bands. The coat of arms from the stern Capt. Nickols has brought here and deposited in the Harbor Master's office. The fair inference is, that the ship in question was the Hudson Bay Company's ship *Canton,* chartered by the East India Company, perhaps, in 1832, or the wrecks now to be seen there may be those of two distinct vessels. On the shield, which is certainly a curiosity and well worthy of inspection, are first, the royal arms of England—three lions, &c., surrounded by the crown. Under this are evidently the arms of the Hudson's Bay Company, a beaver and a bear. On the outer circle of the shield are a succession of elephants and castles. Then comes a cypher which Captain D. Smith, an experienced British shipmaster, interprets to signify 1799, the date at which the ship was built. There are few probabilities that the fate of the crew of that ship will ever be ascertained. The only sign that men had ever been on the island, beside the remains of the wreck, were some pieces of woodenware. The unfortunate men who were thus cast on a barren island may have perished there of starvation, or, what is more likely, have gone away in the ship's boats and foundered at sea, or fallen a prey to the savage inhabitants of the neighboring islands.

[*For C.P.I. Ed. Note see TAONGI 1.*
Text has been taken from original newspaper as report was shortened by C.P.I. worker.]

TARAWA 1

Daily Evening Traveller, Boston, Mass.
Nov. 23, 1853: 9, 1, 5
MBAt

ATTACK UPON A VESSEL BY SAVAGES

A San Francisco paper says that the brig Rosa, while on a trading voyage among the South Pacific Islands, was attacked at Tauroa by savages, and the Captain and several of the crew murdered. The natives of whom a large number had been admitted on board the vessel, commenced a simultaneous attack upon the crew of the brig, killing or overpowering six of their number, and forcing the survivors to seek refuge in the cabin. They there procured arms and ammunition, and succeeded in shooting several natives from the sky-light. The crew finally left their place of refuge, and after a sharp conflict, succeeded in overpowering the natives—driving most of them overboard. On the deck were found the lifeless bodies of Jacomo Ferreo, the Captain; Emanuel Pancho, boatswain, Wm. Speen, Cooper, and Samuel Bolls, a seaman. There were also missing—having been either thrown overboard or carried away by the savages—Charles Temmins; the chief mate, and Harry Wilson, a seaman—both Americans. Others of the men received severe injuries. Mr. Maiden, the second mate, upon whom the command of the brig devolved, bore the vessel up for Sydney, where she arrived in safety.

C.P.I. Ed. Note: The text of this report is one item in a newspaper column headed "ATTACK UPON A VESSEL BY SAVAGES," the rest of which is irrelevant. Tauroa is probably another spelling for Tarawa. (Tauroa) (Cook) Tarawa Island is Lat. 1°28'N. Lon. 172° 59' E., H.O. Chart No. 125, lies 19 miles northward of Maiana Island. *(H.O. Pub.* No. 166, Vol. II, 4th ed., 1933, p. 458.)

TARAWA 2

The Friend, Honolulu
Mar. 1, 1854: 11, 22, 2
MSaP

MASSACRE AT HALL'S ISLAND

A late San Francisco paper says that the brig Rosa, while on a trading voyage among the South Pacific Islands, stopped at Tauroa, where she was attacked by about one hundred and fifty savages from the north end of Hall's Island, Joseph Maiden, chief surviving officer, thus narrates the fight:—

The captain was also on deck; he (Mr. Maiden) took the several clubs from the savages. He then went to the main hatch to speak to the men left in the hold, when he received a severe blow on the head from a club, which knocked him down the hatchway. While in the act of falling he saw two natives attacking Wm. Sheen, a cooper, who shipped at Sydney. The war whoop was then raised and Maiden recovering from the effects of his blow, and not being injured by the fall, directed the men in the hold to make for the cabin, there being a door through the bulkhead, with a view to getting arms. They could not find any ammunition for some time; at length Emmanual Ramose discovered a keg of powder, and afterwards a parcel of shot. Having now loaded some musket, they shot some natives from the cabin sky light, and Maiden, standing at the foot of the companion ladder, and seeing the King's son passing on the deck, ran him through with a bayonet. They then left the cabin and attempted to rush the natives overboard. The natives were struggling with the captain, one with the cook's hatchet and the other with a piece of sharpened iron, like a long knife. Maiden raised his musket at the men, but it missed fire, and he killed one of them with his bayonet. In falling the native dropped the hatchet on Maiden's foot, which cut severely; both in the struggle went down the hatchway together, till the savage was overpowered and killed.—Maiden afterwards shot another native. By this time many of the natives were driven overboard and having hoisted the jib and cut the cable, the vessel stood off from the land. After getting the vessel under weigh, Maiden found that the captain, the boatswain, the cooper and one of the seamen, were lying on the deck, their bodies being mutilated in a horrible manner, by wounds from the hatchets and clubs. The steward, also, was lying on deck, almost dead. He then stood N.E. to endeavor to fetch Tauroa, with the hope of finding the schooner Black Dog, and getting assistance to navigate the vessel. The current, however, drove the vessel to the Westward, and eventually Maiden bore up for Sydney, under the circumstances detailed in our report of the wreck. The murdered men were buried at sea.

The following is a list of the crew at the time of the Massacre, showing those saved and those killed: Capt. Jacomo Ferreo, Italian; Emanuel Pancho, boatswain, Italian; Wm. Sheen, cooper, Englishman;—all killed: Chas. Temmins, chief mate, American; Henry Wilson, seaman, American—missing. either killed or left among the natives; Joseph Maiden, second mate, Englishman; Michael Black, seaman, Irishman; Emanuel Ramose, seaman, Chilian; San Francisco, cook, Portuguese: Eugenio Carbone, steward, Italian, and Joe. a native—all now in Sydney.

C.P.I. Ed. Note: Tauroa is possibly another spelling for Tarawa. Tarawa (Cook) Island is 1° 28' N., 172° 59' E., H.O. Chart No. 123, lies 19 miles northward of Maiana Island. (H.O. Pub. No. 166, Vol. II, 4th ed., 1933, p.458.)

Maiana (Hall) Island is 1° 00′ N., 173° 01′ E., H.O. Chart No. 122. *(H.O. Pub.* No. 166, Vol. II, 4th ed., 1933, p. 457.)

TASMANIA 1

Salem Gazette
Oct. 13, 1795: 9, 3, 1
MSaE

Among the Voyages of Discovery we find that Capt. Hayes has given the name of Puen Streights to the Streights 3 leagues broad between Van Dieman's Land and New South Wales, and has explored them.

C.P.I. Ed. Note: The text of this report is one item in a news column headed "SALEM, OCT 18—SUMMARY," the rest of which is irrelevant.

"Bass Strait, separating Australia from Tasmania, [Van Diemans Land] was discovered by the surgeon of that name, of H.M.S.Reliance, in 1796. On the South side is a group of islands, of which Flinders is the principal." *(Directory of the South Pacific Ocean,* Findlay, Fifth Ed. 1884, p. 1028.)

Puen Streights, mentioned in text, are possibly Banks Strait, which is between the Furneaux Group, of which Flinders Island is a part, and Tasmania. On H.O. Chart No. 825 Banks Strait appears to be not over 20 miles wide at any point.

Banks Strait at Swan Island light is 40° 43′ S., 148° 07′ E. *(American Practical Navigator,* No. 9, Bowditch, 1917 ed. p. 352.)

TASMANIA 2

Salem Gazette
July 27, 1803: 17, 3, 2
MSaE

From the New York Gazette

Extract from a letter received in this city from Capt. Eliphalet Smith, of the brig Fanny, of Boston, dated at sea, lat. 5, 30 S. long. 102, O E. Jan. 25, 1802.

"This will inform you that I am on my passage from Port Jackson to Batavia, and am within a few days mail of that place. My rout was through Bas's streights, which separates Van Dieman's Land from New South Wales on New Holland.—I am the first American ship that ever made this passage, and I flatter myself from the observations which I have made, that this passage which has hitherto been impracticable by all seamen, owing principally to the western winds, which prevail in that latitude, will be rendered not only safe, but expeditions, and of considerable advantage to the mercantile world."

[*For C.P.I. Ed. Note see TASMANIA 1.*]

Hobart-Town, Tasmania. From Dumont D'Urville, *Voyage au Pole Sud*, 2nd expedition, 1837-1840, plate 156.

TASMANIA 3

The Essex Gazette, Haverhill, Mass.
Jan. 30, 1836: 10, 2, 2
MSaE

Another dreadful loss of life occurred on the 14th, of May by the wreck of the Neva convict ship, near the entrance of Bass's straits. There were on board 230 persons in all of whom 150 were female convicts, and 55 children. Only 22 persons reached the shore, and of these seven died soon afterward of exhaustion. Of the fifteen survivors, six were female convicts; the others were the captain, chief mate and seven of the crew. This is the third convict ship lost within two years, causing an aggregate destruction of 528 lives.

C.P.I. Ed. Note: The text of this report is one item in a news column the rest of which is irrelevant.

[*For additional C.P.I. Ed. Note see TASMANIA 1.*]

TASMANIA 4

The Daily Herald, Newburyport, Mass.
Aug. 6, 1858: 27, 3, 2
MNe

Whaleship Menkar, (of New Bedford), Bloomfield, was condemned at Hobart's Town, Van Dieman's Land, in Mch last.
On the 1st of March, on the coast of New Zealand, struck a
sunken reef and knocked off false keel from the stem to the after
part of the fore channels; part of ground tier casks of oil were
stove, and the oil leaked out of them. The ship was much
strained all over. The oil, 1100 barrels of sperm and whale, was
shipped to London in ship Heather Bell, in which Capt. Bloomfield would take passage. The hull and rigging were sold for
L372; the provisions, sails, boats, anchors, chains, &c. sold in
lots, brought L600. The Menkar was owned by Phillip An-
thony, Esq. of Dartmouth, and others, and sailed from New Bedford Aug. 8, 1854. The amount of insurance on the ship, and
cargo in New Bedford, is $31,000

C.P.I. Ed. Note: The text of this report is one item in a news
column headed "SHIPPING JOURNAL," the rest of which is irrelevant. Re: The Island of Tasmania: " . . . It was first discovered by Tasman, in 1642, who named the island Van Diemen's
Land . . . The change of name to Tasmania took place in 1856
. . . ." (Findlay, *Directory of the South Pacific Ocean,* Fifth
Edition, 1884, p. 1031.)

TAUMAKO GROUP 1

Salem Register
June 9, 1803: 4, 2, 1 & 2
MSaE

NEWLY DISCOVERED ISLANDS

We have some important communications from Port Jackson, consisting of observations made in North and South Pacific, by Mr. Simpson, Commander of the Nautilus. This Gentleman has discovered in S lat. 11 deg. 17 min. and E. long. 167 deg 58 min. and island which he has called Kennedy's Island. From its beautiful appearance, united to its being well inhabitated, Mr. S. is of the opinion that it may prove a valuable acquisition to our new colony, as it produces hogs in abundance. The natives (he says) are savage, artful, and treacherous upon Dexter's Group, or Duff's Group, which obliged me to fire upon them; and this may be a necessary precaution to any person who may wish to land upon them hereafter. Upon the Island Disappointment I landed some fowls; sowed several sorts of feed, and put some plants in the ground. In two previous voyages I passed this island, without the precaution of looking for land, as I am sure many other navigators have done. We found upon it the remains of a very large lower mast, next the keel; which led us to think some large Spanish ship had been wrecked upon it, but it must have been long since, as the timber was greatly decayed.

"Though these islands are thinly inhabited, we scarcely saw one in the whole of this group but had natives upon it; and when our distance sunk the reefs below the horizon which extend from island to island, the natives, as they crossed from one to the other, presented the appearance of a regiment of soldiers marching round the horizon on the surface of the sea.—all the islands are exceedingly low, and shew at first, like all the rest of this labyrinth, a few scattered trees above the horizon. This circumstance will demonstrate their danger to a seaman; who can not be to much on his guard, on so perilous a navigation. I am fully persuaded, that not one hundreth part of them are known to navigators. They appeared to us to be formed of coral and sand, lightly covered by a thin black soil; the stones on the shore had the appearance of having been burnt; they were black porous and light." To the above remarks of Capt.Simpson, we add his description of the island Alamagan one of Mariana Islands.

Nautical observations, and Description of the Island of Almagan.

"Ship Nautilus, Oct. 28, 1800.

"Running down along the north part of this island when the East point of it (a small distance from which stands a very high remarkable perforated rock) bore by compass S. 8 deg. E. the island of Sarigan was on with it. "While lying to in Howel's Bay, the island Pagan bore by means of our compasses N. 14 deg. W.

I must regret that commercial interest forbids me running along these islands as far as Urac; as connecting and examing this chain of Islands, is an object, in my opinion, of some consequence to those who navigate these seas; all that I have seen of them are extremely fertile and pleasant. The island produces, in uncommon abundance, Papaw apples, sugar cane, a nut which eats much like an almond, and is enclosed in a light green rhind, a root which is distinguished at Sandwich Islands by the name of Peea, and grows and looks much like a potatoe, but very different stalk, a drawing which accompanies this, and will best explain it. "In its crude state it is considered by the Owhjneans as a poison; they prepare it in the following manner; the root is first well washed, then marked and mixed up with fresh water to about the consistence of butter; after which they let it settle and draw the water off. They let it undergo this operation several times, it then stands in the sun, they then draw the last water off, and it soon dries and resembles flour; it then may be cooked the same as Sago, and I much query if many persons could tell the difference between it and Sago; at Owhee I have often eaten it in preference to Sago. A Malay woman that accompanied Captain Coolage to one of his visits to Owhyhee, attempted to prepare and form it in the manner the Malays do, but did not succeed; however, she owned herself unequal to the task, but said if her countrymen had it, they would with much ease give it the form that we generally see Sago in. It must, of course, make a good substitute for bread. "This island produces a number of plantain or banna trees, but I never saw much of their fruits, and cocoa nuts. In addition to these we have added, by planting and sowing in this bay, in different parts along the shore, water and musk mellons and pumpkins; yams, landed and planted in a state of vegetation; cabbage plants and European potatoes; we also landed a male and female kid, in very high order, about six weeks old; also two cocks and two hens. "Mr. John Howel, in the Lady Washington, 1786, landed some hogs here; and although in visiting this island twice since, we have not seen any of them, yet there is no doubt but what they exist, as the print of their feet has always been seen; some of our party thought they saw the print of the feet of some large animal that east grass (by its dung) as large as a horse. "The birds are of the acquartic kind, and pretty numerous. There are a species of land crabs, known in the West Indies by the name of soldier; they are very large and nice eating.

"There is also an abundance of all kinds of fish, sharks are numerous particularly near the shore. "From the form of this island, I conceive a landing may always be effected on some part of it, however, when possible, Howel's Bay should certainly have the preference; at all events it cannot be worse landing than at most of the West India islands.

"The climate and air must be judged of its situation, as our usual visits and short stays cannot determine them. Our thermometer in the bay at noon stood at 84 degrees upon deck in the shade, but upon the whole I am inclined to think them very salubrios. Our anchorage 1799, is marked by an anchor in Howel's Bay; but we were too near the shore to term it safe anchorage, and we could get no soundings further off. Although this island is situated in the line of the N.E. trade wind, yet as I (and others) have often met westerly winds, and some times very strong ones, I would not reccomend anchoring so near the short, unless a strong trade wind and clear weather should warrant it safe; In that case I would trust it safe, as the westerly winds are always (at least that I witnessed) indicated by heavy clouds, light variable airs, and unsettled weather. "The North mountain burns very much: the Southern ones just smoke, but very little. "Having filled the ship with cocoa nuts, firewood, crabs, and Papaw apples, and accomplished our business at sunset, we hoisted the boat, in and made sail for China.

We were not in want of fresh water, and too much otherwise occupied to seek for it, except what the party wanted for their drink, of which they found sufficient, and very good."

C.P.I. Ed. Note: The above text is a complete copy of a newspaper article . . . .

"Mattoetee *(Motu-iti?)* or *Kennedy Island,* was discovered by the Nautilus in 1801; it is stated to be in lat. 8° 36′ S., long. 167° 5′ E., but the position requires confirmation. Another authority places it in 167° 48′ E." (Findlay, *Directory of the South Pacific Ocean,* Third Edition, 1886, p. 837.)

[*The latitude given in text, 11° 17' S., 167° 58' E., is close to that for Utupua, 11° 20' S., 166° 30' E, at Basilisk Harbour entrance, (P.I.P., Vol. II, p. 261) and Vanikoro, 11° 42' S., 166° 49' E., at Pointe Baoure (P.I.P., Vol. II, p. 261).*]

"DUFF (WILSON) ISLANDS—[TAUMAKO GROUP]— This group, lying about 55 miles east-north-eastward of Matema Islands, was discovered by Quiros. They are 11 in number, extend 17 miles in a northwesterly and southeasterly direction, and consist apparently of volcanic rocks, and easternmost being columnar and covered with trees.

"Disappointment (Netepa) Island (9° 57' S., 167° 12' E., H.O. Chart 1985, the largest of the group, is about 1,200 feet in height." *(H.O. Pub.* No. 165, Vol. I, 4th ed., 1938, p. 287.)

Alamagan Island is 17° 36' N., 145° 50' E., H.O. Chart 5358. *(H.O. Pub.* No. 165, Vol. I, 4th ed., 1938, p. 568.) No mention of Howel's Bay is found in available reference material.

Sarigan Island is 16° 43' N., 145° 47' E., H.O. Chart 5358. *(H.O. Pub.* No. 165, Vol. I, 4th ed., 1938, p. 568.)

Pagan Island, southwest end, is 18° 03' N., 145° 43' E., H.O. Chart 5358. *(H.O. Pub.* No. 165, Vol. I, 4th ed., 1938, p. 568.)

Urac is possibly another spelling for Uracas.

Farallon de Parajos (Uracas Island) is 20° 32' N., 144° 54' E., H.O. Chart 5358. *(H.O. Pub.* No. 165, Vol. I, 4th ed., 1938, p. 570.)

TAUMAKO GROUP 2

Gazette of the United States for the Country,
Philadelphia, Pa.
May 31, 1803: 3, 2, 1
MH

NEWLY DISCOVERED ISLAND

We learn from Port Jackson that Mr. Simpson, commander of the Nautilus, has discovered in S. lat. 11 deg. 17 min. and E. lon. 167 deg. 58 min. an island which he called Kennedy's Island. From its beautiful appearance, united to its being well inhabited, Mr. Simpson is of opinion that it may prove a valuable acquisition to our new colony, particularly as it produces hogs in abundance. The natives (he says) are savage, artful, and treacherous, which obliged him to fire upon them; and this may be necessary precaution to any person who may wish to land upon it hereafter.

(Lon. paper.)

[*For C.P.I. Ed. Note see TAUMAKO GROUP 1.*]

TAUU 1

Columbia Centinel, Boston, Mass.
Aug. 31, 1831: 10, 1, 7
MBAt

[Reports in *American Traveller*, Boston, Sept. 2, 1831 (M) and *New Bedford Mercury*, Sept. 2, 1831 (MNBedf) are similar except that former has ' . . . at N. York last Friday evening, has . . .' and latter has ' . . . at New York 26th ult . . . .']

Schooner Antartic, arr. at N. York, has been absent on a voyage in the North and South Pacific Ocean two years; during which time she has lost nineteen men, six of them died natural deaths, and the other thirteen were massacred by the natives of a newly discovered island in the South Pacific, long. 160 East, while they were on shore trading—eight others were wounded who have since recovered. Capt. Merrell took one of the natives prisoner, whom he has brought home with him.

C.P.I. Ed. Note: The position 160° East given in above article is probably in error.
    " . . . This anchorage is in lat. 4° 50' 30" S., long. 156° 10' 30" E." (Morrell, Four Voyages to the South Seas, 1832, p. 395) "Tauu (Marqueen) Islands, about 90 miles eastward of Kilinailau Islands, are probably identical with the group seen and named Cocos in 1790, and also with those named Massacre Islands from an incident occurring in 1830." *(H.O. Pub. No. 165, Vol. I, 4th ed., 1938, p. 424.)*
    "Kilinailau (Cartaret) Islands (west end, 4° 44' S., 155° 16' E., H.O. Chart 2896), . . ." *(Ibid., p. 423) [Feb. 20, 1968: It ap-*

pears from the description given in TAUU 2 of an atoll with six islands that the events described took place on Kilinailau rather than Tauu.]

TAUU ₂

New England Palladium, Boston, Mass.
Sept. 2, 1831: 73, 2, 3
MBAt

[Report in *Boston Daily Advertiser,* Sept. 7, 1831 (MB) is apparently similar although shortened by C.P.I. worker. Report has in fifth sentence, ' . . . he fell in on the 23d of February with a group . . . .' Report in *Columbian Centinel,* Boston, Sept. 3, 1831 (MH) apparently similar but typescript begins at 'On the 22nd May an incident . . .' the earlier section having been omitted by the C.P.I. worker. The same is true of report from *New Bedford Mercury,* Sept. 2, 1831 (MNBedf) but in this case the first sentence is included. In all these three reports, Captain's name is given as 'Morrell.']

CRUISE OF THE SCHOONER ANTARTIC

On Saturday last was announced the arrival at this port of the schooner Antartic, under the command of Capt. Morrill, after an absence of two years, with a statement that while trading in the South Pacific, he had lost nineteen of his crew, in an encounter with the natives of a newly discovered island.

The circumstances attending the voyage of this vessel are of too remarkable a character to be dismissed with a passing notice.

The Antartic sailed from New York in September 1829, on a voyage to the South Seas, for the purpose of collecting a cargo of fur seal skins. In October following she touched at the Cape de Verd Islands, and obtained the salt necessary for the preservation of the skins expected to be taken; from thence she shaped her course for New Zealand, but being disappointed in procuring skins there, the captain determined on altering his voyage, and sailed for Manilla. Whilst proceeding thither, he fell in with a group of Islands, he named Nesterfield's group. They are small, and a reef of rocks runs from one island to the other. On the day following he discovered land again, and found it to consist of another group of islands, extending about seventy seven miles north and south; these being not mentioned on any chart, he called them Berght group. Here he had some intercourse with the natives, but it was impossible for him to obtain any information from them as to the inducements to trade which their islands afforded, and he therefore continued his course. On the 25th he again saw land, a long low island, which appeared to be loaded with cocoa nuts, without however, the least trace of inhabitants; this island he called Livingston island.

On the 9th of March, he arrived at Manilla, and there made up his mind to fit out the vessel for a voyage to the Fogee Island, in search of a cargo of Beach le Mar, Tortoise shell, &c, &c.

In the prosecution of this voyage he sailed from Manilla on the 12th April. Passing Ives Island Wallace's Island, he, on the 9th May, made six low islands called Los Maticas, where the natives came off to trade with him, but finding they possessed nothing worthy of his notice, his stay with them was short. They indicated to him that further north he would find a large quantity of the article of which he was in search—Beach le Mar.

In shaping his course in that direction he passed a group of islands called by the natives Tama Tam, another group denominated on the chart, Young William's group and the islands of Mondeverdesant.

Captain Morrill appears to have had but little intercourse with the natives of these places, merely enough to obtain from them cocoa nuts and bread fruit, and ascertain that they possessed nothing more. He describes the men as being remarkably robust and tall, sometimes by their conduct leading him to apprehend that they had hostile intentions; at others perfectly peaceable and having no war weapons about them.

On the 22d May an accident occurred to which we should have attached no importance, but which has been carefully noted down amongst the remarkable events of the voyage. "A little bird, as black as ink" came on board the schooner, and could not be induced to leave her. Some of the men, with the credulity common to seamen, thinking it was a bird of ill omen, wanted to kill it, but the captain, pleased with its perfect tameness, determined on preserving its life. On the following day the islands to which the name of Massacre Islands was afterwards given, were discovered and the little bird immediately flew to the land. Numerous no doubt, have since been the regrets on board, that the bird was allowed to escape; for to it have many of their subsequent misfortunes been strangely enough attributed.

On the 23d May, then, the schooner was in sight of six islands, all small with a reef of rocks running from one to the other, through which there was here and there a small channel about 100 yards in width. The islands appeared fruitful, and several large canoes were seen inside the reef, the boat was sent to the reef, and plenty of Beach le Mar, of excellent quality being found there, the captain determined on endeavoring to procure a cargo of that commodity at this place. After anchoring and making other necessary preparations, part of the crew were sent on shore on the 26th, for the purpose of clearing away the trees and bushes and building a house where the Beach le Mar, when taken, might be cured and rendered fit for transportation.

It is perhaps necessary that we should state here, that Beach le Mar is a fish of which the Chinese are particularly fond, and for which they pay a high price.

The natives had come off to the schooner in several large

canoes, bringing with them cocoa-nuts and shells. They were negroes of large stature and some of them appeared to possess considerable acuteness. No white men had ever been seen by them before; they thought the crew of the Antarctic were painted white, and endeavored by rubbing to bring their skins to the complexion of their own. Their ideas were all confined to the little group of islands on which they lived, they had however some imperfect notions of another group at some distance from them, and from those they presumed the schooner now came.

We abstain from noticing the surprise they exhibited on seeing their visitors: the conduct of savages in similar circumstances is probably always alike, and there are few of us who have not, at some time or other dwelt with deep interest on the details of the first meetings between civilized and uncivilized man.

The boat's crew had gotten the forge ashore and set it up; the natives stole some of the armorer's tools, which induced the captain to send another boat with a crew well armed; they compelled a restoration of the things stolen; but the natives now appeared hostile—they drew their bows, and stood ready to discharge their arrows. The crew then determined on seizing the person of the head chief, which they effected, and carried him on board, with many of the natives, he in the evening, however, jumped overboard and swam ashore, and in the course of the night the others followed his example.

On the following morning the people went ashore to work, as usual. At 8 o'clock they returned to the schooner to breakfast, leaving three men on shore to watch their tools; thirty three of the natives collected around these men, and were on the point of commencing an attack, which they only desisted from, on seeing that the boat had come back from the vessel and touched the shore. At midday a number of canoes put off from the is-

lands—the captain being apprehensive of hostilities reinforced
the hands on shore till they amounted in number to twenty-one.
Beads were also sent by him to the officer commanding them,
and he was particularly cautioned to be on his guard, a caution,
however, which he disregarded, for shortly after the natives
made a general and successful attack on them from the
wood,—two of the crew that were in the jolly boat had just time
to shove her off.—When out of the reach of the arrows, they laid
by and took on board three of the crew that had saved themselves in the water. The whale boat dispatched by the captain,
with ten armed men, on hearing the war whoop of the natives,
saved two more of them, the remainder were all massacred, with
the exception of one whose fate we shall hereafter mention.

Capt. Morrill with a diminished crew, found it impossible
to prosecute the objects of his voyage, and he therefore determined to return to Manilla, to obtain a reinforcement of men.
He arrived there on the 25th June, and having shipped fourteen
more men sailed again on the 8th August. On the 13th September he once more reached the islands where he had lost so many
of his crew, and which, from that circumstance, he called Massacre Island; but he had no sooner come to an anchor than he was
attacked by the natives in their canoes; a brisk fire from the
schooner, however, compelled them to retreat.

Shortly afterwards a small canoe put off from the shore, in
which to the great joy of all on board the schooner, they found
one of their old crew, Leonard Shaw, who at the time of the massacre, had hidden himself in the woods and escaped. He had remained concealed fifteen days, subsisting on only four cocoa
nuts when he was discovered by the natives and cruelly
wounded.

From this man, Captain Morrill learned, that the skulls of
thirteen of his men that were killed, were hanging at the Chief's
door, and that a few days before his return to the Island, the na-,

tives had consulted together on killing and eating Shaw himself, but delayed it in consequence of the absence of some of their chiefs. They afterwards sent him on board with proposals it was supposed of a pacific nature.

Shaw, while on this Island, was employed by the natives in manufacturing knives out of the iron they had obtained from the vessel. He was badly treated by them they giving him hardly enough to live upon. He represents the whole of the island as under the sway of one chief who rules with absolute power; each of the other islands has a sub-ordinate chief with many others dependent upon him. He says he could discover amongst them no traces of religion, no appearance of anything like a reverence for a superior power. The chiefs indulge in polygamy, but the generality of the men have but one wife, the women are reserved and chaste, their husbands killing them without any scruple on the least suspicion of infidelity. Shaw thinks they kill all the children except those of the chief, he having perceived none other amongst them. Their huts are made of Bamboes and the leaf of the cocoa nut trees, on the fruit of which, the banana and fish, they entirely subsist. The islands are entirely covered with wood, a few foot paths only running thro' them, the huts are built in small clusters on the seacoast for the convenience of fishing.

The length of this article warns us to bring it to a close, we therefore confine ourselves to but one other encounter with the natives. Capt. Morril, in order to protect the people at work on shore, caused a kind of battery to be constructed on the top of two large trees, about forty feet from the ground, and mounted it with four brass swivels, sixteen of his best men were placed in it with muskets and provisions, but it was hardly completed when the natives came down in large force and attacked the men below, the fire from the battery to their great surprise, opened upon them and compelled them to retreat with severe loss.

We pass over the purchase of the Massacre Island from its chief, his death and many other details. No exertions of Capt. Morrill could pacify the natives, they continued to persevere in their hostilities notwithstanding the great loss of lives they sustained, and the burning of their huts, and eventually compelled him to give up the hope of obtaining a cargo of fish from the reef of rocks which bounds their shores.

Capt. Morrill still prosecuted his voyage and made many other important discoveries, they are, however, his property, and we therefore abstain from noticing them in the hope that he will at another day reap that advantage from them which during this voyage has been denied him.

One of the natives from the Massacre Island, and another from another Island subsequently discovered have been brought home by Capt. Morrill. As may be supposed, they are objects of much curiosity.

His intention is to return with them to their homes, when he hopes that the treatment they have received at his hands will ensure him a better reception from their countrymen, and that the knowledge they will have acquired here, will be the means of introducing amongst them some of the advantages of civilization.

N. York Courier and Enquirer.

C.P.I. Ed. Note: The above text deals with the adventures of Capt. Morrill and discovery of Massacre Island. Rest is irrelevant.

Location: lon. 156° 10′ 30″ E., lat. 4° 50′ 30″ S. (Findlay's *Directory of the South Pacific Ocean,* 5th Ed. 1884, p. 873.) [*Feb. 20, 1968: It appears from the description given in TAUU 2 of an atoll with six islands that the events described took place on Kilinailau rather than Tauu.*]

TAUU 3

New York Observer
Sept. 3, 1831: 9, 3, 4-5
MBC

VOYAGE OF THE ANTARCTIC—*Massacre of* 13 *men.*—The schooner Antarctic having just arrived at this port after a voyage of two years, during which she has lost nineteen of her crew—6 by sickness and 13 by massacre,—the Rev. Mr. Chase, of the Mariner's church, in Roosevelt-street, improved the occasion which a large audience of seamen afforded him on the last Sabbath, of giving a relation of the bloody transaction which precipitated 13 men into eternity.—Mr. Chase had given notice of his intention during the morning services; and, as might have been expected, an audience, over which solemnity reigned, crowded the church, and listened to a sermon from those words:—*But truly, as the Lord liveth, and as thy soul liveth, there is but a step between me and death."* After the sermon, Mr. Chase gave in substance the following relation:—

The schooner Antarctic, captain Benjamin Morrell, sailed from this port September 2d, 1829, with a crew numbering 23, including men and boys. They were principally, however, young men from different parts of the United States, from England, and other countries. They were for the Pacific Ocean, in pursuit of a cargo of pearl, turtle shell, beach la mar; or fur, if they should find a more flattering prospect of success in that branch of trade.

As the voyage was expected to be a long one, the schooner was amply stored with provisions and the necessaries for comfort and health. Bibles and tracts were also put on board, that the means of religious instruction might not be wanting when they should be far from the doors of a Christian sanctuary, and the voice of the living preacher be lost in unmeasured distance. No ardent spirits whatever had been admitted on board as an article of drink, and the happiest results followed this regulation, in the order, harmony, and cheerful obedience of the men. The captain emphatically pronounces his crew *to have been a good one.* This exclusion of ardent spirits was a peculiarly happy circumstance as it regards the reputation of those concerned in this disastrous voyage, as now the unhappy circumstance of losing a part of the crew cannot be attributed to the imprudent use of strong drink.

There is a group of seven small islands, about fifty miles in circumference, lying in the South Pacific, not more than 5 degrees from Solomon's Archipelago, inhabited by savage tribes who had never before seen white people. To one of these islands, of about three miles in extent, situated in lat. 4 56 South, lon. 156 30 East, our adventurers came on the 26th of May, 1830, having previously increased the crew to 33 men, and found the prospects encouraging for obtaining a cargo of Beach la Mar, a species of fish of high value in the Chinese trade. Here anchors were cast and preparations made for building a house, to be used in curing the fish and for other purposes.

At first, the natives, who were negroes of large stature and considerable acuteness, appeared very friendly, and measures were taken to confirm their friendship, by the distribution of presents and the seeds of useful vegetables, while the crew proceeded to erect a house. By the fourth day they had nearly completed the frame—and while 19 of the crew, in company with many of the natives, were at work, some on the building and some in the surrounding wood, all perfectly unsuspicious of any danger, suddenly the natives gave a savage yell or war-whoop, and rushed upon them with bows and arrows, war-clubs, and spears. Those of the crew who were not immediately despatched, ran to the shore, and five of them plunged into the water. Of these five, three were badly wounded with arrows before they were saved by the boats of the schooner. Those who came to the rescue now rowed back with heavy hearts, leaving a number of their companions in sight on the shore, transfixed with spears and weltering in their blood. But they were not permitted long to grieve over their misfortunes, or for the loss of their shipmates. The sudden demonstrations of a preparation for a general attack on the schooner convinced the weakened crew that there was no safety but in flight. Cutting their cables, they hastily sailed from the scene of murder; and Captain Morrell gave the islands the name of "The Massacre Islands," in commemoration of the bloody transaction.

He then directed his course to Luzon, one of the Phillippine Islands, and entered the Spanish port, Manilla. Here he shipped a large number of men, and sailed again for the "Massacre Islands," where he arrived in about three months from the time of the massacre. Having come to anchor near the place where so many of his crew had been murdered, he soon discovered that the natives were still for war. They again made a general attack, but as the crew were now numerous and well armed, the enemy were driven back. Soon after this the natives sent one of the crew, supposed by the captain to have been murdered, on board the schooner, with a request that the firing should cease. He was received by his astonished companions as one raised from the dead, and the request of which he was the bearer was instantly complied with.

From this man, whose name is Leonard Shaw, and whose life was saved by little less than a miracle, the captain was able to learn many of the particulars respecting the fate of the slain. He stated that the bodies of his shipmates were eaten by the cannibals who had put them to death, and that their skulls were hanging as ornaments over the doors of the chiefs. He had been knocked down by a war-club which fractured his scull, but as he was not killed by the blow, he was allowed time to recover, and was reserved for a future feast. He had been compelled to paint and live after the manner of the islanders during the three tedious months of the schooner's absence, without the faintest hope of being rescued from their hands. About a week before the Antarctic returned the time appointed for him to be slain had arrived—the chiefs were invited to assemble, and he was sent to collect the wood necessary for the occasion, having been given to understand that his body was to be roasted for the feast. But some accident occurring in the family of a chief, the feast was put off to a future day; meantime the schooner arrived and he was delivered out of their hands.

The names and places of residence of the deceased are as follows:—*Died*—Francis Patterson, of Yorkshire; Daniel Spinney, of New York; Samuel Gerry, of New York; John Martin, of England; John May, do; John Hamer, do.; *Massacred*—John A. Wallace, of England; George Cartright, do.; Thomas Parker, do.; Geo. Webb, do.; Samuel Wood, do.; Thomas Barnard, do.; Henry Wiley, of Massachusetts; Joseph Hicks, of N. York; Alexander Mooney, do.; George Strong, of Albany, N. W.; James Butter, of Liverpool; Stephen De La Cruz, of Manilla; Polycarpeo Sylvestre, do.—*Badg. Week. Mess.*

C.P.I. Ed. Note: The text of this report is [*from a*] . . . news column headed "VOYAGE OF THE ANTARCTIC." . . .

The unidentified islands mentioned in text are probably Kilinailau Islands.

"Kilinailau (Cartaret) Islands West end, 4° 44' S., 155° 16' E., H. O. Chart 2896, . . ." (Ibid, p. 423)

[*Report has been checked against original newspaper.*

Feb. 20, 1968: It appears from the description given in TAUU 2 of an atoll with six islands that the events described took place on Kilinailau rather than Tauu.]

TAUU 4

Baltimore Patriot Mercantile Advertiser
Nov. 29, 1831: 33, 3, 6
MB

THE TWO SAVAGES FROM THE SOUTH PACIFIC ISLANDS

. . . "The schooner Antarctic, Captain Morrell, arrived at the
port of New York, from a Voyage of Discovery. During the voyage Captain M. discovered several islands in the South Pacific
Ocean inhabited by a singular race of savages.—He landed with
his cres, and endeavoured to cultivate a friendship with the natives in order to traffic with them for mother of pearl, beach-
le-mar, and other articles with which the islands abounded. At
first the savages seemed disposed to cultivate a spirit of amity,
but they finally turned upon the crew of the Antarctic, while on
shore and massacred thirteen of the crew. One of the sailors,
Leonard Shaw, who is now with the savages as kind of inter-
preter, was left on Massacre Island for 3 months. He has
published a pamphlet, which may be had at the exhibition
room, in which his suffrages, while among the savages, are narrated.

These South Sea Islanders are objects of the deepest curiosity. They have with them Bows, arrows, spears, paddles, clothing fishing lines made of the bark of trees, Neck ornaments, etc.,
etc. Their appearance is unlike that of any other human beings
that have ever been in this country. One of them is a Chief at
home—and both are strong muscular men and well
limbed.—The have been visited by thousands in New York, with
wonder and gratification. There is nothing in their appearance
that may prevent the most fastidious from beholding them.
They will remain in this city but a short time, and part of the

proceeds of their exhibition will be appropriated to the expense, of a voyage by which they may return to their own country, somewhat enlightened and improves."

C.P.I. Ed. Note: The text of this report is one item in a newspaper headed "The Two Savages from the South Pacific Islands."

The Antarctic anchorage at the "Massacre Islands" was 1st. 4°, 50′, 30″ S., lon. 156° 10′ 30″ East. (Morrell, *Four Voyages to the South Seas*, 1832, p. 395.) [*Feb. 20, 1968: It appears from the description given in* TAUU *2 of an atoll with six islands that the events described took place on Kilinailau rather than Tauu.*]

TAUU 5

Boston Advocate
Dec. 28, 1832: 1, 2, 1
MB

MORRELL'S VOYAGES AND DISCOVERY

This is another volume just added to this description of literature, which, to a large class of readers, has all the charms of romance. The narrative is drawn up with ease of an accomplished writer, and carries with it internal evidence of being the result of actual observation and adventure: it cannot fail to be very popular. Everyone remembers the prodigious run which Capt. Riley's Narrative had, although some of its marvels have not stood the test of investigation. The present Narrative is better drawn up, more instructive, and scarcely distinguished, with, "moving accidents by flood and field"

In his last voyage Capt. Morrell visited the MASSACRE ISLANDS, and there lost thirteen men of his crew, who were eaten by the Cannibals. This is perhaps the most direct and authentic detail we have, of the actual existence of cannibalism, which has been often doubted and as often asserted. Mrs. Morrell was the companion of her husband, during these frightful ventures.

C.P.I. Ed. Note: The above text possibly refers to Captain Morrell's "FOUR VOYAGES TO THE SOUTH SEAS," published in 1832, and containing a detailed account of his travels. The Antarctic anchorage at the "Massacre Islands" was 4° 50′ 30″S., 156° 10′ 30″ East. (Morrell, *Four Voyages to the South Seas,* 1832, p. 395.)

[*For additional C.P.I. Ed. Note see TAUU 1.*
Feb. 20, 1968: It appears from the description given in TAUU 2
of an atoll with six islands that the events described took place
on Kilinailau rather than Tauu.]

TEMATANGI 1

Sacramento Daily Union, San Francisco, Cal.
Apr. 1, 1857: 13, 3, 1
MB

The British schooner Archimides, Blair, of Sydney, from Valparaiso, bound for Sydney with a full cargo of flour and Panama hats, was wrecked on the 27th of January, on Tekee or Margaret Island, situated in lat. 20 36 S. long. 143 20 W. The Captain and crew arrived at Papetee, all well. The vessel was a total wreck.

C.P.I. Ed. Note: The text of this report is one item in a news column headed "FROM THE SOCIETY ISLANDS," the rest of which is irrelevant.

Nukutipipi (Margaret) Island is 20° 21′ S., 143° 04′ W., H.O. Chart No. 84 *(H.O. Pub.* No. 166, Vol. II, 4th ed. 1933, p. 136.)

[*The wreck was later found to have occurred on Tematangi. See TEMATANGI 2.*]

TEMATANGI 2

Weekly Bulletin, San Francisco, Cal.
Aug. 11, 1857: 2, 5, 1
MH

Two Wrecks.—A few days before the departure of the Roscoe, news had been received by the Government of the discovery of two wrecks of vessels on an island, called Bligh's Lagoon—one of which was supposed to be that of a German vessel, which left the Gambiers for Tahiti, in April 1856, since which nothing had been heard of her; and the other to be that of the British three-masted schooner Archimedes, which was lost in December last. The captain of the Archimedes supposed the vessel to have been lost on Margaret Island; but on examination, no traces could be found of her there. The natives of Bligh's Lagoon having resisted the attempts of parties to land to ascertain the particulars of the wrecks, the Government of Tahiti has dispatched the French steamer Milan, which would probably return a few days after the departure of the Roscoe.

C.P.I. Ed. Note: The text of this report is one item in a news column headed "Later from Tahiti," the rest of which is irrelevant. "Tematangi, or *Bligh Island,* was discovered by Captain Bligh, in 1792, and named by him *Lagoon Island.*" (Findlay, *Directory of the South Pacific Ocean,* Fifth Edition, 1884, p. 606.)
"Tematangi Island (21° 41′ S., 140° 39′W., H.O. Chart No. 77), 90 miles westward of Mururoa, was discovered in 1792 and named Lagoon Island. The atoll is about 7 miles in diameter." *(H.O. Pub.* No. 166, Vol. II, 4th ed., 1933, p. 135.) Report . . .

[*TEMATANGI*] taken from *Sacramento Daily Union,* of **April** 1, 1857, places the wreck of the *Archimedes,* at Nukutipipi, **or** Margaret Island.

TEMATANGI 3

Boston Post
Sept. 4, 1857: 51, 59, 9
MB

CALIFORNIA NEWS

The schooner J. H. Roscoe, 45 days from Tahiti, arrived at Panama. News had been received by the government of the discovery of two wrecks of vessels on an island, called Bligh's Lagoon,—one of which was supposed to be a German vessel, which left the Gambiers for Tahiti in April, 1856, since which nothing had been heard of her; and the other to be that of the British three-masted schooner Archimides, which was lost in December last.

C.P.I. Ed. Note: The text of this report is one item in a news column headed "LATER FROM TAHITI," the rest of which is irrelevant.

Archimides, mentioned in text is probably another spelling for the schooner Archimedes.

[*For additional C.P.I. Ed. Note see TEMATANGI 2.*]

TEMATANGI 4

Weekly Bulletin, San Francisco, Cal.
Sept. 5, 1857: 2, 5, 3
MH

By the Tahitian schooner, Eliza Dunnett which arrived here yesterday from Tahiti 60 days out we have dates to 1st July last. The following extracts of a letter from a private correspondent, written when the schooner was about to sail, gives the latest news from that quarter.

The Milan (French Steamer) has returned from Bligh's Lagoon, without having succeeded in getting any more information of the wrecks recently discovered on the above island. The natives having disappeared, they (the steamer) burned their canoes and houses, and tried to set fire to the herbage on the Island, but on account of the heavy and continued rains could not succeed. Bligh's Lagoon is covered with the Roa tree, which produces the thatch in which oranges are wrapped in Tahiti for this market. This thatch not being used, lies and rots upon the ground, and affords good shelter or concealment; when dry, it burns readily.

The schooner Emma L. Simpson landed at the Island and recovered some articles from the wrecks, and has identified the wrecks as being those of the schooners Sarah Ann and Archimedes. Mrs. Stevens, (of Papeete,) who had two sons on board the Sarah Ann has made arrangements with Hort Brothers to go still to the same Island and seek for her sons, some clothing of theirs being found by the above schooner.

Trade generally is very dull here, and there is little shipping in port.

C.P.I. Ed. Note: The text of this report is one item in a news column headed "LATER FROM TAHITI," the rest of which is ir-relevant.

"Tematangi, or *Bligh Island,* was discovered by Captain Bligh, in 1792, and named by him *Lagoon Island.* The natives seen by Captain Beechey are darker than the Lagoon Islanders of Cook, and were all provided with stones, clubs, and spears. A portion of these hostile natives were removed to Tahiti in 1858. They were strongly suspected of having eaten the shipwrecked crew of the *Sarah Anne.* "Findlay, *Directory of the South Pacific Ocean,* Fifth Edition, 1884, p. 606.)

[*For additional C.P.I. Ed. Note see TEMATANGI 2.*]

TEMATANGI 5

Daily Globe, San Francisco, Cal.
Dec. 27, 1857: 3, 2, 4
MH

Massacre at Bligh's Lagoon

Bligh's Lagoon, one of the circular reefs which abound in the South Pacific, is in South lat. 18 West Long. 172 and is generally considered as belonging to the Paumotu group. We are indebted to Capt. Bell, who came passenger from Tahiti in the Emma for the following statement of facts. About eighteen months ago a brigantine belonging to Bremen, name unknown, with a German captain and crew on board, together with a French priest, and two children of a Mrs. Stevens, of Tahiti, as passengers, sailed from Gambia Island for Tahiti. She never arrived at the latter place. Some time in June last, Captain Dunham of the schooner Julia landed on Bligh's Lagoon and found the natives in possession of several articles of women's clothing, and wearing necklaces braided from the hair of white men; besides which there were remnants of a wreck on the reef. On this being reported at Tahiti, the French war steamer Melan was dispatched to the island, but upon her approach the natives secreted themselves, and after burning a single hut the steamer returned to Tahiti. Mrs. Stevens at once chartered the Julia, and with a party of Society Islanders proceeded to the Island, where they landed, and by means of setting fire to the pandanus trees, which is the only vegetation there, succeeded in driving the people from their hiding places and taking sixteen out of the twenty-two, which comprised the entire population. Two were killed and four escaped. They found the skulls of the two children, respectively six and eight years of age, in the morae or sacred enclosure. The wreck had been so broken up that it could not be identified, though no doubt existed that it was that of the missing vessel. The natives were taken to Tahiti, and the women were in the families of the English missionaries.

—Com. Ad.

C.P.I. Ed. Note: The text of this report is one item in a news column headed "LATER FROM THE SANDWICH ISLANDS," the rest of which is irrelevant. Longitude 172° W. mentioned in text is probably in error.

[*For additional C.P.I. Ed. Notes see TEMATANGI 2 & 4.*]

TIKEI 1

Boston Patriot and Morning Advertiser, Boston, **Mass.**
May 14, 1817: 17, 2, 1
MSaE

[Reports in *Salem Gazette,* May 16, 1817 (MHi) and *Niles'
Weekly Register,* Baltimore, Md, May 17, 1817 (MNBedf) both
omit dateline and latter has 'Rorik'. Other wise both are identical.]

St. Petersburg, March 15—Lieut. Kotzebue, commander of the
ship Rurik, has discovered on his voyage round the world, several new islands, which he has named Romanzow's, Speridow's,
Krusenstern's, Kielurow's and Suwarrow's islands.

C.P.I. Ed. Note: The text of this report is one item in a news
column headed "FOREIGN," the rest of which is irrelevant.

Romanzow's is identified as Tikei or Romanzoff Island, was
discovered April 20, 1815, by Otto van Kotzebue, and was
named after the munificent author of his voyage. *(Directory of
the South Pacific Ocean*, Findlay, Fifth ed. 1884, p. 621.)

Tikei Island, is 14°57′S., 144°32′W., H.O.Chart No.77
(H.O. Pub. No. 166, Vol.II, 4th ed. 1933, p. 159.)

Speridow's is identified as Takapoto or Spiridoff.
Directory of the South Pacific Ocean, Findlay, Fifth ed. 1844, p.
621.)

Takapoto is 14°38′ S., 145° 12′W., H.O. Chart No. 81
(H.O. Pub. No. 166, Vol.II, 4th ed. 1933, p.160.)

"Tikahau, or Krusenstern, was discovered by Kotzebue,

April 24th, 1815." *(Directory of the South Pacific Ocean,* Findlay, Fifth ed. 1884, p. 624.)

Tikehau (Krusenstern) Atoll is 14°59'S., 148°08'W., H.O..Chart No.85 *(H.O.Pub.* No.166, Vol. II, 4th ed. 1933, p.164.)

Kielusow's cluster is identified as Utirik or Kutusoff Islands, and Kotzebue considered them a fresh discovery, May 21, 1815, on his passage to Kamchatka. *(Directory of the North Pacific Ocean,* Findlay, Third ed. 1886, p.960.)

Utirik (Kutusov) Atoll, at southeast end, is 11°14' N., 169°52' E., H.O.Chart No. 5427 *(H.O. Pub.* No. 165, Vol. I, 4th ed. 1938, p.505.)

Suwarrow's Cluster is identified as Taka or Souworoff Islands. *(Directory of the North Pacific Ocean,* Findlay, Third ed. 1886, p. 960.)

Taka (Suvarov) Atoll at south end is 11°05'N., 169°42'E., H.O. Chart 5427 *(H.O. Pub.* No. 165, Vol.I, 4th ed. 1938, p. 505.)

TIKEI 2

New England Palladium and Commercial Advertiser,
Boston, Mass.
Aug. 1, 1817: 65, 2, 2
MB

[Report in *Independent Chronicle and Boston Patriot,* Aug. 4, 1817 (MB; MBAt) has 'Spiridow' for 'Spiridour', 'Behring's' for 'Berkrings', and 'not yet 30 years of age' but is otherwise identical. Report in *Salem Gazette,* Nov. 4, 1817 (MSaE) has 'Spiridou', 'Behrings', 'not yet thirty years of age', and 'Wormskiold' for 'Wormskrold'. Otherwise the report, which cites 'the Literary Panorama' as source, is similar.]

OTTO VON KOTZEBU'S VOYAGE ROUND THE WORLD

From a London Paper:—The Berlin Gazette gives the following account of this expedition, which has been received from Kamtschatka.

Letters of an earlier date, which, after having doubled Cape Horn, he sent from the coast of Chili, have been lost, or at least have not yet come to hand, Mr. V. Kotzebue discovered three new islands in the South Sea, 14 of lat. and 144 of long.

To these islands he gave the names of Romanzow, (the author and equipper of the whole expedition.) Spiridour (an admiral under whom Kotzbue formerly served several years) and Krusentstern; (with whom he made his first voyage round the world.) Besides these he discovered a long chain of islands in the same quarter, and two clusters of islands in the 11th degree of lat. and 190th deg. of lon. (It is not specified whether the lat.

is N. or S. or the lon. E. or W.) These he called after the ship, Rurick's Chain; the two latter Kutusow's Cluster.(a group) and Suwarrow's Cluster.

All these islands are very woody, partly uninhabited, and dangerous for navigators.

The discoverer has sent to Count Romanzou a great many maps and drawings.

On the 12th of July, O.S. Kotzebue, designed to sail from Kamtschatka to Berkring's Straits, according to his instructions. He hopes to return to Kamtschatka in Sep. 1817. On the whole voyage from Chili to that place, he had not a single person sick on board.

He touched at Easter Island, but did not find the inhabitants so friendly as Peyrouse describes them. He thinks that something must have happened since that time, which has made them distrustful of the Europeans; perhaps it may be the overturning of their surprisingly, large statues, which Kotzebue looked for in vain, and found only the ruins of one of them near its base, which still remains.

He saw no fruits from the seeds left by La Peyrouse, nor any sheep or hogs, which by this time must have multiplied exceedingly. A single fowl was brought him for sale. It seems we may hope much from this young seaman, who is not yet 60 years of age.

He was obliged, for many reasons to leave the learned Dane Wormskrold behind, in Kamtschatka.

[For C.P.I. Ed. Note see TIKEI 1.]

TIKEI 3

Niles' Weekly Register, Baltimore, Md.
Aug. 2, 1817: 12, 365, 1
MNBedf

Russia

We have some account of Kotzebue's voyage round the world. He has discovered several new islands in the South Sea. At Easter Island he saw no fruits of the seeds left by Peyrouse, nor any sheep or hogs—a single fowl was brought to him for sale.

C.P.I. Ed. Note: The text of this report is one item in a news column headed "FOREIGN ARTICLES," the rest of which is irrelevant.

Easter Island or Rapa Nui (Great Rapa) at La Perouse Point, is lat. 27°8'46"S., long. 109°24'36"W., according to Admiral Beechey. *(Directory of the South Pacific Ocean,* Findlay, Fifth ed. 1884, pp. 515–519.)

Report . . . [*see TIKEI* 2] already submitted contains a detailed account of voyage mentioned in text and gives name of vessel not shown in text as *Rurick.*

TINIAN 1

Salem Gazette
May 17, 1799: 13, 3, 1
MSaE

[Report in *Columbian Courier,* New Bedford, May 22,1799 (MNBedf) apparently similar but C.P.I. worker has omitted the third to sixth sentences inclusive.]

PROVIDENCE—MAY 15

Extract of a letter from the Surgeon of the ship Ann and Hope, of this port, dated Whampoa, (China) Dec. 17, 1798.

"I wrote you (via London) from Port Jackson, in New Holland, and gave a circumstantial account of the voyage, till our arrival there. I will add, that after beating several days off Port Jackson, and finding it in vain to contend with adverse wind and a strong current, we fell to leeward, and ran into Botany Bay", the southern realm, and land of rogues," where we anchored Oct. 21. Next day, Messrs. Snow, Thompson, Page, jun, and myself, went to Sydney, a British settlement about 9 miles distant, where we waited on Governor Hunter, and were politely received. After tarrying two days, we returned to the ship, accompanied by some of the first characters at Sydney, who dined on board. On the 25th after having completed our wooding and watering, we again put to sea.

"On the 9th of Nov. off New Georgia, spoke the ship Jenny, Capt. R. Brown, from Boston, formerly of New York, bound for Canton. He informed, that agreeable to his orders, he had touched at the island of New Amsterdam, and taken off a number of the crew of a Boston sloop, that had been wrecked there; the rest of the crew preferred remaining on the island.

On the 30th of Nov. at half past 4 P.M. we made the island of Tinian, 7 leagues distant. Next day came to anchor in the road, and the Captain, with 25 men, went ashore. As we lay at anchor, we discovered, by means of a glass, two flags flying at Lord Anson's beach, and a man walking backward and forward, seemingly in great agitation. When the pinnace drew near the shore, he hailed her, and inquired what country men we were. Being told, he was questioned in turn. He replied that he was an unfortunate Lascar, cast away there about 18 months since, in the Brig Bramin, from Macao, Capt. Swain, formerly of Providence, R. I. When the captain went on shore, he prostrated himself at his feet, in the oriental manner. He informed us that he was the only human being on the island, and begged to be taken on board, and delivered from death. The scene was affecting. Capt. Page consoled him, by assuring him that he should return to Macao in the ship, where he would find vessels bound to Bengal, and be restored to his friends. He is about 25 years of age, had been the surang, or head of the gang, (a term answering to boatswain with us) and is a man of abilities. He converses in English, French, Spanish, Portuguese and Malay, besides his own language. He informed us that the brig was originally commanded by Capt. McClennan, an Irishman, who died at Lenconia; that the mate, whose name was Swain, succeeded to the command; that they arrived at Tinian about 18 months since, and, preserving no order, the Captain and his mistress being on shore, and the people on board intoxicated, she parted her cables in the monsoon at night, and struck on a reef, where she went to pieces. The people were all saved except one, and part of her cargo was preserved. The crew lived some months in huts, after which The Lascars, 9 or 10 in number, remained till the arrival of a Spanish vessel, when they were confined in irons, and all carried off, except this unfortunate man, who escaped into the woods. When the Spaniards had sailed, he returned to the huts, which he found plundered of everything saved from the wreck. Here he had spent his time in solitude and tears till our arrival.

"Tinian abounds with fruit, such as oranges, limes, guavas, the bread fruit, cherries, plumbs, beans, cocoas, and cabbages; cotton and indigo are also in a great plenty. The cattle are numerous and large, and hogs and fowls abundant. We saw some remains of the pyramidical pillars mentioned by Lord Anson, but none of them are standing. This island, even in its present uncultivated state, appears to be one of the finest and most desirable spots on earth. We remained there about 12 hours, got a supply of vegetables, and then departed. It lies in lat. 15 North, long. 146 East."

C.P.I. Ed. Note: Tinian Island, mentioned in text, may possibly be "Tinian Island (south end, 14° 55′ N., 145° 38′ E., H. O. chart 5359). . . ." *(H.O. Pub.* No. 165, Vol. I, 4th ed. 1938, p. 564.)

Ship *Ann and Hope* of Providence.

TINIAN 2

New England Palladium, Boston, Mass.
Jan. 23, 1827: 64, 3, 1
MBAt

Captain Alfred P. Edwards, of N. York, who came passenger in the ship Champion, at the Vineyard, from Canton and Manilla, states that he was at the Island of Guam, the Capital of the Ladrone or Mariana Islands, in April last, and that while there he learnt from the Governor that he had, a few days before, dispatched a Sergeant's Guard to the Island of Tinian, and that on their arrival there, they found that the Island had, a short time before, been visited by the British whale ship George the Fourth, Capt. Buckley, of London, and that, after replenishing his ship with refreshments, he commenced a general devastation on the Island, by burning all the houses built there, cutting down and destroying the Bread Fruit, Cocoa Nut Trees, Vines, &c, &c, and left the Island. Two of his crew, however, deserted, and were found in the Island by the Soldiers, and from them the facts were confirmed. No reasons were assigned for his conduct.

The Island of Tinian is the spot in which Lord Anson, when on his voyage round the World, stopped for refreshment, when his crew was in the most distressed situation, from the effects of the Scurvy, and the Island is described by the writer of Anson's Voyage, as being one of the most fertile and delightful spots on the face of the Globe; and from that time it has been a favorite stopping place for the ships which visit the Pacific, particularly the American Whale Ships.

The Governor of Guam had taken measures to have the houses rebuilt, and the Fruit Trees renewed.

C.P.I. Ed. Note: Tinian Island is south end, 14° 55′ N., 145° 38′

E., H.O. Chart 5359. *(H.O. Pub.* No. 165, Vol. I, 4th ed., 1938, p. 564.)

Guam Island is south end, 13° 15′ N., 144° 43′ E., C.S. Chart 4202. *(H.O. Pub.* No. 165, Vol. I, 4th ed. 1938, p. 556.)

TINIAN 3

New Bedford Mercury
Oct. 9, 1829: 23, 3, 1
MNBedf

NEWS COLUMN

A whaler, lately in weighing her anchor at the Island of Tinian, hooked up the anchor of the Centurion, 64 guns, which was left there by that ship in the year 1742, when Com Lord Anson touched there to refresh his crew. It was comparatively little corroded, having merely on it a thick coat of rust. The wooden stock was completely rotted off. The anchor was carried over to the island of Guam, where the natives immediately commenced beating it out into bars and belts, with which they are now building a brig.

[*For C.P.I. Ed. Note see TINIAN 2.*]

TINIAN 4

Boston Daily Evening Transcript
Oct. 12, 1852: 23, 1, 4
MBAt

RUINS OF AN ANCIENT AND MAGNIFICENT CITY AT TINIAN ISLAND, IN THE NORTH PACIFIC

Capt. Alfred R. Fisher, of this town, informed us that when on his last whaling voyage, in the ship America, of New Bedford, (which was about 8 years ago,) he had occasion to visit the island of Tinian, (one of the Ladrone Islands,) to land some sick men. He stopped there some days. One of his men in his walks about the island, came to the entrance of the main street, of a large and splendid city, in ruins. Capt. Fisher, on being informed of the fact, entered the city by the principal street, which was about three miles in length. The buildings were all of stone, of a dark color, and of the most splendid description. In about the center of the main street he found 12 solid stone columns, six on each side of the street; they were about 45 or 50 feet in height, surmounted by cap stones of immense weight. The columns were 10 feet in diameter at the base, and about three feet at the top. Capt. F. thinks the columns would weight about 60 or 70 tons, and the cap-stones about 15 tons. One of the columns had fallen, and he had a fine opportunity to view its vast proportions and fine architecture. From the principal street, a large number of other streets diverged. They were all straight, and the buildings were of stone. The whole of the city was entirely overgrown with coco-nut trees, which were 50 and 60 feet in height. In the main street, pieces of common earthenware were found. The island has been in possession of the Spaniards for a long time. Six or seven Spaniards resided on the island when

Capt. F. was there. They informed him that the Spaniards had had possession about 60 years—that they took the island from the Knackas, who were entirely ignorant of the builders of the city, and of the former inhabitants. When questioned as to the origin of the city, their only answer was—"There must have been a powerful race here a long time ago." Capt. F. also saw on the island immense ledges of stone, from which the buildings and columns had evidently been ejected. Some portions of them exhibited signs of having been worked. There is food for speculation. Who were the founders of this once magnificent city in the North Pacific and what has become of their descendants? Whatever the answer may be, they were evidently a race of a very superior order.

C.P.I. Ed. Note: The text of this report is one item in a newspaper column headed "RUINS OF THE ANCIENT AND MAGNIFICENT CITY AT TINIAN ISLAND IN THE NORTH PACIFIC," the rest of which is irrelevant.

[*For additional C.P.I. Ed. Note see TINIAN 2.*]

TINIAN 5

Salem Gazette
Nov. 23, 1852: 94, 2, 5
MSaE

[Identical report in *Essex County Mercury* (W), ˙Salem, Nov. 24, 1852 (MSaE).]

RUINS OF ANCIENT CITIES IN THE ISLANDS OF THE NORTH PACIFIC

The ruins of ancient cities of immense magnitude and extent, have long been known to exist in several islands of the Pacific ocean, the origen and existence of which, history furnishes no account. In one of the Ladrone islands, a group lying in latitude 16 deg. north, longitude 170 east, some two thousand miles from the coast of China, are the stupendous ruins of one of these ancient cities.

The Vineyard Gazette, published at Edgartown, gives an account of a visit to these ruins by Capt. Alfred K. Fisher, of the Nantucket whale ship America. The principal street was three miles long, and the buildings all of stone of a dark color, and of the finest material. Near the centre of the street were twelve solid columns, near fifty feet in height, and ten feet in diameter at the base, surmounted by stone Caps of immense weight. From the principal avenue other streets diverge at regular intervals and at right angles. The ruins of the whole city were overgrown with trees of ancient and gigantic growth. The native inhabitants, nor the Spaniards in whose possession the island is at present, could give no account of the founders of the city. It seems to be a counterpart of those Central American cities, the record of whose people is blotted from the memories of men. Boston Journal.

TONGA 1

Massachusetts Mercury, Boston, Mass.
Aug. 1, 1797: 10, 3, 1
MSaE

From an English paper, May 30.

Our last advices from the coast of France, afford us some very cautions and interesting particulars: Two ships, who sailed on a voyage of discovery from L'Orient early in the summer of 1794, and supposed long since to have perished, arrived in safety at that port, after having explored a considerable part of the Southern hemisphere. They remained at the friendly Isles nearly six months, and were so cordially received by the natives, that five of them solicited, and obtained permission to visit the Lobotato, or heavenly world, as they now call Europe, and have also arrived in perfect health at L'Orient. The French navigators have brought the pleasing information, of the natives both in the Sandwich and Friendly Islands, having at length succeeded in finding a remedy for that tremendous disorder, which had for several years desolated each country.

C.P.I. Ed. Note: Tonga (Friendly) Islands consists of over 100 islands and islets, lying between 18° 01′ and 21° 28′ S., and 173° 54′ and 175° 33′ W. (*H.O. Pub.* No. 166, Vol. II, 4th ed. 1933, p. 192.)

TONGA 2

Columbian Centinel, Boston, Mass.
June 28, 1806: 45, 2, 1
MHi; MWA

New Speculation

A letter from *Canton (China)* dated *Jan.* 9, 1806, informs that a Nantucket ship had arrived there from the *Friendly Islands,* with three thousand picol of *Sandal Wood,* which sold at twenty seven dollars the *picol.* The first object of the voyage was seal skins, which not succeeding, the Captain turned his attention to collecting the Sandal Wood; in which he succeeded so well, that the wood which cost, it was said, only 1500 dollars, sold for 78,000.

The number of *Dollars* imported into *China,* by American vessels, in 1803 and 1804-1805, amounted to 4,857,300!

C.P.I. Ed. Note: The text of this report is an item in a newspaper column headed "New Speculation." . . .

[*The text of this report has been checked against original newspaper held by MWA. The last sentence was omitted by the C.P.I. worker.*]

TONGA 3

Columbian Centinel, Boston, Mass.
Nov. 24, 1827: No. 4552, 2, 5
M

ARRIVED

Edgartown, Nov. 17, Arr. ship Franklin, Coffin 120 days from Coquimbo, with 2050 bbls. oil for Nantucket, Ship North America, was to leave Tonga, 20th, July for Nantucket. The Franklin, Oct. 17, reports no late news from any whale ships in South Seas. 18th. arr. ship Loan, from Mattapoisett, where she had been undergoing repairs. 20th, 8 o'clock P.M. arr. ship Ganges, Coffin, 4 months, from Society Islands, full cargo of oil for Nantucket.

C.P.I. Ed. Note: The text of this report is one item in a newspaper column headed "ARRIVED," complete text is given. . . .
The Society Islands lie approximately between Motu-Iti, (Tubai) Island, Lat. 16° 17′ S. and Mehetia Island, Lat. 170 53′ S., and between Mehetia Island, Lon. 143° 05′ W. and Fenua Ura (Scilly) Islands. Lon. 154° 43′ W. H.O. Charts, No. 2023-2065. *Ibid.* pp. 120, 72, 121.

[*For additional C.P.I. Ed. Note see TONGA 1.*]

TONGA 4

Boston Daily Atlas
Sept. 30, 1834: 3, 2, 3
MHi

Intelligence has been received at Salem by the owners of a brig, that while fourteen of the crew were employed at the Feejee Islands, they were attacked by a body of the natives, who killed nine of them. It has often been recommended to mariners not to trust too much to savages, lest they should abuse the confidence placed in them, and giving way to their horrible propensities and passions commit outrages. About thirty years ago the master of an English vessel anchored near one of those islands, and admitted the natives on board without restriction. What was the consequence? At a concerted signal they attacked and murdered the English and made themselves masters of the vessel.—A boy, however, whose name was Mariner, having concealed himself in the hold, escaped the fate of his comrades, and remained four years in the country, after which he was received on board a ship which touched there, and conveyed home. Shortly after his return a narrative of his adventures was published, it having been compiled with care and judgement by Dr. Martin. Prior to this publication, the cluster of islands now called the Feejes, or, as Dr. Martin spells the word, Fiji, had been laid down in maps as the Friendly, the name given to them by Capt. Cook, to commemmorate his kind and hospitable reception by the natives.—That great navigator however, was completely deceived by them, Mr. Mariner having learned that it was their design to assassinate his whole party, and that nothing prevented its execution but the time.—Their treachery, accordingly was neither discovered nor suspected by Cook, but having been made known to Mr. Mariner, there appeared sufficient reason to substitute the name by which they themselves designate the islands, for the one bestowed by Capt. Cook. His narrow escape, and the fate of the crews mentioned above, should teach those who visit the islands, not to lay aside precaution in their intercourse with them and other uncivilized nations who have seldom been visited by Europeans or Americans. The master of the Salem brig afterwards touched at the Pelew Islands, where also he was attacked by the natives, whom, however, he repulsed, though with the loss of one of his crew, a Sandwich boy, in the conflict. Either, then, the Pelew Islanders must have become changed in character since the time of Abba Thul. who protected and supported Capt. Wilson after his shipwreck amongst them, or they must have received some provocation from other navigators. The old chief showed his confidence in his guests, by placing his son, Lee Bee, under the care of Capt. Wilson, who took him to England. Lee Bee gained so much the affection, not only of his patron, but of all those to whom he was introduced, that his memory is still preserved in England with respectful association.

C.P.I. Ed. Note: The text of this report is taken from an article for a separate report on the island mentioned. Pelew (Palau) Islands lie in lat. 7° 19'N., lon. 134° 28'E. *(H.O. Pub. No. 165, Vol. I, 4th ed. 1933, pp. 548-9.)*

TONGA 5

The Sailor's Magazine and Naval Journal, New York
Nov. 1840: 13, 90, —
MNBedf

Australia and Pacific Islands

On the 19th July left the Bay of Islands. Wind S. W., steered direct for Toga, which after baffling winds we saw on the 28th. I tried to make Pylstart Island, but not having seen it, I concluded it lies to the westward of 184 5'E. The wind hanging to the westward, I rounded the west end of Tonga, and hove to for the night. Having rounded the west end of the Island, avoiding some reefs off it, all of which I believe are visible, I ran to the E. N. E. until past the island of Atata. The passage into which I entered is to the northward of the middle reef, which is circular, and lies N.E. from Atata. The passage is about half a mile wide, with another reef about that distance north from the circular one. Having entered betwixt these two, it is necessary to keep to the south-east for about a mile and a half, to avoid some stones that lie off the middle reef, and then haul up south by compass for Nukualofa, which may be distinguished by the church, built on the only rising ground near. I anchored in 14 fms. with the small reef bearing north, the church south, Panghai Motu E. by N. just shutting in the distant main land. With the prevailing S. E. winds the usual passage in, is between the east end of Toga and Ena Island to the anchorage under Panghai Motu. The north passage is to be preferred in going out, the passage west of Atala being narrow and intricate, and therefore should not be attempted without a leading wind.

Nukualofa is the principal christian town and the residence of the missionaries. The population of the island is 5000, of which 1000 are christians. The principal heathen settlements are Bea about 5 miles from Nukualofa, and Mua about the same distance up the creek, round Panghai Motu. The water is bad and not plentiful. Pigs, yams, &c., may be obtained. The landing is awkward, as a reef extends a quarter of a mile from the shore; but just to the eastward of the church a cut has been made, which admits a boat to approach the shore at high water. King Josias promised me that he would build a wharf out into deep water. A pilot will come off on a signal being made.

Toga to Hobai—Left Toga at 1h. 20 m. on the 3rd August, and the regular breeze blowing, ran out by the northern passage at 7 h. 30 m. having run N. 51 E. (true) 29 miles perceived two small islands and tacked off. At daylight made the land and ran round Haano the N. E. island of the Habai group; found we had been set north 15 miles; attempted to find an anchorage under it, but not liking its appearance, stood off. These islands are very low; the reefs do not extend more than a quarter of a mile on the eastern of the northernmost islands. In rounding Haano it is necessary to give the N. W. point a berth of half a mile to avoid a reef off it. From the point N. 41 E. (true) 6 miles, lies a bank with only 3 fms. on it, which does not appear to have been before noticed. Went up to Lifuka, the residence of the missionaries, in my boat, and during my stay got observations for the time and the latitude. The ship was in the mean time employed in making a rough survey of the coast, and while standing off and on for the night she discovered the bank above mentioned.

The Habai Islands are subject to King George of Vavan, and Lifuka is his favorite residence; the population is about 4000 to 4500, three-fourths Christians. The only place likely to afford an anchorage is upon the shoal patch to the west of Foa, with the space between Lifuka and Foa open. Nothing but a few yams or fowls is to be procured.

Koa is a perfect pyramid about 5000 feet high.

Tofoa has an active volcano at the north end, and is about 2800 feet high. A remarkable lake is spoken of on Tofoa, the islanders bring from it numbers of small black pebbles of igneous origin, which are much in request to cover the graves of their friends. About thirty persons reside at Koa and seventy at Tofoa.

Habai to Vavan.—Vavan lies N. E. about 60 miles from Haano. We ran in by the S.W. passage. No directions are necessary, the water being very deep and there being no hidden danger. The finest yams in the universe are grown at Vavan. During my stay, King George acquainted me that he had chosen a flag for his dominions; white bordered with red, bearing a St. Andrew's cross of the same colour. Should a ship require a refit, there may be found a snug berth under a small island on the south side of the harbour, bearing about S.W. one mile and a quarter from the usual anchorage. A ship of 400 tons has been hove down on the beach opposite.

C.P.I. Ed. Note: The above text is a complete copy of an article. . . .

Pylstart is possibly another spelling for Pylstaart (Ata) Island.

Ata, also known as Pylstaart Island, is 22° 20′ S., 176° 12′ W., H. O. Chart No. 2016. (*H.O. Pub.* No. 166, Vol. II, 4th ed., 1933, p. 196.)

The position assigned in the text of above report should possibly read 175° 55′ W., instead of 184° 05′ E. Toga, or Tonga Island, may possibly be another name for Tongatabu, the largest of the Tonga Islands.

A portion of the above text, describing the rounding of Atata and anchoring off Nukiualofa, by the *Conway,* is men-

Night dance at Hapai, Tonga. From Cook's *Voyages.*

tioned in Findlay's *(Directory of the South Pacific Ocean,* Fifth Edition, 1884, p. 538.)

There are three channels by which Nukualofa Anchorage can be reached—Lahi (Great) Passage, Biha (Eastern) Passage, and Egeria Channel. *(H.O. Pub.* No. 166, Vol. II, 4th ed., 1933, p. 198.)

Tongatabu Island is 21° 10′ S., 175° 15′ W., H.O. Chart No. 2016. The towns of Mu'a, Bea and Nukualofa (the capital of the Tonga Group) are on this island. *(Ibid,* p. 197) The circular reef mentioned in above report is possibly Hakau Mamao.

Hakau Mamao is an oval, coral, reef lying northeastward of Niu Aunofo. *(H.O. Pub.* No. 166, Vol. II, 4th ed., 1933, p. 199.)

Lahi Passage is 20° 57′ S., 175° 12′ W., H.O. Chart No. 2013 and is entered from the northward, passing eastward of Hakau Mamao and Monro Rock. *(Ibid,* p. 199)

Monro Rock is possibly the second reef mentioned in text. Monro Rock is a small coral head with 4 fathoms of water over it, located 1,800 yards northeastward of Hakau Mamao, in approach to Lahi Passage. *(Ibid,* p. 199)

Atata Island is 21° 03′ S., 175° 16′ W., and is located westward of Lahi Passage. *(H.O. Pub.* No. 166, Vol. II, 4th ed., 1933, p. 199.)

The small reef mentioned in above report may possibly be Pangaimotu Reef.

Pangaimotu Reef is mentioned, in the description of the Eastern Passage, as having a beacon on its northwestern point. *(H.O. Pub.* No. 166, Vol. II, 4th ed., 1933, p. 201.)

Panghai Motu is possibly another spelling for Pangaimotu. This island should not be confused with another of similar name (in two words) located in the Vavau Group of the Tonga Islands. A separate report on the *Conway's* visit to this other island is included in . . . this account.

Kava-drinking ceremony, Friendly Islands. From Cook's *Voyages*.

Pangaimota Island is mentioned in the directions for approaching the Eastern Passage from the north, or south. *(H.O. Pub. No. 166, Vol. II, 4th ed., 1933, p. 201.)*

Ena is possibly another spelling for Eua Island. Eua Island is 21° 20′ S., 174° 57′ W., H.O. Chart No. 2010. *(H.O. Pub. No. 166, Vol .II, 4th ed., 1933, p. 196.)*

Habai is possibly another spelling for Haapai Group. Haano Island, the northernmost island of the Hapai Group is 19° 40′ S., 174° 17 W. *(H.O. Pub. No. 166, Vol. II, 4th ed., 1933, p. 229.)*

A barrier reef follows the eastern coast line of the chain of islands. Northward of Haano it projects over 1,000 yards. *(Ibid, pp. 229 to 230)*

Bethune Bank is possibly the bank referred to in above text. Bethune Bank extends 7 miles in a northerly direction with depths of 7 to 10 fathoms, its center being about 5 miles northeastward of the northern extremity of Haano Island. *(H. O. Pub. No. 166, Vol. II, 4th ed., 1933, p. 231.)*

Lifuka Island is 19° 48′ S., 174° 21′ W., H.O. Chart No. 2009. *(H.O. Pub. No. 166, Vol. II, 4th ed., 1933, p. 224.)*

Habai is possibly another spelling for Haapai Group. Haapai Group is composed of numerous small coral islands, 19° 54′ to 20° 10′ S., 174° 16′ to 174° 48′ W., H.O. Charts Nos. 2007 and 2008. *(H.O. Pub. No. 166, Vol. II, 4th ed., 1933, p. 211.)*

Foa Island is the next island northward of Lifuka, standing on the same reef, H.O. Chart No. 2007. *(H.O. Pub. No. 166, Vol. II, 4th ed., 1933, p. 229.)*

Koa Island lies northward of Tofua, separated by a channel two miles wide. It rises to a peak, 3,380 feet high, which appears as an almost perfect cone from every direction. *H.O. Pub. No. 166, Vol. II, 4th ed., 1933, p. 222.)*

Tofoa is possibly another spelling for Tofua Island. Tofua

Double canoe of the missionaries, Vavau, Tonga. From Dumont D'Urville, *Voyage au Pole Sud*, 2nd expedition, 1837-1840, plate 79.

Island is 19° 45′ S., 175° 05′ W., H.O. Chart No. 2016. It is an active volcano, 1,500 to 1,660 feet high, there is a remarkable fresh water lake in the center of the island. Tofua is uninhabited but is frequented by the natives of other islands, who take away the black volcanic stones to decorate graves. *(H.O. Pub. No. 166, Vol. II, 4th ed., 1933, p. 222.)* Vavan is possibly another spelling for Vavau Island. Vavau Island, 18° 37′ S., 174° 01′ W., is the principal island of this group of the Tonga Islands. *(H.O. Pub. No. 166, Vol. II, 4th ed., 1933, p. 238.)*

The small island mentioned in above text is possibly Pangai Motu.

This island should not be confused with another of similar name (combined in one word), located off Tongatabu Island.

Pangai Motu, a fantastically shaped island, forms with the main island the harbor and ports of Neiafu. *(H.O. Pub. No. 166, Vol. II, 4th ed., 1933, p. 241.)*

Neiafu Harbor, between the northeast coast of Pangai Motu and the southwest coast of Vavau, is 18° 39′ S., 173° 59′ W., H.O. Chart No. 1983. *(Ibid, p. 242)*

Stone archway, Tonga.

TONGA 6

Daily Mail, Boston, Mass.
Dec. 22, 1840: —, 1, 2
MB

Disatrous affair with the natives of Tongo, one of the South Sea Islands.—Sydney papers of the 25th July furnish us with the details of an affair between the natives of Tongo and the crew of Her Majesty's ship Favorite, Captain Crocker, in which the Captain was killed and several of the men were wounded. It appears that the heathen portion of the natives had again exhibited a spirit of persecution and the Missionaries, Messrs. Tucker and Ravone, with their families, were obliged to fly for their lives to a small fort belonging to the Christian natives. Just at this crisis, Her Majesty's ship Favorite appeared off the island, and the missionaries sent a letter to the captain, informing him of their perilous circumstances, and requesting him to afford them protection.

Captain Crocker immediately, landed with a number of armed men and proceeded to the headquarters of the heathen party, with the humane intention of acting the part of a mediator, and effecting a reconciliation between them and the native Christians.

To the surprise of the captain he found that the heathens had a strong fortification, surrounded by a moat filled with water, 40 feet wide.

The place had all the appearance of having been constructed by persons acquainted with engineering, having regular loop-holes for musketry, while the entrance was guarded by a carronade.

Some Europeans were associated with the heathens and one of them long known in the island by the significant title of

"Jimmy the Devil", took an active part in the negotiation which ensued. Captain Crocker endeavored to convince them of the desirableness and advantages of peace, and proposed that both parties should destroy their forts, and live in amity with each other.

For a time, he entertained the hope that this mediation would be successful; but at length, impatient of the delay which took place, he ordered a musket or two to be fired for the purpose of intimidation. This unfortunate step produced, however, the opposite result.

The carronade was immediately discharged, accompanied by a heavy fire of musketry, by which the captain and two officers were killed; and the first lieutenent and nineteen men were wounded. Lieut. Dunlap shortly ordered his men to retire, and returning to the spot where the missionaries and their families were, took them on board the Favorite and conveyed them in safety to the neighboring island of Vanou.

C.P.I. Ed. Note: The above text is a complete copy of an article in a newspaper column, the rest of which is irrelevant.

[*For additional C.P.I. Ed. Note see TONGA 1.*]

Double canoe in its house, Tonga. From Dumont D'Urville, *Voyage au Pole Sud*, 2nd expedition, 1837-1840, plate 78.

TONGA 7

Boston Daily Advertiser
Feb. 7, 1851: 77, 2, 7
M

WHALERS

At Friendly Islands, Sept 3, Canton Packet, Howland, New Bedford, 8 mos. out, 140 sp, all well, bound to New Zealand; reported by letter from the first officer. A letter from the second officer, dated July 27, reports her 150 sp.

C.P.I. Ed. Note: The text of this report is an item in a newspaper column headed "WHALERS," . . . the rest of which is irrelevant.

[For additional C.P.I. Ed. Note see TONGA 1.]

TONGA 8

The Commonwealth, Boston, Mass.
Sept. 16, 1854: 8, 2, 3
MH

[Report in *Salem Evening Journal—D*, Sept. 16, 1854 (MSaE) is identical to the first two sentences.]

Loss of a Whaleship

The New Bedford Mercury mentions the loss of the whaleship Sally Anne, of that port, Capt. Hathaway, which was lost on Friendly Islands on the 2nd of April last. All hands were saved. The natives took possession and stole everything. The vessel was insured in New Bedford, at the Union Mutual Marine Insurance office for $1688; Commercial Mutual Marine $7625; and at two offices in Boston for $11,000.

C.P.I. Ed. Note: The text of the above report is one item in a newspaper column headed "Loss of a Whaleship," the rest of which is irrelevant.

Friendly Islands are identified as Tonga Islands.

[*For additional C.P.I. Ed. Note see TONGA 1.*]

TONGA 9

Boston Daily Courier
July 3, 1863: 29, 4, 2
MB

DEATH BY SHIPWRECK

Information has just been received by letter from Sydney of the death by shipwreck of Edward W. Gardiner Esq. and wife of Nantucket. In 1862 he received the appointment of Government Commercial Agent to Navigator's Island, and sailed from New York in May of that year. The vessel was wrecked on or about the 11th of January, near the Friendly Islands. The British Consul to Navigator's Islands was also on board and the English authorities have since made every search for him or any survivors, if any there might be but without avail. Mr. Gardiner was the father of Thomas 73, Gardiner Esq. of this city.

C.P.I. Ed. Note: The text of this report is one item in a newspaper column headed "DEATH BY SHIPWRECK," . . . the rest of which is irrelevant.

[For additional C.P.I. Ed. Note see TONGA 1.]

TONGA 10

The Friend, Honolulu
Sept. 1, 1863: 20, 72, 1
MSaP

WRECK OF THE "ANITA," AND LOSS OF LIVES

From our valued correspondent, Mr. A. Unshelm, Hamburg, Consul at Apia, Samoan Islands, we have received the following particulars relating to the wreck of the Anita, and the probable loss of several passengers and the crew. Among the passengers we notice with feelings of deep sorrow the names of our old friends and acquaintances, Captain and Mrs. Gardner, of Nantucket, and also two children of Mr. Pritchard. Hereafter should additional particulars come to light, we hope our correspondent will not fail to communicate the same.

The Hamburg schooner Anita, bound from Fejee to Samoa with a cargo of cocoanut oil, was lost in a tremendous hurricane on the 12th of January last. The vessel is supposed to have been lost between Vavou and Savage Island, (Friendly Island Group.) On board of the Anita were Captain and Mrs. Gardner, of Nantucket, proceeding to Samoa, where Captain Gardner had been appointed U.S. Consul. On board were also a sister and two children of Mr. W.P. Pritchard, H. B. M. Consul at Fejee (son of the Consul formerly of Tahiti.) Mr. Pritchard was sending his family to Samoa, to proceed in one of Mr. Unshelm's vessels to England. In the meantime, in happy ignorance of the fearful blow impending over their heads, Mr. and Mrs. Pritchard subsequently took passage in the Cheetah, of Sydney, to rejoin their family, as they hoped, in Samoa, with the view of all proceeding together homewards. On the trip from Fejee to Samoa, the Cheetah called at Haapai, Friendly Islands, and while receiving cargo, Mr. and Mrs. Pritchard were invited to remain at the mission house. On the morning after their arrival, they took a walk on the beach, along the seashore. They had not gone many yards when they observed something floating over the reef. They watched it as it came nearer. "It is a box," they said. A moment more and it was washed to their feet. They recognized it. "It is our Patty's box from the Anita," said the husband to his wife. This was the only thing washed ashore on this island from the wreck—and here Mr. and Mrs. Pritchard first heard of their fearful loss. This box seems to have been sent a silent messenger from the lost, to whisper "the mighty sea has engulphed us—the fearful hurricane has swept over us!" And this is all they have been able to trace of those so dear and so precious to them. Subsequently the hull of the vessel was drifted ashore, on one of the neighboring islands, dismasted, full of water, without a trace of the fate of the unfortunate crew, but with cargo intact. Altogether it is a most mysterious case. The only hope that now remains—after a most thorough search on all the islands anywhere within the scope of the hurricane—is that some passing vessel may have taken the people off the wreck, and with his "forlorn hope," Mr. Pritchard and his most amiable lady proceeded to England in the Cesar Godeffroy. To a fond mother and an affectionate father, how terrible has been this blow.

C.P.I. Ed. Note: Vavou mentioned in text is probably another spelling for Vavau.

Vavau Island is 18° 37′ S., 174° 01′ W. *(H.O. Pub.* No. 166, Vol. II, 4th ed. 1933, p. 236.)

Niue (Savage) Island is 19° 02′ S., 169° 51′ W., H.O. Chart No. 1986 *(H.O. Pub.* No. 166, Vol. II, 4th ed. 1933, p. 251).

TONGA 11

The Friend, Honolulu
July 2, 1866: 23, 54, 3
MSaP

WRECK OF THE "JOHN WESLEY"

The London *Watchman* gives an account of the loss of the Mission brig *John Wesley,* on the coast of Tonga, in November last. She had on board four Missionaries, who were going to the District Meeting, and was wrecked on a coral reef, on which she was cast by a violent ocean current. This current was produced by an earthquake, which extended hudreds of miles, and caused much damage on the islands. The brig has done good service to the cause of Missions, having been used for twenty years, conveying our Missionaries and Mission stores from island to island, and was fully insured in England. No lives were lost, and the cargo was all saved. The *Watchman* states that the Jubilee schooner will soon be ready, and able to perform most of the trips necessary for Mission purposes, and that steps will soon be taken to supply a temporary successor to the John Wesley.

C.P.I. Ed. Note: Tonga Island mentioned in text is probably Tongatabu Island, which is the chief island of the Tonga group.
Tongatabu Island is 21° 10′ S., 175° 15′ W., H.O. Chart No. 2016 *(H.O. Pub.* No. 166, Vol. II, 4th ed. 1933, p. 197.)

TONGA 12

National Intelligencer, Washington, D.C.
Apr. 4, 1866: 66, 1, 7
MB

AN EARTHQUAKE AT SEA

The English papers received by the City of Paris contain the following—:

"Captain Morse, of the ship Syren, Boston, United States, which recently arrived at Birkenhead, states that on the 18th of November, 1865, at six o'clock A.M., in latitude 24° S., longitude 173° 30′ W., while on his passage from Baker's Island to the port of Liverpool, he experienced what he supposed to be a shock of earthquake. At first was heard a heavy, deep, rumbling sound, accompanied by a vibration of the ship, which increased in violence until the vessel seemed as though driving over a reef. There was a strong breeze, with rather heavy clouds; the sea in the vicinity of the ship appeared as if suddenly fixed, a phenomena which lasted apparently between three and four minutes. The compass card during the time of the shock was rapidly revolving. The man at the wheel was violently and visibly shaken, and those on deck generally were scarcely able to keep their feet. One man engaged in connecting the hose pipe to a force pump upon the top gallant forecastle was thrown backwards against the bitts. The sound at first resembled distant thunder, and increased in intensity till at its height it could be only compared to the deafening roar of innumerable pieces of the heaviest artillery. Two sailors on the fore royal yard at the time, stated afterwards, that they did not hear the noise nor feel the vibration.

C.P.I. Ed. Note: The text of this report is one item in a newspaper column headed "AN EARTHQUAKE AT SEA," the rest of which is irrelevant. Baker Island is 0° 13′ N., 176° 33′ W., H.O. Chart No. 1198. *(H.O. Pub.* No. 166, Vol. II, 4th ed., 1933, P. 473.)

[*The location given is southeast of Tongatabu & Eua.*]

TONGATABU 1

Salem Gazette
Oct. 25, 1805: 19, 3, 3
MSaE

The ship Portland, formerly of Boston, Capt. Mellin, is said to have been cut off at the Friendly Islands, in the Pacific Ocean. The accident is supposed to have happened about 18 months since.—The Portland left Batavia nearly three years ago, when the Dutch Government, having claims on the ship, wished to detain her. Captain Mellin proceeded to the Isle of France, the Cape of Good Hope, and then passed round Cape Horn, and touched at the Friendly Islands. Upon the boats landing, the natives suddenly seized her with the crew, and then got possession of the ship. It is conjectured that no person on board was spared by the natives, save a Malay woman, who was seen on the islands by a ship which sailed from Manilla under American colours. The ship lost her boat's crew there, and came near being captured by the islanders, who made a desperate attempt against her.—The account of the loss of the Portland is given on the authority of the Malay woman. Vessels touching at any of the Islands in the great Southern Ocean, ought to be always on their guard against the designs of the natives.

C.P.I. Ed. Note: The text of this report is one item in a column headed "MARINE INTELLIGENCE," the rest of which is irrelevant.

A later account in the "Salem Gazette," Sept. 16, 1806, covered in [*TONGATABU 4*] . . . places the wreck of the "PORTLAND," at Tongatabu, one of the Friendly, group.

TONGATABU 2

Columbian Centinel, Boston, Mass.
Oct. 26, 1805: 44, 2, 4
MLy

[Identical report in *Boston Gazette,* Oct. 28, 1805 (MBAt).]

NAUTICAL AND SHIPPING MEMORANDA

The ship Portland, formerly of Boston, Captain Mellin, is said to have been cut off at the Friendly Islands, in the Pacific Ocean, by the natives, about 18 months since; and every person on board, it is conjectured, were massacred.—The account of the loss of the Portland, is given on the authority of a Malay woman, on the islands, who said she was on board the Portland at the time.—This information was given to a ship from Manilla, under American colours, and which lost her boat's crew there, and came near being captured by the islanders, who made a desperate attack upon her.

C.P.I. Ed. Note: The text of the above report is a copy of an article in a newspaper column headed "NAUTICAL AND SHIPPING MEMORANDA." . . .

Friendly (Tonga) Islands are situated in lat. between 18° 01'S., and 21° 28'S., lon. 173° 54' W. and 175° 33' W., H.O. Chart No. 2016. *(H.O. Pub.* No. 166, Vol. II, 4th ed. 1933, p. 192.)

TONGATABU 3

United States' Gazette For The Country, Philadelphia, Pa.
June 9, 1806: 6, 1, 1
MH

DEPOSITIONS

Respecting the ship Union, of America: Daniel Wright, Chief Mate of the ship Union of New York being sworn, says, that on or about the 29th of August, 1804, he sailed in the said ship from the harbour of Port Jackson under the command of Captain Pendleton, having taken on board Mr. John Boston, whom this deponent understood to be Supercargo; that they touched at Norfolk Island, and from thence proceeded to the Island of Tongataboo, one of the friendly Islands, where they arrived on or about the 30th of September; that soon after they came to anchor a number of canoes visited them, but left them at sun-set; that on the following morning they came off in great numbers, among whom was a Malay that spoke broken English, who informed them they could get plenty of wood, water, and refreshments there, and was very urgent for the ship's boats to be sent on shore; that one of the ship's boats was accordingly hoisted out mann'd with 6 men, 4 muskets, and 2 cutlasses; in which boat the Captain and Mr. Boston went; that soon after the departure of the boat from the ship, the natives became very troublesome from their numbers on board and round the vessel; that this deponent stationed all his remaining hands about the ship to prevent their coming on board; but they succeeded in getting up, contrary to his wish, to the number of thirty, who this deponent observed had passed a number of clubs in the ship's channels ready to be handed in: and from his observations he had no doubt but that they meant to take the ship; that the chief frequently urged this deponent to let more men come on board, which he positively refused, telling him, that he should be obliged to turn out those who were already on board, which he did the greater part without any resistance or much trouble; that the chief did not seem in any wise dissatisfied with this proceeding, but remained on board some time after, to eat and drink with this deponent; that he shortly after took leave of the ship, and was accompanied by the whole of the canoes alongside; that immediately after the departure of the natives from the vessel this deponent hoisted the colours of the ship, and fired a gun to put those on shore upon their guard, from his observation of the conduct of those that were on board; but soon after taking up the spy glass and looking towards the shore, he perceived the ship's boat on the beach lying broadside up, in the hands of the natives, and a number of natives about her; that this might have been between one and two o'clock, the boat having been gone about four hours; that this deponent then put the ship in the best order he could, expecting an attack from the natives,—but no canoes came off that night;—that the next morning two canoes came within hail, but would not come on board; and from several gestures which they made the people on board wanted this deponent to fire on them, having constructed those gestures to that of the boat's crew being murdered, also wishing him much to get the ship under way, and leave the place immediately—but which this deponent would not allow of; that no further intercourse passed that day.

That the day following several canoes came within hail, in one of which this deponent discovered the Malay, who asked this deponent to come on shore, for that the Captain and Mr. Boston wished him; that he endeavoured to get the Malay alongside, but could not prevail upon him to do so though he promised to accompany him; the Malay then went on shore again. The same afternoon he came off again, accompanied by several canoes in one of which the deponent observed a European woman, who spoke to them in English, as did also the Malay, inviting him on shore; but by particular signs from the white woman, when unnoticed by the natives, she forbid them to comply with the request;—That finding they could not prevail in getting another boat from the ship, they took their departure, and nothing further occurred that day.

The next morning being the third after the boat in which the Captain and Mr. Boston had gone on shore, several canoes again came off, in one of which was the white woman, and in the other the Malay, repeating the former request; that the deponent endeavoured to get him, (the Malay) along side by offering presents for the chief, but without effect; that the white woman stood up in the head of one of the canoes, cried out that those on shore were murdered by the natives, and then leaping into the water, swam towards the ship, the men on board presenting their muskets, and thereby deterring the natives from picking her up, by which means she reached the vessel, and was taken on board; that the said woman informed the deponent, that the Captain and the boat's crew had been murdered on shore; upon which information he ordered the natives to be fired on, and saw two fall in one of the canoes, that he immediately directing the cables might be cut, and putting out to sea, shaped his course for Port Jackson, where, he arrived in 19 days without accident.

C.P.I. Ed. Note: The above text is an excerpt taken from a lengthy article in a newspaper column headed "DEPOSITIONS," the rest of which is irrelevent. Tongatabu is another spelling for Tongataboo lat. 21° 10′ S., lon. 175° 15′ W. H.O. Chart 2016 (H.O. Pub. No. 166, Vol. II, 4th ed. 1933, p. 197.)

TONGATABU 4

Salem Gazette
Sept. 16, 1806: 20, 2, 3
MSaE; MHi

SHIP NEWS

From the Sydney Gazette and New South Wales Advertiser dated Oct. 28, 1805.

On Tuesday arrived the Union, American ship, which left this for China, the 29th of August; came last from Tongataboo, one of the Friendly Islands, which she left the 5th instant. By a young woman named Elizabeth Morey, the mate of the Union, and others on board, the following melancholy statements were deposed to:—

DEPOSITION

Respecting the loss of the American ship Portland. Elizabeth Morey, being sworn, says, that she left the Cape of Good Hope, with Mr. Lovat Mellon, captain of the American ship Portland, bound to Lima; that on or about the 1st of June, 1802, she touched at an island in the Pacific Ocean, called Toongataboo; that Capt. Mellon received a message from a white man named Doyle, then residing on the island (and who, the deponent afterwards learnt, had got there from some vessel that had been cast away on another island, and the captain and crew killed); that the chief wished him, Capt. Mellon, to send one of his boats manned to assist him in repelling some invaders that had landed from another island; that a boat was sent armed with 8 men, and the second mate(Mr. Anderson); who, after he had performed the duty alloted to him, returned on board in the evening.

That previous to Mr. Anderson's return on board, Mr. Gibson, the chief mate, with a boat manned with 4 men, went on shore for the purpose of bringing the former boat's crew on board; which he did, and both boats came together; that soon after the return of the boats on board, the chief of that part of the island, named Ducava, came on board to return the captain's thanks for the assistance he had received, stopped on board the ship all night, and on the morning following went on shore; that the night after, the chief sent word on board for the two boats to be sent to shore for refreshments the next morning; that the captain ordered the mate not to do so; but the following morning, before the captain was up, the mate had sent them both manned and armed, with the second mate; about two hours after the small boat returned, with two boys in her, accompanied by several canoes and natives, with yams and the white man Doyle;

That after unloading her, she was again sent on shore woth the two boys—and the natives, with the white man Doyle before mentioned, remained on board. That shortly afterwards, the Natives, with the said Doyle, took an opportunity of surrounding the captain, chief mate, and sailors then on board, 7 in number, and killed them all, except the two boys, this deponent, and a black woman, her servant, and threw the dead bodies overboard.

That the deponent seeing the massacre, attempted to jump overboard, but was prevented by the white man Doyle, who told her not to be frightened, for she should not be hurt; that she was sent soon after on shore in one of the Native's Canoes, and given to the Chief's wife; that this deponent, after she had got on shore, learnt from the boys, five in number, that were left alive, with a white man of diminutive stature, that the whole of the ship's company that were on shore had been killed except themselves; that the ship, after the deponent's departure was kept by Doyle; that the chief himself went off to get her unloaded, for three successive days; but not being able to accomplish the unloading of the ship, he ordered the five remaining white persons to go on board to render assistance in landing her cargo, which consisted chiefly of bales of calico, and different piece goods, which they accomplished in six days following; that all the sails were unbent and landed, except two; that after the cargo was so landed, the four white boys and man took an opportunity of driving the Natives overboard, killing Doyle, cutting the cable, and standing out to sea with the ship; and that what further became of the vessel the deponent cannot say.

[*For C.P.I. Ed. Note see TONGATABU 3.*]

TONGATABU 5

The Friend, Honolulu
Apr. 1849: 31, 1
MBAt

LOSS OF THE UNITED STATES

This ship sailed from the United States, December 10th, 1845. In November, 1848, she left Lohaine, ran down to *FANNING'S* Island for wood and water. There she took on board the family of Mr. Foster, and with all, his son-in-law, Mr. Halstead, 13 passengers in all and was bound to *SUNDAY* Island.

On the 13th December passed the Navigator Islands where three sperm whales were taken. On the morning of the 20th December, in that region of the ocean where there are no sunken reefs or rocks if the charts are correct, the vessel was stove, and in five minutes, filled and sunk. The place where it struck was about 57 miles N.W. of Tongataboo, in the few minutes allowed for getting clear of the rock. All were successful except four children of Mr. Halstead, who were drowned. Capt. Worth, and his boat's crew, after 28 hours of hard rowing succeeded in reaching Tongataboo. The mate, Mr. Cressy, with the remainder of the crew and surviving passengers, succeeded in reaching a small island, about 20 miles distant, where they remained two days, and for want of provisions, put away for Tahiti.

[*For C.P.I. Ed. Note see TONGATABU 3. It is not clear whether this is a separate account from that in TONGATABU 6, or an incorrect copy from the same source.*]

TONGATABU 6

The Friend, Honolulu
Apr. 2, 1849: 7, 31, 1
MSaP

[Reports in *Boston Daily Advertiser,* Aug. 17, 1849 (M), *New Bedford Mercury,* Aug. 17, 1849 (MNBedf) and *Whalemen's Shipping List,* New Bedford, Aug. 21, 1849 (MDarHi) are all similar to first three paragraphs but all then end, ' . . .struck a whale. Capt. W. came to the Sandwich Islands on board the Brooklyn, Cpt. Jeffery. The crew and passengers of the United States will remain in Tongataboo, till they can procure a conveyance thence. Honolulu Friend of 2d. April'.]

LOSS OF AMERICAN WHALE SHIP "UNITED STATES"

This vessel sailed from U. S. December 10, 1845, and had taken 700 barrels sperm and 1700 barrels whale oil. In November, 1848, she left Lahaina, run down to Fanning's Island for wood and water. There she took on board the family of Mr. Foster, and that of his son-in-law, Mr. Halsted, 13 passengers in all, and was bound to Sunday Island. On the 13th of December passed the Navigator Islands, where three sperm whales were taken. On the morning of the 20th December, in that region of the ocean where there are no sunken reefs or rocks, if the charts are correct, the vessel was stove and in five minutes filled and sunk.

It was at 3 o'clock in the morning when the sad catastrophe took place. The spot where she was stove was about 57 miles N. W. of Tongataboo. In the few moments allowed for getting clear of the wreck all were successful, except four children of Mr. Halsted who were drowned. Capt. Worth and his boat's crew, after 28 hours of hard rowing, succeeded in reaching Tongataboo. The mate, Mr. Creasy, with the remainder of the crew and surviving passengers, succeeded in reaching a small island about 20 miles distant, where they remained two days, and for want of provisions put away for Tongataboo.

Capt. Worth and his ship's company received every attention from the Rev. Mr. Webb, an English Wesleyan Missionary residing in Tongataboo. We are requested by Capt. Worth to bear his public testimony to the kind attention which he received from both Rev. Mr. and Mrs. Webb.

In the account of the wreck furnished by Mr. Creasy for the Sandwich Island *News,* he gives his opinion that the vessel struck a rock. Capt. Worth is of the opinion that the vessel was stove by a whale. Capt. W. and his mate left Tongataboo in the French Sch. "Clarion", and after a passage of 38 days reached Tahiti.

Agreeable to the request of Capt. Worth, we insert the following:—

"Mr. Damon—In publishing the account of the loss of my ship, you will do me the favor to insert the following statement.—On my passage from Tongataboo to Tahiti, in L. 24° S., and L. 153° W., I spoke the H. B. Company's Bark, "Cowlitz", Captain Weynton. I told him my circumstances. I had no shoes, and our small vessel was in distress; all that Capt. W. would furnish me was one small pig and a few potatoes. His conduct I considered most unkind and ungenerous. He seemed to view me as an imposter! While Capt. Nott, who was a passenger on board the "Cowlitz", and had lost his vessel, the "Vancourer", at Columbia River, manifested the kindest feelings; gave me two shirts, and what was of vastly more consequence, a kind look.

("Signed)
"Galvin G. Worth,
"Late Master of the "United States".
"Honolulu, March 27, 1849."

Capt. W. came to the Sandwich Islands, on board the

"Brooklyn", Capt. Jeffrey, from whom, and whose lady, he desires us to state, that received every kindness. Mr. Creasy came here on board the "James Monroe", Capt. Bowman. The crew and passengers of this ill-fated "United States" most probably remain on Tongataboo, although it is to be hoped they may have found some means of conveyance to a part of the world where their wants can be better supplied. They were in rather a suffering state when Capt. Worth left them.

[For C.P.I. Ed. Note see TONGATABU 3.]

TONGATABU 7

Boston Daily Journal
June 22, 1849: 17, 3, 2
MH

[Similar reports in *New Bedford Mercury*, June 22, 1849 (MNBedf) and *Boston Daily Advertiser*, June 23, 1849 (MB) except that latter omits last sentence and acknowledges *New Bedford Mercury* as source.]

A letter received in Nantucket, from C. W. Rand, Esq., dated San Francisco, April 19, reports that ship United States, Capt. Worth, of that port, which left Oahu Nov. 3, struck on the 20th of Dec. a hidden rock some 50 miles WNW of Tongataboo, and immediately went to pieces. The officers and crew barely escaped with their lives. Capt. Worth and his mate arrived at Tahiti, Jan. 20. The mate arrived at Oahu, March 17, on board ship James Monroe, and Captain Worth arrived there the same day, in ship Brooklyn. There is an insurance on the United States at an office in N. Bedford for 10,500.

C.P.I. Ed. Note: The text of this report is one item in a news column headed "DISASTERS," the rest of which is irrelevant.

[*For additional C.P.I. Ed. Note see TONGATABU 3.*]

TONGATABU 8

Boston Herald
June 23, 1849: 6, 668, 3
MB

[Similar report in *Christian Watchman & Reflector*, Boston, June 28, 1849 (MH)]

LOSS OF SHIP UNITED STATES

A letter, dated San Francisco, April 19 confirmed the report that the ship United States, Capt. Worth, of that port, which left Oahu Nov. 3d, struck on the 20th December a hidden rock, some 50 miles W.N.W. of Tongataboo, and immediately went to pieces. The officers and crew barely escaped with their lives.

[*For C.P.I. Ed. Note see TONGATABU 3.*]

TONGATABU 9

Boston Daily Advertiser
July 28, 1849: 74, 2, 8
M

WHALERS

A Correspondent of the New Bedford Mercury, writes from Tahiti, that an American Whaler struck something, supposed part of a wreck, (no date), a few miles North of the island of Tongataboo, and filling went down instantly. All hands, (excepting two children, who were, according to the report in the cabin asleep and perished) were saved, although they had just time to let the boat down, ere the vessel founded. The crew landed at Tonga. The Mercury says, "The above no doubt, refers to the United States, of Nantucket, before reported lost about the same time and place, and in a similar manner.

C.P.I. Ed. Note: The text of the above report is a copy of an article in a newspaper column headed "WHALERS." . . .

[*For additional C.P.I. Ed. Note see TONGATABU 3.*]

TONGATABU 10

Boston Post
Jan. 7, 1860: 56, 3, 5
M

WHALERS

A letter from Capt. Bailey, of Bark, E.C. Cowdin, of Dartmouth, reports her at Tongaboa, Navigator Islands, Aug. 28, with 1240 Bbls. ap. oil, all told, all well.

C.P.I. Ed. Note: The text of this report is one item in a news column headed "WHALERS," the rest of which is irrelevant. Tongaboo is probably another spelling for Tongatabu.

[*For additional C.P.I. Ed. Note see TONGATABU 3.*]

TONUMEIA 1

The Observer, Salem, Mass.
June 28, 1823: 1, 4, 3
MSaE

A letter from New Zealand mentions that the Ceres, whale ship of London, was lost on the desolate Island of Tonamia (one of the Friendly Islands) in 1821. There were 31 persons on board.

The captain sent 12 men in two boats to a neighboring island for provisions. The natives murdered five of them and severely cut the others. At Tonamia, the natives afterwards, killed the captain, cooper and boy.

Fifteen of the crew reached the volcanic Island of Mattao, where they remained 13 months, their food being cocoanuts.

They were at length discovered and taken off the Island by the Missionary Society's ship St. Michael, and landed at Port Jackson.

C.P.I. Ed. Note: The text of this report is one item in a news column, the rest of which is irrelevant.

Tonamia Island, mentioned in report is probably another spelling for Tonumeia Island.

Tonumeia Island, of the Nomuka Group, is in 20°28' S., 174°46'W., H.O. Chart No. 2006 *(H.O. Pub.* No. 166, Vol. II, 4th ed. 1933, p. 208) and is identified as one of the Tonga (Friendly) Islands.

Island of Mattao, mentioned in text is probably Mathew Island (spelled Matthew, on H.O. Chart No. 825) and is in 22°20'S., 171°19'E., H.O. Chart No. 1996 *(H.O. Pub.* No. 165, Vol. I, 1938 ed., p. 50). It is of volcanic formation, composed principally of basaltic rock and is uninhabited *(Ibid.* p. 50).

TORI SHIMA 1

New Bedford Mercury
Jan. 16, 1846: 39, 1, 3
MNBedf

[Report in *Boston Daily Evening Transcript,* Jan. 12, 1846 (MBAt) is similar except for giving '21°1'N., longitude 130°, 42'E.']

SHOALS IN THE PACIFIC

During a late passage of the brig Hannah of Salem, between China and the Sandwich Islands, the following Shoal and Islands were seen, believed by the captain not to be in any book or chart:—A Shoal about 300 yards in diameter, with a breaker on it, lat 21 1N lon. 125 102E, a small low Island, lat. 23 8N. lon. 130 42E.; a small high island, lat. 30 42N. lon. 140 6E.

C.P.I. Ed. Note: The above text is a verified copy of article. *The second* island described in text, . . . is probably Tori Shima (H.O. Chart No. 1500 46th ed. April 1939.) Shoal, mentioned in text, not shown on available charts or publications. Longitude, given in text, appears to be in error.

TORRES STRAIT 1

Daily Atlas, Boston, Mass.
May 31, 1836: 4, 2, 5
MHi

MARINE JOURNAL

A bottle was picked up near Botany Bay, corked and sealed, containing a memorandum written in lead pencil, as follows: "The Ann, from New York for Timor, Williams, master, was abandoned by the officers and crew in Torre's Straits—July 18, 1835." On the back of the paper as follows: "Became a total wreck." (The original is in possesseion of the editor of the Salem Register.)

C.P.I. Ed. Note: The text of this report is one item in a newspaper column headed "MARINE JOURNAL," the rest of which is irrelevant.

Torres Straits, mentioned in text is identified as [*lying between or extending between?*] Osprey Reef (lat. 13°, 51', 10" S., lon. 146°, 36' E., and Booby Island the westernmost island in Torres Strait, lies in lat. 10°, 36', 5", S., lon. 141°, 54', 45" E. (Findlay, *Directory of the South Pacific Ocean,* Fifth Ed. 1884, P. 963) and *(Ibid.* p. 952).

TUTUILA 1

New England Puritan, Boston, Mass.
Mar. 24, 1842: 3, 2, 7
MH

FOREIGN SELECTIONS FROM LATE ENGLISH PAPERS

The Missionary Ship Camden, that bore the lamented Rev. John Williams to the fatal island of Erromanga, is now performing a fourth voyage among the islands of the South Seas, to promote the evangelising of the inhabitants. The latest accounts from the Samoas, in which Mr. Williams felt much interested, state that no fewer than 500 natives had become Christian communicants in one of them—Tutulia—in the course of last year—and that after the most careful examination into their principles and conduct by the missionaries.

C.P.I. Ed. Note: The text of this report is one item in a newspaper column headed "FOREIGN," the rest of which is irrelevant. Complete text is used. . . .

Tutulia mentioned in text is probably another spelling for Tutuila Island.

Tutuila Island is 14° 19′ S., 170° 50′ W., H.O. Chart No. 2924, *(H.O. Pub.* No. 166, Vol. II, 4th ed., 1933, p .258.)

Erromanga Island mentioned in text is probably another spelling for Eromanga Island. Eromanga Island, center, is 18° 49′ S., 169° 05′ E., H.O. Chart 2027. *(H.O. Pub.* No. 165, Vol.I, 4th ed., 1933, p. 189.)

Native Missionary Church, Pang-a-pungu Tutuilleh, Navigator Group.

Missionary Church, Tutuila, Samoa. **Sketch by an unknown artist, 1840. Peabody Museum of Salem.**

English missionary's residence, Tutuila, Samoa. Sketch by an unknown artist, 1840.
Peabody Museum of Salem.

TUTUILA 2

Daily American Eagle, Boston, Mass.
Apr. 1st, 1845: 1, 2, 3
MB

FROM THE PACIFIC

The bark Autumn arrived at New York, on Sunday from Vavoo, Friday Islands, bringing an account of the trial and conviction of Henry Lee alias Leonard Bonzy, one of the hands of the Autumn for the murder of a chief of the Toomahlooah (one of the Navigator's Islands), while the Autumn was stopping at that port.

C.P.I. Ed. Note: The above text is a complete copy of a news article. . . .

Toomahlooah is possibly another spelling for Tutuila, or Tootooellah, one of the Samoa, or Navigators, Group. Tutuila, or Tootooellah, Island is almost divided in two by Pago-Pago (Pango-Pango) Harbour.. (Findlay, *Directory of the South Pacific Ocean,* Fifth Edition, 1886, p. 657.) Tutuila Island is 14° 19′ S., 170° 50′ W., H.O. Chart No. 2924. *(H.O. Pub.* No. 166, Vol. II, 4th ed., 1933, p. 258.)

Vavoo is probably another spelling for Vavau Island of the Friendly, or Tonga, Group.

Vavau Island is 18° 37′ S., 174° 01′ W. *(H.O. Pub.* No. 166, Vol. II, 4th ed., 1933, p. 238.)

Friday Islands in above text is possibly another name for the Friendly Islands.

Tonga (Friendly) Islands, H. O. Chart No. 2016, are between 18° 01 S., and 21° 28′ S., and 173° 54′ W., and 175° 33′ W. *(H.O. Pub.* No. 166, Vol. II, 4th ed., 1933, p. 192.)

TUTUILA 3

Boston Daily Journal
May 2, 1861: 29, 1, 8
MH

Ship Metacom, Hinds, of New Bedford, was wrecked at the Navigator Islands Dec. 29, while getting wood, a heavy N.W. gale having come on which parted the larboard chain, dragged the other anchor, and went ashore on the reef, broadside to, and bilged. In one hour and a half after striking she fell over and sunk. The crew took to the boats and landed on the Island in safety. Had on board about 100 bbls, sp. (50bbls. being on deck) and about 900 bbls. whale oil—no bone. All the sp. oil and from 600 to 700 bbls. of the whale oil floated ashore, the ship having broken up, which, together with some provisions etc, were saved, all hands arrived at Upola, where they remained until, Jan.29, when ship Artic of Fairhaven from Baker's Island for New York came in. and Capt. Hinds and wife, the 1st mate, Mr. Z. L. Doane of New Bedford, the 3d mate, took passage, and arrived at New York 30th ult. The oil etc. saved from the ship was sold at auction at Upola being bought in parcels by different parties. The Metacom was owned by Messrs. J.B. Wood & Co., and others, and sailed in July 1857, being valued with outfits at $37,000. She was insured for $26,000. Sent home on voyage 90 bbls, sp,200 do,wh,oil, and 11,300 lbs, bone.

C.P.I. Ed. Note: The text of this report is one item in a news column headed "WHALERS," the rest of which is irrelevant.

TUTUILA 4

Boston Daily Courier
May 2, 1861: 74, 3, 5
M or MB

[Similar reports in *Boston Daily Advertiser,* May 2, 1861 (MBr) and *Boston Post,* May 2, 1861 (MB). Both give '$37,000' and the *Boston Post* has '$26,600' instead of '$26,000'. Report in *Daily Evening Standard,* New Bedford, May 1, 1861 (MNBedf) omits last four sentences but is otherwise similar. Report in *Boston Daily Courier,* May 2, 1861 (MBAt) omits passages between ' . . .island in safety.' and 'All hands. . .'; '. . .Hinds and wife. . .' and ' . . .took passage'; and also the last four sentences. This is probably a C.P.I. worker's error.]

MEMORANDA

Whaleship Metacom, (of New Bedford) Hinds, was wrecked at the Navigator Islands in December under the following circumstances:—Sailed from Honolulu Nov. 24 for home, and put into the Tutuilla Islands, Navigators, Dec. 22, taking two sp whales at the mouth of the bay, making 50 bbls. of oil. On the 29th, while getting wood, a heavy N. W. gale came on, parted larboard chain, dragged the other anchor, and went ashore on the reef, broadside to, and bilged; a large hole being stove in the starboard bow and another in the starboard quarter. In one hour and a half after striking she fell over and sunk. The crew took to the boats and landed on the island in safety. Had on board about 100 bbls. spm. (50 bbls. being on deck) and about 900 do. wh.—no bone. All the sperm oil and from 600 to 700 bbls. of the whale oil floated ashore, the ship having broken up, which together with some provisions etc., were saved. All hands arrived at Upolu, where they remained until Jan 29, when ship

Arctic, of Fairhaven, from Baker's Island for New York came in, and Capt. Hinds and wife, the 1st mate, Mr. Z.L. Doane, of New Bedford, the 3rd mate, C.T. Moulton of Maine, and a seaman, M. Morse of Maine, took passage, and arrived at New York on Tuesday. The oil etc., saved from the ship, was sold at Upolu at auction, being bought in parcels by different parties. The M. was owned by Messrs. J. B. Wood and Co. and others, of New Bedford, and sailed thence in July 1857, being valued, with outfits at $37,006. She was insured in New Bedford for $26,000. Sent home on the voyage 90 bbls. sp. 200 do. wh. and 11,300 bbls. bone.

C.P.I. Ed. Note: The text of this report is an item in a newspaper column headed "MEMORANDA," . . . Navigator Islands are identified as Samoa Islands. Samoa Islands are in Lat. 13° 31′ S. to 14° 30′ S., Lon. 168° 00′ W. to 173° 00′ W. H.O. Chart No. 87. *(H.O. Pub.* No. 166, Vol II, 4th ed., 1933, p. 253.)

TUTUILA 5

The Daily Mercury, New Bedford, Mass.
May 2, 1861: 29, 3, 3
MNBedf

Ship Metacom of this port, was totally wrecked at Tutuilla (Navigator's) Island, during a gale of wind in December last, having parted her cables, and went on to a reef and bilged, after which fell over and sunk. The officers and crew took to their boats and all landed safely on the Island. She had taken 50 bbls sperm oil since leaving Sandwich Islands, and was bound home. About 700 bbls oil were saved and got on shore, which together with the wreck, were sold at auction. The crew then proceeded to Upola, where they remained until Jan. 29th, when ship Arctic, of Fairhaven, touched there and took on board Capt. Hinds and wife, Mr. Zebina L. Doane, of this city, 1st mate,—Chas. T. Houlton, 3d mate, and Melville Morse, seaman, and brought them to New York. The balance of the crew have gone to Sydney, N S W. The Metacom was owned by J.B.Wood & Co., and others. Insurance in this city to amount to $26,000.

C.P.I. Ed. Note: The text of this report is one item of a news column headed "MARINE JOURNAL," the rest of which is irrelevant.

[*For additional C.P.I. Ed. Note see TUTUILA 1.*]

TUTUILA 6

Massachusetts Ploughman, Boston, Mass.
May 4, 1861: 20, 2, 6
MH

MARINE ITEMS

Whaleship Metacom, (of New Bedford) Hinds, was wrecked at the Navigator Islands in December. Sailed from Honolulu Nov.24 for home, on 29th, a heavy NW gale came on; went ashore on the reef, broadside to, and bilged; a large hole being stove in the starboard bow and another in the starboard quarter. In one hour and a half after striking she fell over and sunk. The crew took to the boats and landed on the Island safely.

C.P.I. Ed. Note: The text of this report is an item in a newspaper column headed "DISASTERS," . . . the rest of which is irrelevant.

[*For additional C.P.I. Ed. Note see TUTUILA 4.*]

TUTUILA 7

Massachusetts Ploughman, Boston, Mass.
May 25, 1861: 20, 2, 1
MH

MARINE ITEMS—WHALERS

Arrived at Honolulu 16th, ult., Tamerlane, Winslow, of N.B., 120 sh 250 sp oil and 1200 lbs. bone this season. She reports the loss of whaleship Metacomet, Hinds, at Navigators Island in January, a total loss. Also reports the massacre at Auckland, New Zealand, of 800 foreigners by the natives.

C.P.I. Ed. Note: The text of this report is an item in a newspaper column headed "Whalers," . . . the rest of which is irrelevant.

[*For additional C.P.I. Ed. Note see TUTUILA 4.*]

TUTUILA 8

Boston Post
Feb. 6, 1872: 80, 2, 6
MB

PACIFIC COAST

San Francisco, Feb. 4,—A coaling station for the San Francisco and New Zealand line of steamers has been established at the harbor of Raza, on the island of Tutuila, one of the Navigator's group. A California Company has also purchased 90,000 acres of land on the same island, where a colony will be established to raise sugar, cotton and coffee.

C.P.I. Ed. Note: Raza Harbor is not mentioned in available reference material.

[For additional C.P.I. Ed. Note see TUTUILA 1.]

TUTUILA 9

Boston Post
July 17, 1872: 83, 2, 4
MB

FOREIGN NEWS

South Sea Islands—Commander Meade, of the United States steamer Narragansett has formally assumed the protectorate of Tutuilla Island, where a private company has been formed to work the plantations. The promoters of the enterprise allege that they have received promises of differential duties on produce shipped to the United States. Gordon, a missionary to Errominga has been murdered by the natives. The Figi Islands are undergoing an incipient revolution. The Government is powerless against it.

C.P.I. Ed. Note: The text of this report is one item in a news column headed "FOREIGN NEWS," the rest of which is irrelevant.

[*For additional C.P.I. Ed. Note see TUTUILA 1.*]

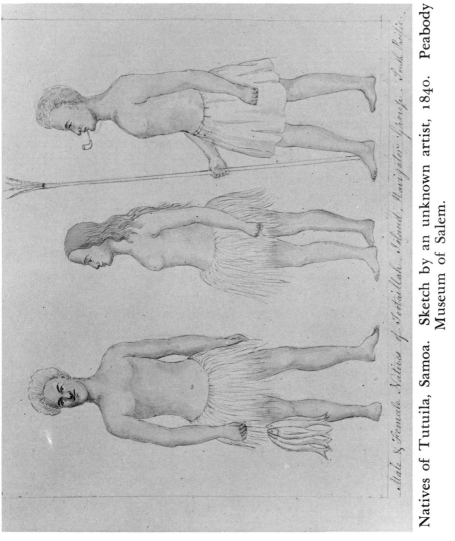

Male & Female Natives of Tortuellah Island, Navigator Group, South Pacific.

Natives of Tutuila, Samoa. Sketch by an unknown artist, 1840. Peabody Museum of Salem.

UA HUKA 1

Boston Daily Advertiser
Oct. 11, 1854: 84, 2, 7
M

WHALERS

Sld from Marquesas Islands, June 20, Pantheon, Hazzard, N.B. for Arctic Ocean, While at anchor at Uahuga, her crew set fire to her, but it was discovered and extinguished with but trifling damage.

C.P.I. Ed. Note: The text of this report is one item in a newspaper column headed "WHALERS," the rest of which is irrelevant. Complete text is used. . . .

Uahuga is probably meant for Ua Huka. Ua Huka (Washington) Island is 8° 54′S., 139° 33′W., H.O. Chart No. 1792. It is 7.5 miles long, east and west, and about 5 miles wide. . . . *(H.O. Pub.* No. 166, Vol. II, 4th ed., 1933, p. 167.)

Marquesas Islands, southeastern group, was discovered in 1595, and named the Isles de Marquesas de Mendoco. . . . The northwestern group was not discovered until 1791, when the islands were sighted by the American Ship Hope, of Boston, Mass. . . . *(H.O. Pub.* No. 166, Vol. II, 4th ed., 1933, P. 167.)

UA HUKA 2

The Salem Observer
Nov. 20, 1858: 36, 2, 6
MSaE

MORE CASTAWAYS DISCOVERED

Commodore Sinclair of the United States ship Vandalia, while searching for three men belonging to the ship Wild Wave, which had been wrecked on the island of Oeno, and who afterwards reached Tahiti in a boat of their own construction, visited the little island if Sooahoogah, where he found six white men—three Americans and three Englishmen—who have lived there fourteen years, and had so completely identified themselves with the natives as not to desire to leave.—Richmond Whig.

C.P.I. Ed. Note: The island mentioned in above text is not found in available reference material.

[*It is probably Ua Huka.*]

UA POU 1

Salem Gazette
Mar. 21, 1817: 31, 2, 2
MSaE

INTERESTING NARRATIVE

From the London Courier, Jan. 2.

By the Governor Macquarie, have arrived Capt. Fowler and part of the crew of the Indian brig Matilda, which sailed from this colony in August, 1813, bound on a voyage to the Derwent and Eastern Islands, and from thence to China; but was cut off and plundered on the night of the 10th of April last, while lying at anchor in Duff's Bay, at the Island of Rooapoah, one of the Marquesas, on a sandal-wood voyage. Five of the crew (Poomootoo men) had previously deserted and joining with some of the Rooanoah natives took the opportunity of a dark night, and the wind blowing fresh right on the land, to cut the vessel adrift, by which means she drove ashore through a heavy surf, and was soon bilged and filled with water. When the cannibal natives saw that it was impracticable to get the vessel afloat, they concurred universally in the design of putting the whole of her crew to death; which appears to have been a constant practice among the different natives towards one another, when their canoes happen to fall upon a strange shore, through stress of weather, or from any other accident.

Capt. Fowler had formed an intimacy with their Chief, or King, Nooahetu, who presided at the tribunal that had devoted the unfortunate mariners to instant slaughter. He witheld his assent to the murder; but had no hesitation in permitting the plunder of the vessel. The crew were informed by such expressions as they could understand, as well as by gesticulations, that accompanied their vehement debate on the occasion, that their lives were dependent on the issue; The good Chief was opposed by many other chiefs; who, though somewhat inferior in rank, were very far superior in number, supported by the common usages of the island, from which the exhibition of clemency appeared an insufferable deviation.

He was seated, with his son by his side, on a mat in his own dwelling; he had been called to the supremacy of the island by the general will of the people, as it was not an hereditary right, but an elective dignity. His people pressed their solicitations earnestly, and at length peremptorily demanded his assent to the sacrifice; which he for a length opposed by the force of words, which not seeming likely to prevail, he adopted a method which silenced the whole in an instant, and saved the lives of Capt. Fowler and his crew. Finding that all his expostulations were defeated upon the principle of undeviating custom, he deliberately took up two ropes that were near him, and fixing one around the neck of his son, and the other round his own, called the chief next in command, who immediately approached him. His conference was short and decisive; he first pointed to the cord that encircled the neck of his son, and then to the other, which he had entwined round his own. "These strangers are doomed to death," said he, "by my Chiefs and my people, and it is not fit that I, who am their King, should live to see so vile a deed perpetrated. Let my child and myself be strangled before it is performed; and then it never will be said that we sanctioned, even with our eye-sight, the destruction of these unoffending people."

The magnanimity of such conduct could not do less than produce, even in the mind of the unenlightened savage, a paroxism of surprise, mingled with a sentiment of admiration, in which the untaught man may possibly excel his fellow creatures, whose conceptions are moulded by tenets calculated to guard him from the extremes of passion. For a moment the people looked wildly on their King, whose person they adored, because his principles were good, and his government just and mild. They saw the obedient Chief, to whom the order of strangulation had been imparted, staring with horror and amazement at the change which a few moments had produced; the mandate which had proceeded from the King's own lips must be obeyed; and, commanded to perform the dreadful office, he proceeded to obey; when a sudden shout from the multitude awed him to forbearance. "The King! the King! from every lip burst forth: "What! Kill the King! No, no, let all the strangers live; no man shall kill the King!" Thus were their lives preserved, and the vessel plundered of everything on board of her.

The floor of the Greenwich, which was burnt at Nooaheva, still remains, and is dry at low water. All her iron and copper have been taken out by the natives, who have a thorough knowledge of the use of these materials. That they are cannibals is well ascertained. They form distinct factions, and make war upon the ruling Chief; the rebels are denominated the Typees; and the opposite parties are horribly sanguinary towards each. Six of the adverse party were killed and devoured by the rebels while Captain Fowler was among them, and the following detestable circumstance occurred on the occasion.—A native man belonging to Port Anna Maria, who was not tatooed, and in consequence prohibited from the eating of human flesh, on pain of death, impatient of the restraint, fell upon one of the murdered bodies, and darting his teeth into it in all the madness of a voracious fury, exhaled the crimson moisture, which had not yet coagulated.

The Chief of Port Anna Maria, who is very friendly to Europeans, is named Kealtanooe, the first part of the name implying the outrigger of a canoe, and the latter signifying greatness. The dress of the men consists merely of a wrapper about the waist; the women are covered from the shoulders down to the ankles, and are generally fairer than the Tahitean women. The Chiefs have no distinguishing mark or ornament, but in the mode of wearing their hair; which the common orders wear tied up in a large knot on each side of the head, a stripe of which, extending from the forehead to the hollow of the neck, is kept shorn, which practice the Chiefs do not adopt. Captain Fowler supposes the worms to be more prevalent and destructive to ship's bottoms there than he has any where witnessed; and to this cause attributes the caution of the natives in drawing up their largest canoes, some of which contain from eighty to one hundred warriors. They are anxious after every kind of property carried among them for barter, and this is supposed their chief inducement for attacking vessels, when they can do so with a probability of accomplishing their object. They have no knowledge of the use of musquests, and have none among them except a few at Port Anna Maria. A gentleman, at this time in Sydney, who resided among them about 15 years ago, in a missionary capacity, describes them as a people constantly employing their thoughts on plunder, and devising schemes for taking advantage of strangers. Their population is very numerous; which he remarked to some of them, to whom he gave description of Otaheite; observing, at the same time that its inhabitants were less numerous; "Cannot we go and take them? What is to hinder us?" was immediately demanded. This anecdote we notice as a specimen of their natural inclination to hostility, in which all accounts respecting them correspond.

C.P.I. Ed. Note: Ua Pou (Adams) Island is 9° 24'S., 140° 03' W., H.O. Chart No. 1809 *(H.O. Pub. No. 166, Vol. II, 4th ed., 1933, p. 177.)*

UA POU 2

The Recorder, Boston, Mass.
June 24, 1817: 2, 3, 3
MBC

SOUTH SEAS

It is stated in the Sydney Gazette of Nov. 8, 1815, that the Indian Brig, Matilda, lying at anchor at the island of Rooapoah, one of the Marquesas, was seized by the natives who determined to put the whole crew to death. But their Chiefs or King Nooahetu, with whom the Captain (Fowler) had previously formed an intimacy, withheld his consent to the murder, though he agreed to the proposed plunder of the vessel. The people strongly urged the custom of the island, which was to kill and eat prisoners who fell into their hands, but the King would not consent; yet finding that his people were intent upon the murder, he had recourse to the following expedient. He deliberately took two ropes that were near him and fixing one around the neck of his son, and the other around his own, called to him the chief next in command and said, These strangers are doomed to death by my people, but it is not fit that I, who am their King, should live to see so vile a deed perpetrated. Let my child and I be strangled before it is performed, and than it never will be said that we sanctioned the destruction of these unoffending people.

C.P.I. Ed. Note: The text of this report is one item in a newspaper column headed "SOUTH SEAS," the rest of which is irrelevant.

Rooapoah is identified as Ua Pou (Adams) in Lat. 9° 24′ S., Lon. 140° 03′ W. H.O. Chart, No. 1809. (*H.O. Pub.* No. 166, Vol. II. 4th Ed. 1933, p. 177.)

UA POU 3

Salem Observer
Dec. 18, 1841: 19, 1, 3
MSaE

Magnanimity of a Savage Chief

It is related in the Percy Anecdotes that the English brig Matilda, Capt. Fowler, on a voyage from New South Wales to the Derwent and Eastern Islands, was cut off and plundered on the night of the 10th of April, 1815, while lying at anchor in Duff's Bay, at the Island of Roodpoath, one of the Marquesas. Five of the crew, who were Poomatoomen, had previously deserted, and joining with some of the Roodpoath natives, took the opportunity of a dark night, to cut the vessel adrift; when she drove ashore through the heavy surf, and was soon bilged and filled with water. When the natives saw that it was impracticable to get the vessel afloat, they concurred universally, in the design of putting the whole crew to death; which is a constant practice among the different natives towards one another, when their canoes happen to fall upon a strange shore, through stress of weather or any other accident. Fortunately, Capt. Fowler had formed an intimacy with the chief, or king, of these savages, Nooahetoo, who presided at the horrible tribunal that had devoted the wretched mariners to instant slaughter. He withheld his assent to the murder, but had no hesitation in permitting the plunder of the vessel. The crew were informed by the significant gesticulations that accompanied the vehement debate on the occasion, that their lives were dependent upon the issue. The good chief, who was seated with his son by his side, was opposed by many other chiefs, though of inferior rank; he had besides been called to the supremacy of the Island, by the general wish of the people, his dignity not being an hereditary right, but elective, and the people now pressed their solicitations earnestly, peremptorily demanding his assent to the sacrifice. For a length of time he opposed this cruel resolution by force of words; but this not seeming likely to prevail, he adopted a mode, which, while it did honor to his huminity, silenced his people in an instant.

Finding that all his expostulations were defeated, upon principal of undeviating custom, he deliberately took up two ropes that were near him, and fixing one round the neck of his son, and the other round his own, he called upon the chief next in command, who immediately approached him. The conference was short and decisive; he first pointed to the cord that encircled the neck of his son; and then to the other which he had entwined round his own. "These strangers," said he, "are doomed to death by my chiefs and my people, and it is not fit that I, who am their king, should live to see so vile a deed perpertrated. Let my child and myself be strangled before it is performed; and then it never will be said, that we sanctioned, even with our eye-sight, the destruction of these unoffending people." The magnanimity of such conduct, produced, even in the mind of the unenlightened savages, a paroxysm of surprise, mingled with sentiments of admiration. For a moment the people looked wildly on their king, whose person they adored.—They saw the obedient chief to whom the order of strangulation had been imparted, aghast with horror and amazement at the change which a few moments had produced. The mandate which had proceeded from the king's own lips must be obeyed; and commanded to perform the dreadful office, he proceeded to obey, when a sudden shout from the multitude awed him to forbear. "The king! the king!" burst from every lip. "What! kill the king? No, no, let the strangers live—no man shall kill the king." Thus were the lives of Capt. Fowler and his men preserved, and they afterwards reached Sydney in safety.—(Medallion.)

in the Central Pacific

C.P.I. Ed. Note: The text of this report is one item in a news column the rest of which is irrelevant.

[*For additional C.P.I. Ed. Note see UA POU 2.*]

UA POU 4

Boston Daily Advertiser
Dec. 13, 1855: 86, 1, 3
M

WHALER

At. Nukahiva, Aug. 24, Isaac Howland, Hobbs, N.B. with 80 bbls was to cruise to the westward and then to New Zealand, Capt. Hobbs reports that he was obliged to put three men, and the third officer on shore on Roa Poa, one of the Marquesas Islands, for mutinous conduct and intent to destroy the ship by setting fire to a barrel of camphene, or any other way when they made the Leeward Islands.

C.P.I. Ed. Note: The text of this report is an item in a newspaper column headed "WHALERS." . . .

Nukahiva Island mentioned in text is another spelling for Nuku Hiva: Nuku Hiva Island is situated in lat. 8° 52'S., lon. 140° 08'W., H.O. Chart No. 1806 (*H.O. Pub.* 166, Vol. II 4th ed. 1933 p. 182.)

Roa Poa is identified as UaPou.

[For additional C.P.I. Ed. Note see UA POU 1.]

UJELANG 1

The Friend, Honolulu
May 1, 1864: 21, 36, 2
MSaP

VOLCANO ON A CORAL ISLAND

We would call attention to the recent eruption on one of the islets of Providence Island as referred to in the report of Captain James. It ought perhaps to occasion no surprise that a phenomenon of this nature should occur, but it is very unusual, and we do not remember to have met with any record of such an event. If all coral and lagoon islands are the summits of old craters, then we are surprised that such eruptions do not more frequently occur. Captain James, who visited the spot, informs us that the event occured only a short time previous to his visit, and that the trees and leaves were scorched with the hot gases, but at present there are no appearances of active fires. The land, embracing a space of three or four hundred feet square, was torn and thrown in every direction, resembling the breaking up of ice on a river in the Spring.

C.P.I. Ed. Note: Ujelang (Arecifos or Providence) Atoll is 9° 46′ N., 161° 00′ E., southeast end, H.O. Chart 5427. *(H.O. Pub. Vol. I, 4th ed. 1938, p. 518.)*

Captain James in this report is the Captain of the *Morning Star* and a lengthy account of his cruise in 1863-64, which included a visit to "that remarkable island called Providence", appears on Page 37 of the same issue (May 1, 1864) of *The Friend* (Honolulu).

UJELANG 2

The Pacific Commercial Advertiser, Honolulu
July 18, 1868: 13, 3, 6
MH

Give Credit To Whom It Belongs.—Capt. Daniel Smith has called our attention to the following article, taken from the North China News, published at Shanghai, and extensively copied into other papers, reporting the discovery of a group of Islands of which but little appears to be known. The Islands were first discovered in 1864, by Capt. Sam'l James, of the brig Morning Star. His report, as published in our paper, locates one of the atolls in north latitude 9°52′, and east longitude 160°56′. He also reported that it had the form of an irregular parallelogram extending east by south and west by north twelve miles, by five in width, and that there are in the atoll ten small Islands, the largest one on the east side. Two passages lead into the lagoon on the south shore, the best of which is about five miles from the east coast. It is the same group as was seen by the Dundonald three years later, as described below. If not heretofore named they should be called Jame's Islands, in honor of their discoverer:

The Dundonald left Sydney on the 29th of September, and on the 3d of October made Norfolk Island, bearing E. by S. 10 miles. From this date to the 8th instant had light N.N.E., wind, which drove the ship very far to the eastward. At 6 A.M. 24th, made the island Oualan (one of the Caroline Islands). At 6 P.M. took our departure from the island, distance 15 miles, and proceeded on our voyage to the N.W. with with a fresh breeze from N.E. About 10 A.M. on the 26th, when walking on the quarter-deck, was very much surprised to see land dipping on the horizon. At first I could not believe that it was land, as I

knew if my reckoning was right that there was no land known to
Europeans nearer than forty miles; but in half an hour the trees
were distinctly visible. I therefore kept the ship direct for it,
determined to satisfy myself as to its position, &c. At 11 A.M.
four more islands appeared in sight, all covered with trees, and
at noon I got a good observation and found my reckoning quite
correct, so that these islands had not been discovered before. At
1 P.M., we came up to them, and the ship was then rounded to
with the southernmost islands bearing north northwest, distance
two miles. A boat was lowered and I proceeded toward the island accompanied by Mr. M'Kay, passenger. After getting in
within a hundred yards of the shore our progress was suddenly
stopped by an extensive reef. Up to this time we had seen no
signs of life on the island. We then rowed around along the
shore for about five miles, until we came to a break in the reef,
and immediately pulled for it, but on getting closer to it found
there was no possibility of crossing, owing to the water being too
shallow. We then discovered that the reef was a bed of red
coral, completely surrounding the island, inside of which the
water was apparently about six feet deep, and as smooth as a
mirror. We then pulled for the next island, which was connected with the first by a coral reef, but the water did not break
on it; and when about a mile from the second island, saw the
masts of two canoes lying inside the island. Feeling quite satisfied that if those canoes could get in we also could do so, we
pulled along the island for about two miles, and then found an
opening in the reef through which we passed, and found ourselves in the center of a beautiful lagoon with about 14 feet of
water, and the bottom perfectly clear, consisting of corals and
other calcareous productions. We then went alongside of the
canoes, but finding no natives in them, being immediately followed by the crew and Mr. M'Kay. As soon as the boat was
made fast, fired a few shots in the air, having taken the precaution to arm ourselves before leaving the ship, and proceeded to a

large opening in the trees, keeping a sharp lookout for any one that might be concealed in the bush. After walking about fifty yards inland, we came to a beautiful clear space of about 300 yards long, 80 or 100 broad, of which we took a good survey before proceeding further; not thinking it judicious to go into the bush, as there was quite space enough for a large number of natives to be concealed in it. Cocoa-Nut trees were in abundance, with plenty of nuts in immense clusters, and the ground was strewed with those that had dropped down from the trees. There were a great more trees of different kinds, but we could not find any other fruit, though we found a large basket full of potatoes just dug, so that it would seem the natives have been disturbed by our firing when coming on shore. The basket was made out of the cocoanut leaf and the potatoes were similar to ours, only very bitter in taste and very much like quinine. After spending about two hours looking over the island, we returned to the boat loading her with cocoanuts, and regretting very much that time would not allow us to take a further survey. Before getting into the boat the health of Queen and Royal Family was drunk with all honors, and at the request of the crew and Mr. M'Kay, the islands were christened Kowley's Group, and the one I landed on Kowley's Island, as I was the first to land, and feel certain that I was the first white man that ever set his foot on it. We took each a little part of whatever we could get out of the canoes, to keep in rememberance of our visit, and the peculiar figurehead of the largest canoe is now on board of my ship. The position of the islands is-southernmost islands, lat. 9 deg. 47 min. N., long. 161 deg. 15 min. 45 sec. E. The group extends in an E. by S., and W. by N. direction for about thirty miles but cannot say what their extent is north and south, as I had not time to explore them properly. The latitude and longitude may be relied on, as I only left the Island of Onalau two days before, and my instruments were quite correct then.

C.P.I. Ed. Note: The above text is a complete copy of a newspaper article. . . .

"UJILONG, *Arrecifos, Casobos,* or *Providence Islands.*—On the early Spanish charts two groups, under the names of Arrecifos and Casobos or Casbobas, were shown hereabout; but their existence was not verified till 1811, when the ship *Providence* discovered a group, to which the name of the ship was applied. Dr. Gulick, who calls the native name *Ujilong,* says that there is but one reef here, so it must include the two older notices. He says the population of Ujilong is 1,000. It was visited in 1864 by Captain James, in the missionary ship *Morning Star,* who states that, although to the westward of the Ralik chain, the natives speak the Marshall Islands dialect. It was also visited by the Dundonald, Captain Kewley, in 1867; he speaks of the large quantity of cocoa-nuts. . . The N.E. end of Ujelang is in lat 9° 43′ N., long. 161° 19′ E." *(Directory of the North Pacific Ocean,* Findlay Third ed. 1886, pp. 969, 970.)

Ujilong is probably another spelling of Ujelang.

Ujelang (Arecifos or Providence) Atoll, southeast end, is 9° 46′ N., 161° 00′ E., H.O. Chart No. 5427.

Oualan is possibly another spelling of Ualan.

Kusaie (Ualan) Island, northeast end, is 5° 22′ N., 163° 01′ E., H.O. Chart No. 5420. *(H.O. Pub.* No. 165, Vol. I, 4th ed. 1938, p. 522.)

Norfolk Island: Inner end of jetty, is lat. 29° 03′ 45″ S., long. 167° 58′ 06″ E. (Bowditch, No. 9, 1917 Edition, *American Practical Navigator,* p. 350.)

ULITHI 1

The Polynesian, Honolulu
July 18, 1840: 1, 23, 3 & 4

LETTER TO THE POLYNESIAN

March 20th, '40.   Touched at the Mackenie's Group.   Find these islands correctly placed in Lat 10° 5′ N. Long. 139° 40′ E., but their number is much greater than was supposed.   I counted twenty one, there may be more, whereas in the charts they are marked nine only, very low, inhabited by a fine race of men.   There are several passages between the islands to the centre, which forms a large basin six miles by eight.   Joseph M. Metcalf.

[*Ulithi atoll, at Asor islet, is 10° 02′ S., 139° 46′ E. (P.I.P., Vol. I, p. 547). C.P.I. worker has noted in heading of report that vessel is brigantine Rosa.*]

UNITED STATES OF AMERICA ₁

Boston Daily Advertiser
Feb. 8, 1850: —, —, —
M

DISASTERS

Ship Arkansas, Shepard of and from New York, anchored in San Francisco harbor Dec. 19 about 3 O'clock, and during the gale on the following night, dragged her anchors and struck on Bird Island, where she knocked off her rudder. Her fore and mizen masts were out away, and by great exertion the crew finally succeeded in getting the vessel afloat, and she was subsequently towed to a place of safety by boats of other ships in port. She had about 80 passengers including 7 females and several children. No lives were lost.

C.P.I. Ed. Note: The text of this report is one item in a newspaper column headed "DISASTERS," the rest of which is irrelevant. Bird Island mentioned in text is identified as Reitoru, situated in lat. 17°, 48′ S., 143° 06′ W. H.O. Chart No. 77. *(H.O. Pub.* No. 166, Vol. II, 4th ed., 1933 p. 142.)

[*This identification is clearly impossible as the ship was in San Francisco harbor.*]

UNITED STATES OF AMERICA 2

Salem Gazette
July 12, 1853: No. 55, 2, 5
MSaE

The ship Carrier Pigeon, Capt. Doane, from Boston for San Francisco, went ashore on the 9th June, in a fog, on Point New Year, 30 miles south of San Francisco. In fifteen minutes after she struck there were seven feet of water in her hold; and in half an hour water was above her lower deck. Two steamers were sent to the wreck, and 1200 packages of light merchandise saved. The ship will be a total loss, as also much of her cargo. At last accounts the tide water was ebbing and flowing through the wreck, her deck having been broken.

The steamer Sea Bird, which had been sent to the assistance of the Carrier Pigeon, was beached while taking out her cargo. At last accounts, she was breaking to pieces.

C.P.I. Ed. Note: The above is one item in a column headed "ARRIVAL OF THE ILLINOIS AT NEW YORK," the rest of which is irrelevant.

Position of Point New Year not given in available reference material.

UPOLU 1

The Friend, Honolulu
Aug. 15, 1846: 4, 125, 3
MSaP

Samoan or Navigators Islands

For the information of ship masters we insert the following "notice:"

"It is desireable that it should be extensivly known, that the harbor called Fagaloo, on the N. East side of Upolu, affords but very unsafe anchorage. It was carefully surveyed and condemned by Commodore Wilkes commanding the United States Squadron. If masters of vessels, with a knowledge of this fact, comply with the wishes of worthless Foreigners, who contrive to get on board to Pilot them into that harbor, it will be at the risk of losing the insurance. Should anything of a disastrous nature happen, the masters of said vessels will be held responsible.

John C. Williams, U. S. Consul.
Geo. Pritchard, H. B. M. Consul.

Apia Harbor, March, 1846."

C.P.I. Ed. Note: Fagalos Bay on the northeast coast of Upulu Island is 13° 54' S., 171° 28' W., H. O. Chart No. 1136 *(H.O. Pub.* No. 166, Vol. II, 4th ed. 1933, p. 267.)

UPOLU 2

The Friend, Honolulu
Mar. 15, 1847: 5, 46, 3
MSaP

THE MISSING TAHITI SCHOONER

In the Friend of Dec. 15, it was stated that a schooner left the Society Islands, Oct. 2d, for Honolulu, via Raiatea. She was owned by a Mr. Tibbetts, who was coming here with his family. Several passengers were on board, and among them some merchant Catholic priests. The vessel has been supposed to be lost, but Capt. Parker, of the "Elizabeth Starbuck", reports her having touched at Upolu, one of the Navigator Islands, under most distressing circumstances. It appears that she came north, into the vicinity of the Sandwich group, as was supposed, and after a fruitless attempt to find any of the islands, sailed for the south and fell in with the Navigator's group. She went into Apia on the island of Upolu. The schooner's company was in almost a starving condition. After the vessel was refitted by Mr. Pritchard, the English Consul, with rigging, sails, provisions and water, she made the second attempt, having secured, as was supposed, the services of an experienced navigator. She left Upolu on or about Jan. 1847. Capt. Parker confidently expected to have found her in this port. He left there the 5th of February, making the passage direct. The schooner must now have been out more than two months. Serious fears are now entertained that she must eventually have been lost, or else, that she is still searching, in vain, for the islands.

N.B. The above mentioned vessel arrived this morning; heard no particulars.

UPOLU 3

Boston Post
Sept. 13, 1847: 31, 2, 5
M

MARINE JOURNAL
WHALERS

A letter from Capt. Geo. A. Covell of ship Mt. Vernon, N.B. reports her at Upola (Navigator's) Mch. 22, with 100 sp. 100 wh. recruiting for N.W. Coast. Capt. C. writes that "on the 16th Mch. lat. 16° 30′ S., lon. 171° 40′ W., we experiences a tremendous typhoon, in which we lost the mizzen topmast, 2 topgallant masts, flying jibboom, 2 boats and some sails, and had I been any way doubtful of the qualities of the ship I am sure we should have lost all three topmasts. I have heard of several ships which were in the same hurricane, and all of them sustained more or less damage. Two of them arrived here today—the Eliza Adams, of Fairhaven, with loss of topgallant masts and two boats, and the Ganges of Nant., with the loss of foremast, three topmasts, jibboom, and a whole suit of sails." (The quantity of oil on board the E. Adams, and Ganges is not mentioned.)

C.P.I. Ed. Note: The text of this report is one item in a newspaper column headed "MARINE JOURNAL," the rest of which is irrelevant. Complete text is used. . . .

Upola is another spelling for Upolu.

Upolu is one of the Navigator or Samoa Group and lies in lat. 13° 54′ S., lon. 171° 42′ W., H. O. Chart No. 2923. *(H.O. Pub.* No. 166, Vol. II, 4th ed., 1933, p. 266.)

UPOLU 4

Boston Daily Advertiser
Sept. 13, 1847: 70, 2, 7
M

WHALERS

At Upola, Navigator's Islands, March 24, (by letter) Lagoda, Col. N. B., 230 Wh 70 sp recruiting for N. W. Coast. At do March 22, Mt. Vernon, Covell, N. B. 100 sp. 100 wh. recruiting for N. W. Coast. Capt. C. writes that "March 16, lat. 16° 30' S., lon. 171° 41' W., we experienced a tremendous typhoon, in which we lost the mizen top-mast, two top gallant masts flying-jib boom, two boats and some sails, and had I been any ways doubtful of the qualities of the ship, I am quite sure we should have lost all three top masts. I have heard of several ships which were in the same hurricane, and all of them sustained more or less damage. Two of them arrived here today: The Eliza Adams of Fairhaven, with loss of top gallant masts and two boats, and the Ganges of Nantucket, with loss of foremast, three top masts, jib boom, and a whole suit of sails" (The oil on board the E Adams and Ganges not mentioned.)

C.P.I. Ed. Note: The text of this report is an item in a newspaper column headed "WHALERS," the rest of which is irrelevant.

[*For additional C.P.I. Ed. Note see UPOLU 3.*]

UPOLU 5

Boston Post
Oct. 25, 1848: 33, 2, 5
M

[Similar report, except for omission of cargo details and arrival date in first sentence, in *Boston Daily Advertiser*, Oct. 25, 1848 (M).]

WHALERS

A letter from Capt. Brooks, of Ship Sally Anne, of New Bedford, reports her arrival at Upolu, Navigator Islands, April 17th with 750 bbls. (150 sp) oil. Capt. B. writes that on the 13th of April, Upolu 60 miles distant, experienced a tremendous gale of wind in which all the sails were blown from the yards when snugly furled, lost three boats and had two others badly stove, lost top gallant masts, jilboom, galley and cooking apparatus, the bulwarks from main rigging forward, fore and main spencers blown to atoms etc. The gale continued three days, in which the ship drifted 4 degrees under bare poles also reports in port ship Cambria and Harrison of New Bedford. The Cambria lost sails, spars, boats, head of rudder etc. The Harrison got on to a reef near the island, broke rudder pintels and came off with a loss of false keel—would go to Sydney to heave out for repairs.

C.P.I. Ed. Note: The text of this report is one item in a newspaper column headed "WHALERS," the rest of which is irrelevant. Complete text is used. . . .

[*For additional C.P.I. Ed. Note see UPOLU 3.*]

UPOLU 6

Boston Daily Advertiser
Nov. 20, 1848: 72, 2, 8
M

WHALERS

Ar. at Sydney N.S.W. June 8, Harrison, Sherman, N.B. from Upolu, Navigator's Islands. The Harrison has obtained 100 bbls. sp. and 400 black fish oil, since leaving Sydney, March 16, making a total of 140 sp. and 1500 black fish oil, during the 37 months she has been out. She has come on to Sydney for repairs, having been driven ashore in Apia Harbor, in April last, during a heavy N.W. gale of 36 hours duration. At the time she drove she had two anchors out, top masts struck and yards down. When got off again, it was found her false keel had gone, rudder unshipped, and that the vessel was leaky; also that the oil was leaking from the casks.

C.P.I. Ed. Note: The text of the above report is a copy of an item in a newspaper column headed "WHALERS," . . . the rest of which is irrelevant.

[*For additional C.P.I. Ed. Note see UPOLU 3.*]

UPOLU 7

Boston Daily Advertiser
May 8, 1849: 73, 2, 8
M

WHALERS

Touched at Upola, Navigator's Islands Oct 8, Rebecca Sims, Ray,N.B. 1600 sp 200 wh; 21st, Narragansett, Rogers, Nan 900 sp came in to fish her foremast, succeeded, and sld Nov.4, for New Zealand; Nov.18, Barclay, Baker, 130 sp for N. Zealand.

C.P.I. Ed. Note: The text of the above report is one item in a newspaper column headed "MARINE JOURNAL," the rest of which is irrelevant. Complete text is used. . . .

[*For additional C.P.I. Ed. Note see UPOLU 3.*]

UPOLU 8

The Friend, Honolulu
Sept. 1, 1849: 7, 46, 1
MSaP

INTELLIGENCE FROM SAMOA, OR NAVIGATOR ISLANDS

New Iron Seamen's Chapel—Loss of Am. Whaleship Gem—War among Samoans—Whooping Cough—Missionary Barque "John Williams."

Apia, Upolu, Feb. 27, 1849

My dear Sir—Opportunities for sending letters direct from this to your Islands, are but of rare occurrence, so I must take what presents at the present time, to forward by way of Tahiti. We have to acknowledge your kindness in transmitting to us from time to time copies of the "Friend". I fear our little "Reporter" is but a poor return for the trouble you take. Situated as we are, any news is always very acceptable. We are especially glad to hear of good being done among seamen.

I am sure you will rejoice to learn that our Bethel Chapel here is about completed. I trust that many who visit this port will be induced to come and listen to the glad tidings of salvation, which we shall endeavor to preach with all simplicity from Sabbath to Sabbath. It will of course be a great addition to my labors to preach in English and well as in Samoan. But we must try and do good to all.

The Chapel is composed entirely of galvanized corrugated Iron, brought out within the last year from England. The cost of the building in London was about £170.—About £60 of this was raised in the Islands before I left; the rest was subscribed by friends in England. It is 40 feet by 20.—Ten feet is taken off the length for a reading room, where a library will be kept, with what newspaper and magazines we can procure. We have need to do something to counteract the temptations held out to seamen by the grog-sellers on shore. One thing astonished me when travelling through England and Scotland, to see the little interest taken in the spiritual welfare of seamen, in remote parts of the world.

Some would say when begging a little sum from them, "But have we do with Seamen's Chapels in the South Seas?" Others would ask, "Does not the Missionary Society support you and build your chapels?" It is difficult to get Christians at home to understand the real state of matters in this quarter of the earth.

You may recollect the "Gem" of Sag Harbor, being at the Sandwich Islands a short time ago. She was wrecked a month ago on Suwarrow's Islands—which are only a number of sand banks, surrounded by a large reef, about 500 miles to the N. E. of this. It seems that the reef was not laid down correctly on the chart, and the captain not being aware of this, but supposing he had passed them, was going on, no one thinking of danger, when the ship struck the reef about half past 10 at night. About a week after the mate and a number of the crew reached this in a boat. A small vessel was sent to endeavor to save the rest, but they could not find the Island. Capt. Worth, however, and those with him, managed to repair their boats. After being 21 days on one of the sand banks, they left, and got here six days since. All hands were saved.

Our work continues to be hindered by this foolish and wicked war. When or how it will end, is difficult to say. The longer it is continued the more difficult will it be to reconcile the contending parties. A large meeting is being held this week at the next Island, Savaii, of the neutral party, consisting mostly of church members, and steady people, to try some plan to restore peace.—The aggressive party contend for retaining the powers which they gained in former wars. The others say, we wish no superiority—but we fight for equality. The last have certainly so far right on their side, and have ever shown a disposition to settle matters quietly. It was only when they were compelled that they took up arms. It is pity to see what evil they are doing both to soul and body. If ever this war was settled, both sides have had so much of it, that they will think well before they commence the like again. Some of the leading chiefs have been killed.

Whooping cough has been very bad, among children, particularly. It was introduced some months since from Tahiti.— None of the Missionary children have died from it, but vast numbers of the natives.

Our missionary bark, John Williams, has gone to Sydney about a month ago. She is to call at the New Hebrides, to see how our friends Geddie and Archibald are getting on. Mr. and Mrs. Powell, belonging to our Mission, went with them when they settled at Aneitum. They may expect much rough work for a long time.

Praying that the Lord may bless you in your soul, family and labors, believe me

My dear Sir,
Yours very truly,
Wm. Mills.

Rev. S. C. Damon.

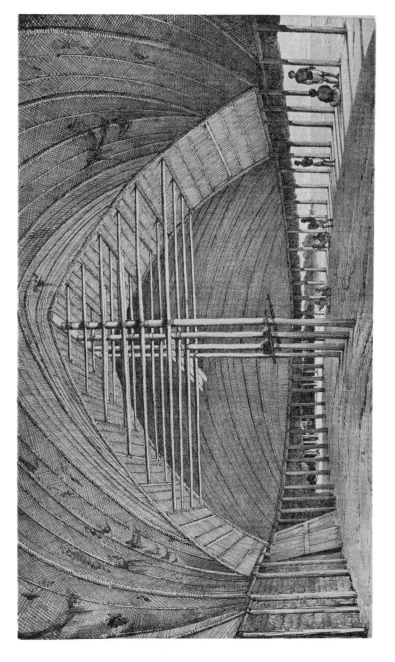

Interior of a meeting house, Apia, Upolu, Samoa. From Dumont D'Urville, *Voyage au Pole Sud*, 2nd expedition, 1837-1840, plate 71.

UPOLU 9

Boston Daily Evening Transcript
Aug. 7, 1850: 21, 2, 5
MBAt

GALE AT THE NAVIGATOR ISLANDS

The British brig Two Friends, which arrived in this harbor from New Zealand on Saturday, experienced a terrific hurricane off Navigator Islands about the 17th April. The vessel was thrown on her beam ends, and lost most of her canvass and top-gallant yards. She put into Apia Bay to repair damages and was detained there 24 days. Such a severe hurricane had never before been felt by the inhabitants; every building on the island having been swept away.

C.P.I. Ed. Note: The text of this report is one item in a newspaper column headed "GALE AT THE NAVIGATOR ISLANDS," the rest of which is irrelevant. Navigator (Samoa) Islands are situated in lat. between 13° and 14°S., lon. between 168° and 173°W. H.O. Chart No. 87. (*H.O. Pub.* No. 166, Vol. II, 4th ed., 1933, p. 253.)

UPOLU 10

The Friend, Honolulu
Sept. 1, 1850: 8, 72, 3
MSaP

By the ship Tobacco Plant.—on the 6th of April, 1850, the ship Hercules of New Bedford, 33 mos. out, with 250 bbls. sp; and the Br. Bk. favorite, of London, 14 mos. 50 bbls; went on shore in a typhoon at Apolo, Pear Harbor, total wrecks. Also a missionary schooner lay high and dry on the reef, June 17th, spoke the ship Phoenix, of Nantucket, 22 mos out, 350 bbls. in lat 1 50 S. long. 169 43 W.

The following intelligence was furnished by the 2d mate of the lady Howden; on the morning of the 22d of June, the British brig Lady Howden, of London, Capt. Chalk, from California for Sydney, went on a reef about 12 miles to the southward of Ongea, one of the Fejee Islands, at a quarter past 3 A.M. With great risk the boats were got out and dragged over a coral reef for upwards of a mile, in passing the outer part of which the cutter was capsized and everything in her lost. The long boat had a narrow escape. The natives plundered the vessel of everything they could lay their hands on.

C.P.I. Ed. Note: The above text is taken from a column headed "MARINE JOURNAL," the rest of which is irrelevant.

UPOLU 11

Boston Post
Feb. 15, 1851: 38, 2, 6
M

DISASTERS, ETC.

Accounts from Upola (Navigator Island) to June 5, 1850, state that Capt. Imbert, (late of ship Hercules, 2d of N.B.), with all his officers were there. Capt. I., in company with the Mexican Counsul, had bought a brig, and would proceed to San Francisco with a full freight, to sail some time in July. When the gale abated in which the Hercules was lost, they were enabled to walk all round the ship at times. The ship was scuttled, the oil taken out (about 400 bbls.) and sold. The ship used up.

C.P.I. Ed. Note: The text of this report is one item in a newspaper column headed "DISASTERS, ETC.," the rest of which is irrelevant.

[*For additional C.P.I. Ed. Note see UPOLU 3.*]

UPOLU 12

Weekly Alta California, San Francisco, Cal.
Mar. 1, 1851: 3, 3, 4
MH

A barque from San Francisco, bound to Sydney with passengers, (supposed from description to be the Adario), was wrecked on the island of Porlu, 20th Oct. There were no lives lost, but the passengers were robbed of all they possessed by the natives.

C.P.I. Ed. Note: The text of this report is one item in a news column the rest of which is irrelevant.

Porlu Island, mentioned in text is probably meant for Upolu Island.

[*For additional C.P.I. Ed. Note see UPOLU 3.*]

UPOLU 13

Weekly Alta California, San Francisco, Cal.
Mar. 29, 1851: 3, 3, 4
MH

BARQUE ADARIO

The Narwhal, English whaler, at Sydney, Dec. 23, had the owner, Captain, crew and passengers of the barque Adario on board, (before reported,) from San Francisco, bound to Sydney, wrecked on a reef about 14 miles distant from Opolu. The Adario was purchased at this port by Mr. Noeks, of Launceston, and commanded by Capt. Gill, of Hobart Town.

C.P.I. Ed. Note: The text of this report is one item in a news column, the rest of which is irrelevant.

Opolu, mentioned in text is probably another spelling for Upolu Island.

[*For additional C.P.I. Ed. Note see UPOLU 3.*]

UPOLU 14

Boston Daily Advertiser
July 8, 1851: 6, 2, 8
M

WHALERS

At Upolu, Navigator's Islands, Jan. 26, Timor, Baker, S.H., 1200 bbls.

C.P.I. Ed. Note: The text of the above report is an excerpt from a copy of an item in a newspaper column headed "WHALERS," . . . the rest of which is irrelevant.

[*For additional C.P.I. Ed. Note see UPOLU 3.*]

UPOLU 15

Boston Daily Adv[ertiser]
Nov. 4, 1851: 78, 2, 7
M

WHALERS

As at Apia, Navigator's Islands, Mch. 8, Friends, Low, N.L. 80 sp. 70 wh;

At Upolu, Aug. 9, Phocion, Nichols, N.B. 1000 sp. (her carpenter was killed June 25, in an affray, with a Portuguese, who stabbed him in the side);

C.P.I. Ed. Note: The text of the above report is one item in a newspaper column headed "WHALERS," the rest of which is irrelevant. Complete text is used. . . . Apia, mentioned in text is a harbor on the northern side of Upolu Island; one of the Navigator Group, and is 13° 49′S., 171° 46′ W. H.O. Chart No. 95. *(H.O. Pub.* No. 166, Vol. II, 4th ed., 1933, p. 271.)

UPOLU 16

Boston Daily Advertiser
Nov. 5, 1851: —, —, —
M

[Report printed here as UPOLU 17 gives different quantities of oil. See also UPOLU 20 for correction.]

WHALERS

A letter from San Francisco Sept. 30, reports at Upolu, Navigator's Island, last of June, Ganges, Nant., 1400 sp. Lion, Prov., 300 sp., Phocion, N.B., 1100 so. on board, (and adds subsequently that each of the two latter took 150 bbls. sp. day they came out, making the Lion 950 and the Phocion 1250: the P. has however, been reported Aug. 9, 1000.)

C.P.I. Ed. Note: The text of this report is one item in a newspaper column headed "WHALERS," the rest of which is irrelevant. Complete text is used. . . .

[*For additional C.P.I. Ed. Note see UPOLU 3.*]

. UPOLU 17

Daily Evening Traveler, Boston, Mass.
Nov. 5, 1851: 6, 84, —
M

WHALERS

A Letter from San Francisco Sept. 30, reports at Upolu, Navigator's Islands, last of June, Ganges, Nan, 900 sp., Lion, Prov. 300 sp., Phocion N B, 1000 sp., on board. (And adds subsequently that each of the two latter took 150 bbls. sp. day they came out, making the Lion 950 and the Phocion 1250; the P. has, however, been reported Aug. 9, 1000 sp.

C.P.I. Ed. Note: The text of the above report is a copy of an item in a newspaper column headed "WHALERS," . . . the rest of which is irrelevant.

[*For additional C.P.I. Ed. Note see UPOLU 3.*]

UPOLU 18

Boston Post
Nov. 6, 1851: 39, 2, 4
M

WHALERS

A letter from Capt. Nichols, of ship Phocion of New Bedford, reports her at Upolu, Navigator Islands June 7 with 650 bbls. sperm oil on board (sent home 150 sp). Capt. N. reports the death of his carpenter (not captain as misprinted in the Post) Henry Bernharst, a German, June 5th who was killed on shore by a stab in the side, in an affray with three Tonga natives and a Portuguese one of the crew. The Phocion was bound to King's Mill Group.

C.P.I. Ed. Note: The text of this report is one item in a news column headed "WHALERS," the rest of which is irrelevant.

[*For additional C.P.I. Ed. Note see UPOLU 3.*]

UPOLU 19

Boston Daily Advertiser
Nov. 6, 1851: 78, 2, 7
M

WHALERS

A letter from Capt. Nichols, of the Phocion, N.B. reports her at Upolu, Navigator Islands, June 7, with 850 bbls, sp oil on board (sent home 150 sp, subsequently took 150 sp). Capt. N. reports the death of his carpenter, Henry Bernharst, a German, June 5, who was killed on shore by a stab in the side in an affray with three Tonga natives and a Portuguese, one of the crew. The Phocion was bound to the King's Mill Group.

At Upolu Aug. 6, Martha, Chase, N.B. 525 sp (before reported 250).

C.P.I. Ed. Note: The text of the above report is one item in a newspaper column headed "WHALERS," the rest of which is irrelevant. Complete text is used. . . .

[*For additional C.P.I. Ed. Note see UPOLU 3.*]

UPOLU 20

Boston Daily Adv[ertiser]
Nov. 6, 1851: 78, 2, 7
M

WHALERS

The Lion of Providence before reported at Upolu, last of June had 800 (not 300 sp as misprinted) and took 150 bbls. when leaving port making 950.

At Sydney N.S.W. June 14, Herald, Terry F. H. refitting.—Reports at Simpson's Island, Mch 21 sch Alfred, Davenport, N.B. 150 sp. Sld from Upolu, Navigator's Island, April 25, Lalla Rookh, N.B. 750 sp. The Herald had a severe gale Je 1, lost jib, flying jibboom, fore top gallant yard, starboard boat and received other damage. Spoken May 10, off Sunday Island, Lewis, Clement, N.B. 700 sp.

C.P.I. Ed. Note: The text of the above report is one item in a newspaper column headed "WHALERS," the rest of which is irrelevant. Complete text is used. . . .

[*For additional C.P.I. Ed. Note see UPOLU 3.*]

UPOLU 21

Boston Daily Advertiser
Nov. 27, 1852: 80, 2, 7
M

WHALERS

Arrived at New Bedford 26th, ship Swift, Vincent, Pacific Ocean, Apia, Navigator Islands, July 2, Upolu, July 9, 1900 bbls. sp. oil on board. Sent home 100 bbls. sp. on the voyage. Reports touched at Apia, May 30, Ganges, Coffin, Nan. 1250 sp.

C.P.I. Ed. Note: The text of this report is one item in a news column headed "WHALERS," the rest of which is irrelevant. Complete text is used. . . .

[*For additional C.P.I. Ed. Note see UPOLU 15.*]

UPOLU 22

Boston Post
Nov. 27, 1852: 41, 2, 5
M

WHALERS

Arrived at N. Bedford, 26 inst., Ship Swift, Vincent, Pacific Ocean, Apia, Navigator Island, July 2, Upolu, July 9, with 1900 bbls. sp. oil on board,—barque Smyrna, Tobey, of N. Bedford, 600 sp., (reported off Sunday Islands, March 6, 750 sp.) all bound for the line. Spoke May 4, N.E. from Sunday Islands ship C. W. Morgan, Sampson of N. Bedford 950 sp.

C.P.I. Ed. Note: The text of this report is one item in a newspaper column headed "WHALERS," the rest of which is irrelevant.

[*For additional C.P.I. Ed. Note see UPOLU 3.*]

UPOLU 23

Boston Daily Adv[ertiser]
Jan. 11, 1853: 81, 2, 8
M

WHALERS

At Apia, Navigator's Islands, June 10, Wm. & Henry, Mayhew, F.H., clean; Ganges, Coffin, Nantucket, 1250 sp. to cruise on the Equator.

C.P.I. Ed. Note: The text of this report is one item in a newspaper column headed "WHALERS," the rest of which is irrelevant.

[For additional C.P.I. Ed. Note see UPOLU 15.]

UPOLU 24

Boston Daily Advertiser
Jan. 15, 1853: 81, 2, 8
M

WHALERS

At Apia, Navigator's Islands, June 10, Emily, Vincent, N. B., 2000 sp. bound home.

C.P.I. Ed. Note: The text of this report is one item in a newspaper column headed "WHALERS," the rest of which is irrelevant.

[*For additional C.P.I. Ed. Note see UPOLU 15.*]

UPOLU 25

Boston Post
June 17, 1853: 42, 2, 5
M

WHALERS

A letter from the first officer of the Atkins, Adams of F.H. dated Oct. 8th 1852 reports her arrival at Upolu, Navigator Islands, and on her way south. Since reported off French Rock with 950 bbls.

C.P.I. Ed. Note: The text of this report is an item in a newspaper column headed "WHALERS," . . . the rest of which is irrelevant.

[*For additional C.P.I. Ed. Note see UPOLU 3.*]

UPOLU 26

Boston Post
July 16, 1853: 43, 2, 6
M

WHALERS

A letter from Capt. White, of ship Triton 2d of N.B. dated Navigator Islands Jan. 18th states that ship has been on a rock in the harbor of Upolu and stove a hole in her bottom—had since discharged cargo, hove down and repaired damage, and was then ready for sea—no oil on board.

C.P.I. Ed. Note: The text of this report is an item in a newspaper column headed "WHALERS," . . . the rest of which is irrelevant.

[*For additional C.P.I. Ed. Note see UPOLU 3.*]

UPOLU 27

Boston Daily Advertiser
Oct. 18, 1853: 82, 2, 7
M

[Reports similar to first two sentences in *Boston Daily Atlas,* Oct. 19, 1853 (MBr), *Daily Commonwealth,* Boston, Oct. 19, 1853 (MH), *Boston Courier,* Oct. 20, 1853 (MB) and *New England Farmer,* Boston Oct. 22, 1853 (MH.)]

DISASTERS

Ship York, M'Kendry, from Honolulu Apr. 6 for New Bedford sprung a leak when two days out, and attempted to return, but was prevented by strong adverse winds, and proceeded to Upolu, Navigator's Islands, where she ar. Apr. 26.—A survey was held and the ship was condemned and sold for $1700. We do not learn any further particulars, as the account comes in a brief letter put on board a vessel which passed the Islands on her way from San Francisco to Australia, whence the letter was sent to Liverpool, and thence to the United States. The cargo was probably then awaiting an opportunity to be reshipped to New Bedford, The York was an old vessel, formerly a New York and Liverpool packet. Much anxiety has been felt in relation to her, as until now, nothing had been heard of her since she left Honolulu.

C.P.I. Ed. Note: The text of this report is an item in a newspaper column headed "DISASTERS," the rest of which is irrelevant.

[*For additional C.P.I. Ed. Note see UPOLU 3.*]

UPOLU 28

Boston Daily Adv[ertiser]
Oct. 22, 1853: 82, 2, 7
M

DISASTERS

Ship York from Honolulu, before reported condemned and sold at Upolu, Navigator's Islands, was bound to New London, not New Bedford. There is insurance on her cargo in New York for $20,000. It is presumed that the cargo was landed without material damage.

C.P.I. Ed. Note: The text of this report is one item in a newspaper column headed "DISASTERS," the rest of which is irrelevant.
    Complete text is used. . . .

[*For additional C.P.I. Ed. Note see UPOLU 9.*]

UPOLU 29

Boston Daily Advertiser
Nov. 11, 1853: 82, 2, 5
M

DISASTERS

Ship York, McKendry, from Honolulu, for New London, which was condemned and sold at Navigator's Islands, arrived at Sydney N S W Aug. 17.—

C.P.I. Ed. Note The text of this report is one item in a news column headed "DISASTERS," the rest of which is irrelevant.

[*For additional C.P.I. Ed. Note see UPOLU 9.*]

UPOLU 30

Boston Post
Nov. 18, 1853: 43, 2, 5
M

DISASTERS

A letter received in New Bedford from Capt. McKendry, of ship York, dated June 28th, at Upolu, states that he sold 250 bbls. sp. oil at 43¢ per gallon, and 1600 bbls. wh. oil at 16¢ per gallon, the balance of the cargo he proceeded to Sydney with, at which port he has since arrived, where it will be shipped or sold as may appear to the best interest of the owners or those concerned.

C.P.I. Ed. Note: The text of this report is an item in a newspaper column headed "DISASTERS," . . . the rest of which is irrelevant.

[*For additional C.P.I. Ed. Note see UPOLU 3.*]

UPOLU 31

Boston Daily Advertiser
Sept. 12, 1855: 86, 1, 2
MB

DISASTERS, ETC.

Barque Elvira,—, from San Francisco for Sydney and Melbourne, with lumber and 70 passengers, put into Upolu, Navigator's Islands, no date, short of provisions and sails, and it was thought would be condemned.

C.P.I. Ed. Note: The text of this report is an item in a newspaper column headed "DISASTERS," the rest of which is irrelevant.

[*For additional C.P.I. Ed. Note see UPOLU 3.*]

UPOLU 32

Boston Daily Advertiser
May 14, 1856: 33, 4, 7
MHi

WHALERS

At Apia, Navigator Islands, no date, ships Rambler, Porter, Nantucket, very leaky,—had been condemned, and was to be sold at auction.

C.P.I. Ed. Note: The text of this report is an item in a newspaper column headed "WHALERS," . . . the rest of which is irrelevant.

[*For additional C.P.I. Ed. Note see UPOLU 15.*]

UPOLU 33

Boston Evening Traveller
Dec. 22, 1856: 12, 4, 8
MBAt

WHALERS

A letter from Capt. Swain, of ship Minerva 2d, of New Bedford, reports her at Upolu June 18, with 160 sp. all well. Had lost 2 men at the island of Manua May 26th by the upsetting of a boat—Edward Phillips, of Fishkill, and Louis Lunnett, residence unknown; was to leave same day for the line and New Zealand.

C.P.I. Ed. Note: The text of this report is one item in a newspaper column headed "WHALERS," the rest of which is irrelevant. Complete text is used. . . .

[For additional C.P.I. Ed. Note see UPOLU 3.]

UPOLU 34

The Friend, Honolulu
Sept. 8, 1860: 17, 68, 3
MSaP

James D. Hague, Esq., Chemist of American Guano Company.

HARBOR OF APIA, NAVIGATOR'S ISLAND

The harbor of Apia, on the island of Upolu, Navigator's, is one of the best in the Pacific. It is capacious, well protected, has a good entrance and sufficient depth of water for large vessels. An experienced pilot is at hand.

This port has been frequented for many years by whaleships that touch to obtain water and supplies, but it is not until lately that merchant vessels have had much occasion to avail themselves of its advantages.

Since the importation of guano has been commenced from Baker's and other islands near the Line, a number of merchant ships, on their way home, have called at Apia for provisions and water. Yams are generally to be had in abundance; pigs and fowls readily obtained; fresh water is close at hand, and a suitable launch or water boat has been ordered from Sydney to facilitate the watering of large vessels.

Mr. August Unshelm, an agreeable and hospitable gentleman of much business experience, is established there, making it the depot of an extensive trade among the various groups of islands in the South Pacific. This gentleman is prepared to furnish to vessels all such ships' stores as are ordinarilly in demand, and will take drafts at reasonable discount. He is ever ready to oblige all to whom he can render any service.

The settlement is not large and there are but few foreign residents. The Rev. A. W. Murray, an English Missionary, has

been established there many years.   Mr. John C. Williams, H.
B. M. Consul, and Mr. Unshelm, reside there, with their families, who extend to strangers visiting there a friendly welcome,
seeking to render their stay agreeable by many kind services
and attentions, and those who have enjoyed their hospitality
must ever hold them in grateful remembrance.

[For C.P.I. Ed. Note see UPOLU 3.]

UPOLU 35

Boston Evening Transcript
Jan. 7, 1861: 32, 4, 4
M

SHIPPING INTELLIGENCE
General Record

Ship Morning Light, Johnston, from Baker's Island for Hampton Roads, put into Apia, Navigator's Island, in Oct. and would have to discharge and recaulk.

C.P.I. Ed. Note: The text of this report is an item in a newspapr column headed "SHIPPING INTELLIGENCE," . . . the rest of which is irrelevant. Baker's, mentioned in text is identified as Baker Island. Baker Island is situated in Lat. 0°13′N., Lon. 176°33′W. H. O. Chart No. 1198. *(H.O. Pub.* No. 166, Vol. II, 4th ed., 1933, p. 473.)

[*For additional C.P.I. Ed. Note see UPOLU 15.*]

UPOLU 36

Daily Eve[ning] Traveler, Boston, Mass.
Nov. 12, 1862: 18, 4, 2
M

WHALERS

A letter from Capt. Grant of ship Japan, of New Bedford reports her at Upola Navigator Islands. July 7 with 1150 bbls. sp. oil on board; had discharged 3rd mate, Mr. Mooney; was bound to the line, thence to New Zealand.

C.P.I. Ed. Note: The text of this report is one item in a newspaper column headed "WHALERS," the rest of which is irrelevant.

[For additional C.P.I. Ed. Note see UPOLU 3.]

UPOLU 37

"Whalemen's Shipping List," New Bedford, Mass.
May 15, 1866: 24, 2, 4
MDarHi

[Similar report in *The Friend,* Honolulu, Sept. 1, 1866 (MSaP) is signed and dated:—"An American. Apia, Upolu, March 6, 1866.]

HARBOR OF ASPIA ISLAND, UPOLU, NAVIGATORS' ISLAND

By an American resident who has had the experience of the islands for nineteen years.

The harbor of Aspia, on the island of Upolu, Navigators', lies in latitude 13° 51′ 20″ S., and longitude 174° 45′ W., a capacious, well protected, and has a good entrance, with sufficient depth of water for vessels of any size. An experienced liscensed pilot is always at hand.

This port has for five and twenty years been frequented by whale ships that touch here to obtain water and supplies; while many merchant vessels have had occasion to avail themselves of its advantages, and since the importation of guano has commenced from Baker's, Howland's, McKean's and other islands, many of the vessels engaged in that trade have called at Aspia for water and provisions. Supplies, both foreign and native, are to be obtained; while fresh water is close at hand.

Several agreeable and hospitable merchants of much business experience are established here, making it a depot of an extensive trade among the various groups of islands in the Pacific Ocean. These merchants are always prepared to furnish vessels with all such stores as are generally in demand, and will take drafts at reasonable discount; and they are ever ready to oblige those whom they can render any service.

It has been the conviction of those well experienced in such matters—persons capable of forming a judgment in the matter,—that Aspia would make a most eligible depot for guano and steam vessels. A wharf could in a short time and at a trifling expense be built, thus rendering every facility for the landing of cargoes.

The attention of ship owners and masters is earnestly called to the many advantages offered them at this port. It is a well known fact that vessels calling at many of the islands in the Pacific are often times delayed, while the masters are put to much trouble and inconvenience by the desertion of their men. Desertion here is a very rare occurrence, and when a case of this kind does happen, the apprehension of the party is certain, just for the mere fact the natives are eager to receive the bounty, thus saving a great amount of trouble to the master; and there is at all times a good supply of wood and water and all other things generally required by vessels, owners and master both would find it to their advantage to send or bring their vessels to this port for refreshments.

To those who would emigrate here with a view of settling on the island, I would say, good land is to be obtained at a fair price, and there are no difficulties whatever attending agriculture. The cotton which is now extensively cultivated is of superior quality and commands a high price in foreign markets.

The foreign population is at present increasing. Settlers would be welcomed here with every demonstration of cordiality.

[For C.P.I. Ed. Notes see UPOLU 3 & 15.]

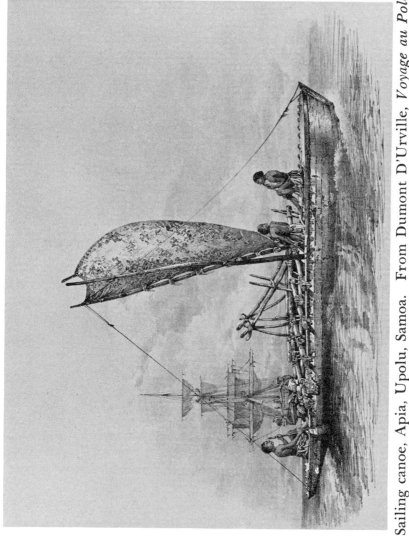

Sailing canoe, Apia, Upolu, Samoa. From Dumont D'Urville, *Voyage au Pole Sud*, 2nd expedition, 1837-1840, plate 72.

Houses and canoes, Apia Upolu, Samoa. From Dumont D'Urville, *Voyage au Pole Sud*, 2nd expedition, 1837-1840, plate 73.

UVEA (WALLIS) 1

Boston Daily Advertiser and Patriot
Feb. 1, 1833: 41, 2, 4
MBAt

The Sydney, N. S. Wales paper of July 2d, states that the crew of the whale ship OLDHAM, of London, has been Massacred at WALLIS Island, by the natives. The greater part of this island has been reduced to subjection by George MININI, a native of WAHOA, and a particular friend of the American traders. He has become part owner of the American schr. CHINCHILLA, which was employed in gathering BECHE LE MER, and was thus engaged when the natives attacked and put him to death. The Oldham made her appearance soon after, when the natives supposing she was an American, and that the crew would avenge the death of Minini, fell upon them by a stratagem, and cut them off to a man.

C.P.I. Ed. Note: The text of this report is one item in a news column, the rest of which is irrelevant.

Uea (Wallis) Island is in lat. 13° 18′ S., long. 176° 10′ W., H. O. chart No.2019. *(H.O. Pub. No. 166, Vol. II, 4th ed., 1933, p. 423.)*

UVEA (WALLIS) 2

Boston Daily Evening Transcript
May 1, 1837: 8, 2, 3
MBAt

[Reports in *Commercial Advertiser and Essex Journal*, Salem, May 3, 1837 (MSaE) and *Lynn Record*, May 3, 1837 (MLy) are similar except for having 'W. M. Barnard.']

HORRID MASSACRE

Mr. M.M. Barnard, formerly an officer of the ship Selma of New Bedford, has arrived home and reports that the English Missionaries at Keepel Island (one of the Friendly group) conceived the benevolent plan of attempting to introduce Christianity at Wallis Island, by sending natives teachers and missionaries, thinking that they would meet with less opposition than foreigners. They procured them a passage to the Islands in August last, but soon after they landed the whole, 70 in number, were murdered. Mr. Barnard was at the Island at the time of the massacre took place and left in a sloop of war Vincennes, when she touched at that place. He left the latter vessel at Cape Town.

C.P.I. Ed. Note: The text of the above report is a copy of an item in a newspaper column headed "HORRID MASSACRE," . . . the rest of which is irrelevant.

[*For additional C.P.I. Ed. Note see UVEA (WALLIS) 1.*]

UVEA (WALLIS) 3

Daily Atlas, Boston, Mass.
May 1, 1837: 5, 2, 3
MHi

[Identical report in *Salem Gazette,* May 2, 1837 (MSaE) gives *New Bedford Gazette* as source. Similar reports in *Columbian Centinel,* Boston, May 3, 1837 (MBAt) and *Christian Workman,* Boston, May 5, 1837 (MH).]

HORRID MASSACRE

Mr. William M. Barnard, formerly second officer of the ship Selma, of this port, arrived here in Parachute a few days since and has furnished us with a detailed account of the murder of 70 natives South Sea Island Missionaries in the month of August 1835, at Wallis' Island. It appears from his journal that the English Missionaries at Keppel Island, (one of the Friendly group) conceived the benevolent plan of attempting to introduce Christianity at Wallis's Island by sending native teachers and missionaries thinking they would meet with less opposition than foreigners. They procured them a passage to the island—but, horrid to relate, soon after they landed the whole number were murdered in a most barborous and inhuman manner. Mr. Barnard was at the island at the time the massacre took place and left in the sloop of war Vincennes, when she touched at that place. He left the latter vessel at Cape Town.—New Bedford Merc.

C.P.I. Ed. Note: The text of the above report is a copy of an item found in a newspaper column headed "HORRID MAS-

SACRE," the rest of which is irrelevant. Keppel (Niuatobu-tabu) Island is in lat. 15°58′S., lon. 173°48′W., H.O. Chart No. 2021 (*H.O. Pub.* No. 166, Vol. II, ed. 1933, p. 247.)

[*For additional C.P.I. Ed. Note see UVEA (WALLIS) 1.*]

UVEA (WALLIS) 4

Sandwich Islands Gazette, Honolulu
Feb. 24, 1839: 3, 3, 1
MBAt

Liniar Notices of the Pacific No. 13.
A Cruise among the various Islands
From the Journal of Captain E. Stokes.
By S. D. MacKintoch

The schooner RAIATEA of the burthen of sixty-five tons, under command of Capt. Stokes, left the Society Islands on the 6th of October, A.D. 1837. The Rt. Revd. J. Bte. Francois Pompalier, Lord Bishop of MARONEE (or Marouee)—three priests and three catechists were passengers on board. After losing sight of the Societies, the Captain directed his course towards Palmerston's Island, lying in Latitude 18.16 S., Longitude 163.20 W. This island was discovered on the fourteenth of the month; no landing place suitable for a boat being ascertained, the vessel departed for VAVAO, one of the Friendly Islands, where they arrived on the twenty-fourth. At daylight the entrance to Port Refuge was perceived; at noon the vessel came to anchor in the port. On the next day the Lord Bishop of Maronee visited the shore to get an interview with the King; by whom he was kindly received, and from whom he received permission to remain on the Island. On the thirty-first of October the RAIATEA made sail from the Island, and directed its course towards WALLIS Island. At 5 P.M. the Almaguros were seen; it seemed impossible to weather them, and the Captain judged it proper to bear up and run between them. These islands bear from each other, by compass, N.W. by W., and S.E. by E. off the southernmost island, which is very low; there is a reef extending W.S.W., for three miles; there is also another reef off the N.E. point, but the high island is free from all danger.

November 3d. At daylight saw Wallis Island; at 10 A.M., the RAIATEA, being near the entrance of the harbor, the Captain ran his vessel in and came to anchor. The vessel was shortly visited by a number of natives, many of whom had had former acquaintance with the Captain. At noon, the Captain, accompanied the Bishop on a visit to the King Lavalooa, and permission was granted to land one priest and one catechist with their effects. On November 7th the gentlemen landed.

C.P.I. Ed. Note: This is a complete copy of a newspaper article. . . . Maronee or Marouee may be another spelling for Moorea, one of the Society Islands. Moorea (Eimeo) one of the Society Islands is 17°30′ S., 149°50′ W., H. O. Chart No. 2065. *(H.O. Pub.* No. 166, Vol. II, 4th ed., 1933, p. 102.) Palmerston Islands are 18° 04′ S., 163° 10′ W., H. O. Chart No. 1980, have no safe anchorage. *(H.O. Pub.* No. 166, Vol. II, 4th ed., 1933, p. 67.) Vavao is probably another spelling for Vavau, one of the Tonga, or Friendly Islands.

Port Refuge, 18° 39′ S., 174° 04′ W., is on the western coast of Vavau, *(H.O. Pub.* No. 166, Vol. II, 4th ed., 1933, p. 238.)

Almaguros is possibly another spelling for Amargura (Fanua Lai). The captain may have included Fanua Lai and Toku Islands in a group because of their proximity. Toku Island is 27 miles northwestward of Vavau, 18° 09′ S., 174° 11′ W., H. O. Chart No. 2016. Fanua Lai (Amargura) is 12 miles northwestward of Toku Island. *(Ibid,* p. 244.)

[*For additional C.P.I. Ed. Note see UVEA (WALLIS) 1.*]

UVEA (WALLIS) 5

Niles National Register, Baltimore, Md.
Jan. 18, 1845: 67, 305, 2
MNBedf

PACIFIC ISLANDS

A letter from Tahita of June 2d, states that henceforward the chiefs of Wallis's and the Gambier Islands, and the island of Fontana, are under the Protectorate of France, and government has ordered a vessel to these new acquisitions to notify that they will be forwith occupied.

C.P.I. Ed. Note: The above text is a complete copy of an item taken from a news column headed "FOREIGN," the rest of which is irrelevant.

Mangareva (Gambier) Islands are 23° 08′ S., 134° 58′ W., H. O. Chart No. 2024. *(H.O. Pub.* No. 166, Vol. II, 4th ed., 1938, p. 130.)

Fontana may possibly be another spelling for Futuna.

Futuna or Horne Island is 14° 14′ 20″ S., 178° 06′ 45″ W. (Bowditch, 1917, p. 348)

[*For additional C.P.I. Ed. Note see UVEA (WALLIS) 1.*]

UVEA (WALLIS) 6

Boston Daily Advertiser
July 2, 1850: 76, 2, 8
M

WHALERS

The James Loper, of Nantucket, in coming out from Wallis Island, in Jan, got on a reef of rocks, and she was discharging at Sydney for the purpose of being hove out for repairs

C.P.I. Ed. Note: The text of this report is an item in a newspaper column headed "WHALERS," . . . the rest of which is irrelevant.

[*For additional C.P.I. Ed. Note see UVEA (WALLIS) 1.*]

UVEA (WALLIS) 7

Boston Daily Journal
Feb. 24, 1860: 28, 2, 7
MHi

[Similar report in *Atlas and Daily Bee,* Boston, Feb. 23, 1860 (MBAt).]

SHIPPING JOURNAL

Sydney, N.S.W. Dec. 15.—The Caroline, Trescott, which arrived here yesterday from Fortuna (South Sea Islands) reports the arrival at Wallis Island on Nov. 5, of part of the crew of an American brig, which had foundered at sea nine days previously; the rest of the crew had arr. at Samoa.

C.P.I. Ed. Note: The text of the above report is one item in a newspaper column headed "SHIPPING JOURNAL," the rest of which is irrelevant.
Complete text is used. . . .
Samoa (Navigator) islands are 13° 30′ S., to 14° 30′ S., 168 00′ W. to 173° 00′ W.   H. O. Chart No. 87.   *(H.O. Pub.* No. 166, Vol. II, 4th ed., 1933, p. 253.)

[*For additional C.P.I. Ed. Note see UVEA (WALLIS) 1.*]

VANAVANA 1

Boston Courier
Feb. 10, 1845: 23, 4, 6
MBAt

[Identical report in *American Traveller,* Boston, Feb. 14, 1845
(MB). Reports in *The Daily Mercury,* New Bedford, Feb. 14,
1845 (MNBedf) and *New Bedford Mercury,* Feb. 14, 1845
(MNBedf) are similar except for giving longitude as '138 degrees 44 minutes.' Report in *Daily Evening Transcript,* Boston, Feb. 12, 1845 (MB; MBAt) is similar except for first sentence which reads, 'Capt. Simmons of the Brig Faith at Baltimore reports the discovery of a new Island in the Pacific, to
which he has given the name of his vessel. Capt. Simmons was
on his way. . . .']

DISCOVERY OF A NEW ISLAND

Capt. B. F. Simmons of the brigantine FAITH, which arrived at
Baltimore on Wednesday of last week, has since reached this
city, and informs us of the discovery of an island not laid down
on any chart hitherto published, a knowledge of which may be
of importance to navigators, as well as others. Capt. Simmons
was on his way from Sidney to Valparaiso, and after leaving
OTAHEITE first saw it on the 31st. of October, 1843. Seen
from the deck of the vessel, the island had the appearance of a
mass of rocks, but a nearer approach showed it to be an island,
covered with cocoanut trees, with thick underbrush.

When convinced that it was an island, Capt. Simmons supposed it might be one already known, and at first, mistook it for
Carisfoot. To be sure, however, he lowered his boat, and attempted to land, but was prevented by a reef of black coral
rocks, with heavy breakers, which surrounded the island. He

went completely round it, however, and found it to be about six miles in circumference.

At a short distance from it he found no soundings in sixty fathoms of water. After examining it for two or three hours, as thoroughly as he deemed necessary, he steered for Carisfoot, according to his reckoning, and made it in the course of a few hours, and passed to the south of it. A large lagoon was in the middle of the island, which seemed to be rich and fertile. On reaching Valparaiso, where he remained some months, he waited upon the Commander of the British squadron, and informed him of his discovery. He examined the most recent English charts but no indication of such an island was to be found. He is situated in the track from Otaheite to Valparaiso, in latitude 21 degrees and 10 minutes, and West longitude 138 degrees 54 minutes. He named it the Isle of Faith, from his vessel. The discovery may be of some importance. Capt. Simmons is a native of Vermont, an experienced seaman, and entitled to no little credit for the care with which he examined the island.

C.P.I. Ed. Note: Carisfoot Island, mentioned in text, is probably Tureia Island. "Tureia (20° 46′ S., 138° 31′ W., H. O. Chart No. 77), also known as Papakena or Carysfort Island, 60 miles north by east of Mururoa, was discovered by the British naval vessel *Pandora* in 1791." (*H.O. Pub.* No. 166, Vol. II, 4th ed. 1933,pp. 135, 136.)

Isle of Faith, mentioned in text, may possibly be Vanavana Island as description and location seems to indicate.

"Vanavana (20°45′S., 139°09′W., H.O.Chart No. 77) also known as Kuratake or Barrow Island, 32 miles westward of Tureia, was discovered by Beechey in 1826. The atoll consists of a narrow strip of land about 200 yards wide surrounding a lagoon 1.8 miles in length north and south, and about 1.3 miles wide, . . ." (*H.O.Pub.* No.166, Vol.II, 4th ed. 1933, p.136.)

VANAVANA 2

Evening Mercantile Journal, Boston, Mass.
Feb. 11, 1845: 12, 2, 1
MB

[Identical reports in *Boston Bee,* Feb. 13, 1845 (MB), *Boston American Eagle,* Feb. 13, 1845 (MB), *Daily National Intelligencer,* Washington, D.C., Feb. 14, 1845 (MB), *Salem Gazette,* Feb. 14, 1845 (MSaE) and *Christian Register,* Boston, Mar. 1, 1845 (MH). Report in *Morning Register,* New Bedford, Feb. 12, 1845 (MNBedf) gives longitude as '158 54.' but is otherwise identical.]

AN ISLAND DISCOVERED IN THE PACIFIC

Captain Simmons of brig Faith, who arrived at Baltimore last week, discovered an island in the Pacific, which is not laid down in any chart. He was on his passage from Otaheite to Valparaiso, and fell in with this island in lat. 21. 10, and long 138.54.

It is a few hours sail from Carysfoot, which he afterwards saw. It is about six miles in circumference, surrounded by a reef of black coral rocks, covered with cocoa trees, and apparently rich and fertile, with a lagoon in the middle. He called it the Isle of Faith.

C.P.I. Ed. Note: Isle of Faith, mentioned in text, may possibly be Vanavan Island. "Vanavana (20° 45′ S., 139° 09′ W., H. O. Chart No. 77), also known as Kurateke or Barrow Island,. . ." (*H.O. Pub.* No. 166, Vol. II, 4th ed. 1933, p. 136.)

VANAVANA 3

Niles' National Register, Baltimore, Md.
Feb. 15, 1845: 67, 384, 2
MNBedf

Capt. Simmons

THE "ISLE OF FAITH"

The "Isle of Faith"—so named by Capt. Simmons, of the brigantine FAITH, who has arrived at Baltimore, was discovered by him on the 31st October, 1843, in lat. 21° 10′ N., lon. 138° 54′ W., in the route from Otahite to Valparaiso. It is about six miles in circumference, surrounded by a reef of black coral rocks. A large lagoon in the middle of the island seemed to be rich and fertile.

C.P.I. Ed. Note: The text of above report is a verified copy of one item taken from a newspaper column headed "CHRONICLE," the rest of which is irrelevant. Previous reports mention Capt. Simmons as a native of Vermont, describes the island as discovered by Capt. Simmons after he passed Otaheite (Tahiti) on a voyage to Valparaiso from Sydney. The latitude given in this report is probably a typographical error N. instead of S.

The description of the island, and the proximity to Otaheite (Tahiti), indicates that this is possibly Vanavana.

[*For additional C.P.I. Ed. Note see VANAVANA 2.*]

VANAVANA 4

The Polynesian, Honolulu
May 17, 1845: 1, 212, 3
MBAt

NEW ISLAND

New Island.—In lat. 21 deg. 10 min. S., 138 deg. 54 min. W. in the track of vessels from Tahiti to Valparaiso, a new island, 6 miles in circumference, not laid down any any charts, has been discovered and named Isle of Faith.

C.P.I. Ed. Note: The Isle of Faith mentioned in above report is probably Vanavana. A longer article taken from *The Daily Mercury,* Feb. 14, 1845, describes the island in greater detail giving the ship name, rig, and the date of visit. There is a difference of ten minutes in the longitude, which is given as 138° 44′ W. whereas this text gives longitude as 138° 54′ W.

[*See VANAVANA 1.*]

[*For additional C.P.I. Ed. Note see VANAVANA 2.*]

VANAVANA 5

The Friend, Honolulu
June 2, 1845: 3, 85, 3
MSaP

ISLE OF FAITH

A new Island has been discovered between Valparaiso and Tahiti, South lat. 21 d. 10 min., West. long. 138 d. 54 min., by Capt. B. F. Simmons of the brigantine Faith. He went completely round it, and found it about six miles in circumference. A large lagoon was in the middle of the Island. He named it "Isle of Faith."

[*For C.P.I. Ed. Note see VANAVANA 2.*]

VANAVANA 6

Boston Daily Advertiser
June 5, 1845: 65, 2, 2
M; MB

[Identical reports in *Salem Observer,* June 7, 1845 (MSaE), *New Bedford Mercury,* July 13, 1845 (MNBedf) and *Daily Evening Transcript*, Boston, June 16, 1845 (MB).]

NEW ISLAND DISCOVERED

We learn form a Paris paper, that Capt. Simner of the brig Faith, discovered in the Pacific Ocean after having passed Otaheite, a small island not laid down on any map, to which he gave the name of his vessel, "Faith Island". Capt. Simner was not able to land upon it, because it is surrounded with rocks and large coral cliffs. He however made the circuit of it, and judged it to be about six English miles in circumference. It had the appearance of being upon its shores, very fertile.

C.P.I. Ed. Note: The text of this report is one item in a newspaper column headed "NEW ISLAND DISCOVERED," the rest of which is irrelevant.

Complete text is used. . . .

Tahiti, the largest of the Society Islands, was formerly called Otaheite, (17°38'S, 149°33'W) *(H.O. Pub.* No. 166, Vol.II, 4th ed, 1933 p.72.)

[*For additional C.P.I. Ed. Note see VANAVANA 2.*]

VANUA LEVU 1

Salem Gazette
Apr. 19, 1831: 45, 3, 3
MSaE

Brig Fawn, Bryant, of Salem, was wrecked on the Fegee Islands, 11th August—crew saved and arr at Manilla in the Clay. The vessel and cargo were insured in Boston.

C.P.I. Ed. Note: The text of this report is one item in a news column, the rest of which is irrelevant.

VANUA LEVU 2

Columbian Centinel, Boston, Mass.
Apr. 20, 1831: No. 4906, 4, 5
MH

The brig Fawn, of Salem, was wrecked on the Fejee Islands, Aug. 11.

C.P.I. Ed. Note: The text of this report is one item in a news column headed "SHIPPING JOURNAL," the rest of which is irrelevant.

VANUA LEVU 3

Independent Chronicle & Boston Patriot
Apr. 20, 1831: 68, 1, 6
MH

Patriot Ship News.

The crew of Brig. Fawn, Bryant of Salem, wrecked on the Fejee Islands, 11th Aug. had arrived at Manilla in the Clay. Vessel and cargo insured in Boston.

C.P.I. Ed. Note: The text of this report is one item in a news column headed "Patriot Ship News," the rest of which is irrelevant. Complete text is used. . . . Fejee Islands mentioned in text is probably another spelling for Fiji Islands. Fiji Islands are 15° to 21° S., 178° W. to 176° E., H.O. Chart, No. 2850. (*H.O. Pub.* No. 166, Vol. 2, 4th. Ed. 1933, p. 283.)

VANUA LEVU 4

Independent Chronicle & Boston Patriot
May 16, 1832: 69, 2, 6
MH

MARINE JOURNAL

Ship, Glide, and brig Niagara, of Salem, have been cast away at the Fegee Islands—no date given—officers and crew saved—

The intelligence was received at Canton, 30th Jan. in a letter from Capt. Meek, of Marblehead, at Manilla (Sic).

C.P.I. Ed. Note: The text of this report is one item in a newspaper column headed "MARINE JOURNAL," the rest of which is irrelevant. Complete text is used. . . .

[*For additional C.P.I. Ed. Note see VANUA LEVU 3.*]

VANUA LEVU 5

Salem Gazette
June 8, 1832: 46, 3, 3
MSaE

[Similar report in *Commercial Register,* Salem, June 9, 1832 (MSaE). Report in *Columbian Centinel,* Boston, June 9, 1832 (M; MH; MHi) begins, 'Capt. Archer, of ship Glide, cast away at the Fejee Islands, arrived in town last night, and states: that the Glide. . . .' Thereafter the report is similar. Both these reports acknowledge *Salem Gazette* as source and have 'Niagara' for 'Niagra'.]

Capt. Archer, and Mr. Burnham, 2d officer of ship Glide, cast away at the Fegee Islands, arrived at New York, on Saturday, in the Gov. Clinton, from Manilla. Capt. A. arrived in town last night, and states that the Glide was driven ashore from her anchorage at Tackanova, on the 22d March, 1831, in a severe gale, and totally lost. Shortly after the loss of the ship the 1st and 3d officers together with most of the crew, embarked on board a schooner belonging to the Sandwich Islands, for Wallis' Island, about 250 miles from Tackanova, in hopes of obtaining a conveyance from thence to the U.S. in some of the whaling ships occasionally touch there.

Capt. Archer and the remainder of his crew, after waiting sometime, were taken to Manilla, in the bark Peru, of Salem.

While the Glide was lying at the Island of Ovaloo, on the 26th Dec., 1830, her boat's crew was attacked, while on shore, and two men, Joshua Derby and Edmund Knight, were killed by the natives.

Joseph Morse and J.H.Johnson, two of the crew of the Glide, went from Manilla in the Gov. Clinton, to St. Helena, where they shipped on board the sch. Lallah Rookh, (Capt. John F. Brookhouse, of Salem.)

Brig Niagra was driven ashore in the same gale, at an Island about 140 miles from Tackanova. Capt. Brown and most of his crew also took passage in the schr. for Wallis's Island, in company with the crew of the Glide. Capt. Vanderford of the Niagra, went to Manilla in the Peru, and was to take passage from there in the ship Lotos, Jenks, for Salem.

C.P.I. Ed. Note: The text of this report is one item in a news column headed "FROM OUR CORRESPONDENCE," the rest of which is irrelevant.

Tackanova is identified as Vanua Levu (Findlay, *Directory of the South Pacific Ocean*, Fifth Edition, 1884, p. 701.)

The word "which" was apparently omitted before "occasionally" in the last line of the first paragraph.

[*Tackanova is probably a corruption of Thakaundrove, the name of one of the provinces of Vanua Levu. Vanua Levu, is the second largest island in the Fiji Group. Position at Kumbulau Point is 16° 54′ S. 179° 05′ E.* (P.I.P., *Vol. II, p. 327.*)

Ovaloo is Ovalau, 17° 41′ S., 178° 51′ E. at Levuka (P.I.P. *Vol. II, p. 297*).]

Ship *Glide* of Salem. Built 1811. Wrecked in the Fijis 1832.

VANUA LEVU 6

Salem Observer
June 9, 1832: 10, 3, 3;
MSaE

THE GLIDE AND NIAGARA

Capt. Archer and Mr. Burnham, second officer of the Ship Glide, cast away at the Fegee Islands, arrived at New York on Saturday, in the Gov. Clinton, from Manilla. Capt. A. has arrived in town, and states that the Glide was driven ashore from her anchorage at Tackanova, Fegee Islands, on the 22d of March 1831, in a very severe gale and was totally lost. Shortly after the first and third officers with most of the crew embarked in a schooner for the Sandwich Islands, in hopes of obtaining a passage home in some whaling vessel. Capt. Archer, with the remainder of the crew, after sometime, were taken to Manilla, in the barque Peru, of this port. When the Glide was lying at the Island of Ovaloo, on the 26th Dec. 1830, her boat's crew was attacked by the natives, and Joshua Derby and Edmund Knight, of this town, were massacred. Joseph Morse and J. H. Johnson of the Glide, took passage from Manilla to St. Helena. The brig Niagara was driven ashore in the same gale at an island about 140 miles from Tackanova, Capt. Brown and most of his crew also took passage to the Sandwich Islands. Capt. Vandeford, of the Niagara, went to Manilla in the Peru, and was to take passage from there in the ship Lotus, Jenks, for Salem.

C.P.I. Ed. Note: The text of this report is one item in a newspaper column headed "THE GLIDE AND NIAGARA," the rest of which is irrelevant. Complete text is used. . . .

[*For additional C.P.I. Ed. Note see VANUA LEVU 5.*]

VANUA LEVU 7

Independent Chronicle and Boston Patriot
June 9, 1832: 69, 2, 6
MSaE

[Similar report in *Boston Advertiser,* June 9, 1832 (MB) gives date '29th Nov.' for '26th Nov.'.]

Capt. Archer, late of ship *Glide,* lost at the Fejee Islands, left there 26th Nov. and arrived at Manilla in the Peru. His vessel and the *Niagara* were wrecked 21st March, 1831, in a gale—the G. had 5 or 600 qtls. of beach le mar on board, which was lost—the N. had but little cargo. Capt. Brown, late of the latter, left the Islands in June following, for *Wallace's* Island, in a Sandwich Island vessel. His mate had gone to Manilla to Eng. A boat from the Glide containing 7 persons, was attacked by the natives of the Fejee's in Dec. 1830, and two lads, named Knights and Derby, killed—they had gone on shore to procure wood for an anchor stock.

C.P.I. Ed. Note: The text of this report is one item in a news column headed "MARINE JOURNAL," the rest of which is irrelevant.

Wallace's Island, mentioned in text is probably another spelling for Wallis Island.

[*For additional C.P.I. Ed. Note see VANUA LEVU 5.*]

VANUA LEVU 8

Essex Register, Salem, Mass.
June 11, 1832: 32, 3, 2
MSaE

[Report in *Boston Daily Advocate,* June 11, 1832 (MB) omits sixth and seventh sentences but is otherwise similar.]

Capt. Archer, and Mr. Burnham, 2nd. officer of ship Glide, cast away at the Fegee Islands, arrived at New York, on Saturday, in the Gov. Clinton, from Manilla. Capt. A. has arrived in town, and states that the Glide was driven ashore from her anchorage at Tackanova, Fegee Islands, on the 22d. of March 1831, in a very severe gale, and was totally lost. Shortly after, the 1st and 3d, officers with most of the crew embarked in a schooner for the Sandwich Islands, in hopes of obtaining a passage home in some whaling vessel. Capt. Archer, with the remainder of the crew, after some time were taken to Manilla, in the bark Peru, of this port. When the Glide was lying at the Island of Ovaloo, on the 26th of Dec. 1830, her boat's crew were attacked by the natives, and Joshua Derby and Edmund Knight, of this town, were massacred, Joseph Morse and J.H.Johnson, of the Glide, took passage from Manilla to St. Helena, where they shipped on board the schr. Lallah Roohk, (Capt. John P. Brookhouse, of Salem.) The Glide had from 5 to 600 qtls, of beach le mar on board which was lost, the natives stripped the crew of every article of wearing apparel and adorned themselves with the trinkets, &c. which they found in the vessel. The natives built them a hut and brought articles of food for their subsistence.

The brig Niagara was driven ashore in the same gale, at an Island about 140 miles from Tackanova. Capt. Brown and most of his crew also took passage to the Sandwich Islands. Capt.

Vanderford, of the Niagara, and many of the crew, went to Manilla in the Peru, and were to take passage from there in the Lotus, Jenks, and the Peru, both for this port. The Niagara had not obtained much cargo, which was lost.

[For C.P.I. Ed. Note see VANUA LEVU 5.]

VANUA LEVU 9

Boston Courier
June 11, 1832: 7, 4, 5
MBAt

Salem, June 8, Capt. Archer, who arrived in town last evening, informs us that the ship was driven on shore on Tackanova, 22d. March, 1831, having parted her cables in a severe gale, and was totally lost. Shortly after the 1st. and 3d. officers embarked in a Sandwich Island sch. for Wallis Island, about 250 miles distant, in hopes of obtaining passage to the U.S. The Capt. 2d officer, and the remainder of the men went to Manilla in the Peru. While the ship was lying at the Island of Ovaloo, 26 Dec. 1830, her boat crew was attacked, when on shore, by the natives, and Joshua Derby, and Edward Knight killed. Two of her men (Moore and Johnson) went from Manilla to St. Helena in the Gov. Clinton, when they shipped on board the sch. Lallah Rookh, Capt. John F. Brookhouse.

The Niagara went on shore in the same gale at an island about 140 miles from Tackanova. Capt. Brown and most of his crew went in the same Sch. with the GLIDE'S crew to Wallis Island. Mr. Vanderford was to take passage in the Lotus at Manilla for this port.

[*For C.P.I. Ed. Note see VANUA LEVU 5.*]

VATOA 1

New Bedford Mercury
Sept. 26, 1828: 22, 3, 3.
MNBedf

[Identical reports in *Boston Courier,* Sept. 29, 1828 (MB; MBAt; MH), *New England Palladium and Commercial Advertiser,* Boston, Sept. 30, 1828 (MBAt), *Salem Gazette,* Oct. 3, 1828 (MSaE) and *Salem Courier,* Oct 8, 1828 (MHi). Similar report in *National Gazette and Literary Register,* Philadelphia, Pa., Oct. 2, 1828 (MNBedf). All except the first two of these reports acknowledge *New Bedford Mercury* as source.]

The ship Oeno, of Nantucket, the particulars of whose loss have been involved in uncertainty, it is now ascertained beyond the possibility of a doubt, was cast away on one of the Fegee Islands in April 1825, and the most afflicting anticipations relative to the fate of the officers and crew are, we are sorry to say, but too fully verified. We have seen a letter from Wm. S. Cary, addressed to the owner of the Oeno, dated at the Fegee Islands, Feb. 17, 1828, stating himself to be the only survivor of that ship's company, and relating the manner of her loss, and the destruction of his companions; from which we have only time to gather the following brief outline.

The ship struck upon a Reef, 4 or 5 leagues from Turtle Island, one of the Fegee Islands, on the night of the 15th April, 1825. Finding it impossible to get her off, the crew abandoned her and landed upon the Island, where, it is stated they were well received by the natives, and remained unmolested and well treated for about two weeks, until canoes arrived from another Island, filled with natives, who finding our countrymen without arms or means of defence, fell upon them and put all to death, with the exception of the above mentioned William S. Cary, who escaped by secreting himself in a cavern. After this melancholy catastrophe, a general plunder took place by the natives. The ship it is stated remained three weeks upon the Reef before she went to pieces. Turtle Island is stated as being in S. lat. 17 deg. and lon. 180.

C.P.I. Ed. Note: "Vatoa (19°50'S., 178°13'W., H.O. Chart No.162), the only island of the Fiji Archipelago visited by Captain Cook, and by him named Turtle Island, . . ." *(H.O. Pub. No. 166, Vol. II, 4th ed. 1933, p. 418.)*

VATOA 2

Columbian Centinel, Boston, Mass.
Oct. 1, 1828: No. 4641, 2, 6
M

LOSS OF SHIP OENO, AND MASSACRE

The unpleasant task devolves on us to record the loss of ship Oeno, of Nantucket, which sailed from the Vineyard Nov. 4th 1824, on a whaling voyage to the Pacific Ocean, and was wrecked on one of the Feejees Islands called Turtle Island, in 1825 where all the officers and crew were inhumanly massacred by the natives, excepting William S. Cary. The facts of which are derived from his letter, dated Feejee Island, Feb. 17, 1828 to Aaron Mitchell, Esq. of Nantucket, owner.

C.P.I. Ed. Note: The text of this report is an item in a newspaper column headed "LOSS OF SHIP OENO AND MASSACRE," . . .

[*For additional C.P.I. Ed. Note see VATOA 1.*]

VATOA 3

Boston Daily Advertiser
Oct. 2, 1828: 39, 2, 3.
M; MB

[Report in *Boston Daily Advertiser*, Oct. 8, 1828 (M) ends at
'. . . Vineyard, November 4th, 1824.' but is otherwise identical.
Report in *New Bedford Courier*, Sept. 30, 1828 (MNBedf) has
been abbreviated by C.P.I. worker but apparently is similar except for omission of paragraphs from *Nantucket Inquirer*.]

New Bedford, Sept. 30—Loss of the Ship Oeno of Nantucket

The fate of this vessel and her crew has at length been ascertained. A letter has been received by Aaron Mitchell, Esq., one
of the owners of that ship, from William S. Carey, the only survivor of the crew, dated at the Fejee Islands, Feb. 17, 1828. We
have obtained a copy of this letter, which is given below, with
the omission of a few unimportant particulars.

Sir—This being the first opportunity I have had of relating
to you the loss of your ship Oeno, I embrace it. We were cast
away on the night of the 15th April, 1825, eight days after leaving the Bay of Islands, New Zealand.

We then rowed for the shore, which was four or five leagues
distant. On nearing it we laid on our oars, and the natives on
the shore beckoned us in a friendly manner to land, which we
did, and found them very civil. It was called Turtle Island, one
of the Fejee Islands. We remained here on good terms with the
natives for about two weeks, when there came some canoes from
an island to windward, the crews of which were very friendly,
until finding that we had no weapons or arms on shore they took

an opportunity when one of the boats was absent on board the ship, and killed all but myself. I secreted myself in a rock that had a hole in it which led down to the shore, and remained there two days. On the third, the chief of the island found me and took me by the hand and talked; but not being able to understand him, I made signs that I was hungry and thirsty. He then made signs for me to follow him, which I did; and he carried me to the town and gave me something to eat and drink. In about six days our enemies left the island, and took with them the plunder they had got from the ship. I went on board the ship several times and got provisions and water, which were very scarce on the island. I remained for five or six days, when there came two large canoes from the leeward, and the natives on the island were busily employed burying the things they had got. I was anxious, not knowing who they were; but the islanders told me they were friendly, and that there was a white man lived on the island they came from. On landing, I found one of them could speak some broken English. I went away from the island with them, and remained there some time, when I heard that there was a brig at Ambow, and was anxious to go there, but the natives told me they would be from there and I could get a conveyance. In a short time they came up and brought with them four white men from the brig, which they informed me was from and belonging to Manilla. The crew had mutinied and killed the officers; the rest of the crew were at Ambow the capital of the Fejee Islands. I went to that island, and found David Whippey there and two other white men. They told me they had picked up some pieces of boats which had drifted on shore, with barrels and staves. They supposed by the wood that it was an American vessel, but did not know until I came from Laguaha. I have stopped some time on this island with my townsman, David Whippey, and finding the natives very friendly to me, I can live very comfortably among them. I had been on the island 14 or 15 months, when the ship Clay, of Salem, arrived. It is nearly three years since the ship was wrecked. We were cast away April 15th, 1825, and the ship lay on the reef three weeks before she came to pieces. We had 150 barrels of oil on board. The ship I send this by has been trading among the islands for sandal wood and beach-le-mar, and is bound from here to Canton or Manilla.

William S. Cary.

Turtle Island is in S. lat 17°, lon .180°.

The Nantucket Inquirer say,—"This account is certainly indefinite, for why should the crew of the boat return on shore to share the fate of their unfortunate companions? It is true they might have returned without a knowledge of the massacre, and have been immediately slain; but the statement leaves their destiny in the dark."

The Oeno sailed from the Vineyard November 4th, 1824. The following is a list of her officers and crew, as given in the Nantucket Inquirer.

Samual S. Riddell, Captain; Wm. H. Shaw, first mate; John P. Drew, second mate; William S. Cary, Joseph Worth, John Williams, boat steerers; Brazillai Swain, Charles G. Cash, William Friend, seamen—all of Nantucket;—Joel Knox, Henry Gordon, James Furse, Jacob Thayer, seamen—place of residence unknown—Archelaus Newton, Abraham Freeman, William Potter, Jesse Elliot, Charles Richardson, Laban Caduda, Abraham Smith—people of colour. Henry Artooi, native of Sandwich Islands.

C.P.I. Ed. Note: The text of the above report is an article in a newspaper column headed "Loss of the Ship Oeno of Nantucket," . . .

[*For additional C.P.I. Ed. Note see VATOA 1.*]

VATOA 4

New England Palladium and Commercial Advertiser,
Boston, Mass.
Oct. 3, 1828: 68, 1, 3
MB

Nantucket, Sept. 27

LOSS OF SHIP OENO, AND MASSACRE OF OFFICERS AND CREW

The unpleasant task devolves on us to record the loss of the Oeno, which sailed from the Vineyard Nov. 4th, 1824, on a whaling voyage to the Pacific Ocean and was wrecked on one of the Fejee Islands, called Turtle Island, in lat. 19, 42, S. lon. 178, 12, W. on the 15th April 1825; Where all the officers and crew were inhumanly massacred by the natives, excepting Wm. S. Cary, as will appear by the following narration, the facts of which are derived from his letter, dated Fejee Island, Feb. 17th, 1828, to Aaron Mitchell, Esq. of this town, owner.

Mr. Cary, after stating that this opportunity to write was the first he had had since he was Shipwrecked, details the Melancholy fate of his companions, and his own escape, of which the following is the substance:—

On the 7th of April, 1825, the Oeno left the Bay of Islands, (New-Zealand,) and on the night of the 15th, struck on a reef of rocks. All hands were immediately called and preparations made to abandon the Ship, as there was nothing but a white foam around her, the sea beating heavily against her side, and no hopes of getting her off. The boats being in readiness for leaving the Ship, Mr. Drew, in the waist boat, with a part of the crew, succeeded in clearing The Reef, and got into smooth water. Capt. Riddell, with another portion of the crew, among whom was Mr. Cary, left in the second boat, and got safely over the reef, though nearly filling with water.

Mr. Shaw, next attempted to lower down the weather boat, for himself and the remainder of the crew, and notwithstanding he embraced the most favourable time, when the water was least agitated, in consequence of some of the tackle getting foul, which occasioned a momentary delay, the boat was struck by a sea which forced her from the Ship, upset her, and precipitated Mr. S. and the remainder of the crew into the water; but they were all soon taken up by the two other boats, and they rowed for the shore, which was four or five leagues distant. They steered directly for the Island, and when near enough to discover the inhabitants, laid a while on their oars.

The natives becoming with their hands, and appearing friendly, they all went on shore, where they remained in safety about two weeks, when they were disturbed by a tribe of Indians from a large island to the windward.

At first, the tribe of hostile visitants appeared very friendly, but finding that the ship's company had no arms on shore, and taking an opportunity when one of the boats was off to the ship, they rose upon the remainder of the crew, and killed all except Mr. Cary.* He escaped by concealing himself in a rock, which had a hole in it that led down to the surf, where he remained two days and two nights.

On the third day, he was discovered by the Chief of the Island, who went to him, took him by the hand, and conversed with him. Mr. C. not understanding the language of the Chief, made signs that he was hungry and thirsty. The Chief, then made signs for Mr. C. to follow him, which he did, and was conducted to the town, and furnished with victuals and drink. There Mr. C. remained till the enemy returned to their own island, taking with them the plunder they had got out of the ship.

Mr. Cary, went off to the ship frequently, during his short

stay on the island, to get provisions and water, which were scarce there. After remaining with the natives of Turtle Island 5 or 6 days, two large canoes were seen approaching, from one of the leeward islands, which threw the natives into consternation, and they immediately buried all the things they had procured from the ship. When the people landed from the canoes and went up to the town, Mr. Cary, learned that they were friendly, that one of them could speak a little broken English, and that there was a *White man* residing on their island.

On their return, Mr. C. went with them to their island, and remained there some time—when he heard of a brig at Ambow, (Capital of the Fejees,) and being anxious to ascertain what vessel she was, he wished to visit that island, but had no means of effecting that object.

The natives told Mr. C. that the canoes would be up in a few days from Ambow, and they accordingly arrived with four of the brigs crew.

The brig was found to be of and from Manilla. The four men informed Mr. C. that they had mutinied, and killed the Captain of the brig, and that the remainder of the crew were at Ambow.

Mr. C. went to Ambow, and found one of his townsmen, (David Whippy, who left Nantucket in Nov. 1819, in ship Francis, Fitzgerald—left the F. in Guayaquil, July, 1821—went to England, in Ship Sidney Packet—sailed from Eng. in ship Prudent—left the P. at Valparaise—went two voyages from V. to Port Jackson, in an Eng. brig, and got his discharge from her at Ambow.) And two other white men there, Mr. C. informed them of the shipwreck of the Oeno, &c. and they told him they had picked up some pieces of boat, with barrels and other articles, that had drifted ashore, and that they supposed by the wood, &c. that some disaster had happened to an Am. ship. Mr. C. states that he found the natives at Ambow very friendly, among whom he lived very comfortably; and that after residing there 14 or 15 months, the ship Clay, of Salem, arrived. The Oeno had 150 bbls. of oil when she was wrecked, and lay on the reef three weeks before she went to pieces.

The Clay, by which Mr. C. wrote, had been trading, at the Fejee Islands, for Sandal wood and beach la mer, and was bound thence to Manilla, (Where she was left by the Milo, arrived at this port, which vessel probably brought the letter.)

The following list exhibits the names of the officers and crew of the Oeno, and place of residence, as far as has been ascertained.

Samuel S. Riddell,	Captain	of Nantucket.
William H. Shaw,	Ist Mate,	,, ,,
John P. Drew,	2nd do.	,, ,,
William S. Cary,	boat-steerer	,, ,,
Joseph Worth,	do.	,, ,,
John Williams,	do.	,, ,,
Brazillai Swain,	seaman	,, ,,
Charles G. Cash,	do.	,, ,,
William Friend,	do.	,, ,,
Joel Knox,	do.	Place of Residence unknown
Henry Gordon,	do.	,, ,, ,, ,,
James Furse	do.	,, ,, ,, ,,
Jacob Thayer	do.	,, ,, ,, ,,
Archelano Newton		People of Color
Abraham Freeman		,, ,, ,,
William Potter		,, ,, ,,
Jessie Elliott		,, ,, ,,
Charles Richardson		,, ,, ,,
Taban Caduda		,, ,, ,,
Abraham Smith		,, ,, ,,

Henry Attooi, native of Sandwich Islands.

* This accounty is certainly indefinite—for why should the crew of the boat return on shore, to share the fate of their unfortunate companions?

It is true they might have returned without a knowledge of the Massacre, and have been immediately slain; but the statement leaves their destiny in the dark—

Nan. Inquirer

[*For C.P.I. Ed. Note see VATOA 1.*]

VATOA 5

Christian Watchman, Boston, Mass.
Oct. 10, 1828: 9, 164, 4
MH

SHIPWRECK—LOSS OF SHIP OENO, AND MASSACRE OF OFFICERS AND CREW

The ship Oeno, of Nantucket, the particulars of whose loss have been involved in uncertainty, it is now ascertained beyond the possibility of a doubt, was cast away on one of the Fegee Islands in April, 1825, and the most afflicting anticipations relative to the fate of the officers and crew are, we are sorry to say, but too fully verified.

A letter from William S. Cary, addressed to the owner of the Oeno, date at Fegee Islands, Feb. 17, 1828, states himself to be the only survivor of that ship's company, and relating the manner of her loss, and the destruction of his companions.—The ship struck upon a reef, 4 or 5 leagues from Turtle Island, one of the Fegee Islands, on the night of the 15th of April, 1825.

Finding it impossible to get her off, the crew abandoned her and landed upon the Island, where it is stated they were received by the natives, and remained unmolested and well treated for about two weeks, until six canoes arrived from another Island, filled with natives, who finding our countrymen without arms or means of defence fell upon them and put all to death, with the exception of the above mentioned Wm. S. Cary, who escaped by securing himself a cavern. After this melancholy catastrophe, a general plunder took place by the natives. The ship, it is stated, remained three weeks upon the reef before she went to pices.

Turtle Island is stated as being in S. Lat. 17 deg. and Lon.

180. The Oeno sailed from the Vineyard, November 4th, 1824. The following is a list of her officers and crew, as given in the Nantucket Inquirer: Samuel S. Riddle, captain, Wm. H. Shaw, first mate, John P. Drew, second mate, Williams S. Cary, Joseph Worth, John Williams, boat steerers, Barzillai Swain, Charles G. Cash, William Friend, seamen—all of the Nantucket. Joel Knox, Henry Gordon, James Furse, Jacob Thayer, seamen-place of residence unknown.—Archelans Newton, Abraham Freeman, William Potter, Jesse Elliot, Charles Richardson, Laban Caduda, Abraham Smith—people of colour. Henry Artooi, native of Sandwich Islands.

C.P.I. Ed. Note: The text of this report is one item in a newspaper column headed "SHIPWRECK," the rest of which is irrelevant. Complete text is used. . . .

[*For additional C.P.I. Ed. Note see VATOA 1.*]

VATOA 6

Boston Daily Advertiser & Patriot
Feb. 19, 1834: 42, 2, 4
MB

[Similar reports in *New Bedford Mercury*, Feb. 21, 1834 (MNBedf) and *New Bedford Daily Gazette*, Feb. 24, 1834 (MNBedf).]

SHIP OENO

Of this ill-fated ship, of which so very few vestiges have ever been discovered, we have just obtained another slight memorial, in the following communication made by an officer of the whaling ship American, under date Gallipagos Islands, March 19, 1831.

"At 5 P.M. got a quadrant out of the Charles, of London, which formerly belonged to Mr. Wm. H. Shaw, first officer of the ship Oeno, of Nantucket, which ship was lost over five years ago on one of the Feegee Islands—where this quadrant was purchased of one of the natives, and has his (Mr. Shaw's) name on the case."

"Capt. Buckley of ship Harriett of London, states that fourteen months ago, while at Sydney, he was informed by the master of a Russian brig, that at the Island of Tongataboo he saw a young boy, who said he belonged to the Oeno, and that there was one man living at the Windward Islands, also belonging to the ship—being the only two survivors—the rest having been massacred by the natives. The boy seemed very anxious to leave the island with the Captain of the brig; but the King would not consent."

This was very probably the lad by the name of Swain—

being the youngest individual on board the Oeno. We have hopes that he may yet be recovered.—

Nantucket Inquirer.

C.P.I. Ed. Note: The text of the above report is one item in a newspaper column headed "Ship Oeno," the rest of which is irrelevant. Tongataboo mentioned in the text is another spelling for Tongatabu. Tongatabu is in lat. 21° 10′ S., lon. 175° 15′ W., H.. O. Chart No. 2016. *(H.O. Pub.* No. 166, Vol. II, 4th ed., 1933, p. 197.)

VATOA 7

Essex Register, Salem, Mass.
Feb. 24, 1834: 34, 3, 3 & 4
MSaE

[Similar but shorter reports in *Boston Courier,* Feb. 27, 1834 (MBAt) and *New Bedford Mercury,* Feb. 28, 1834 (MNBedf). Former ends at ' . . . remained until the loss of the ship.' and latter at ' . . . part trading master.' Both give *Salem Register,* Feb. 24 as source.]

The following interesting article relative to the loss of the ship Oeno, several years since, has been communicated to us, by a young man of this town. The facts stated may be relied on:—

Mr. Palfray—noticing in your last paper an article relative to the fate of the crew of the "Oeno", of Nantucket, which vessel was wrecked on a reef contiguous to Turtle Island, one of the Fejees, some years since, I was much surprised to find that no farther information had been received, considering the numerous opportunities which have existed. I therefore, as one of the crew of the Glide, which ship was also lost among the Feejees, deem it my duty to submit all the information in my possession, and which I obtained from one of the survivors of the Oeno's crew—William Carey, of Nantucket. It appears that the massacre took place sometime subsequent to the loss of the ship, and originated from some disturbance between the natives and the ship's company, which resulted in the destruction of the whole crew, save my informant (Carey) who on the alarm being given, escaped and took refuge in some hidden cave, in the vicinity of the town, He says "Two days I spent in this cave without satiating either my hunger or thirst, aware that as soon as I exposed myself to the view of the natives I should be instantly put to death. This deterred me from attempting to remove, until compelled to, to avoid absolute starvation. I made bold to creep out in search of a cocoanut or some water to allay my immoderate thirst; I had not proceeded far before I was discovered by a native. Perceiving him advance toward me, (with as I expected) an intention to take my life, I seated myself on a rock with my back turned towards him and my head inclined forward to enable him, to more effectually accomplish his purpose, and thus rid me instantly of the miseries of my situation; but providentially, coming up to me, he bade me follow him to the town. Here I was ushered into their "Bore", or public hut, where a great number of natives had collected, nor had I remained long before a very warm and spirited talking ensued, somewhat unintelligeable to me at the time, but as I afterward learned, respecting putting me to death. A majority, however, decided in favor of saving my life. I was ever afterward treated kindly by them, and permitted to roam in whatever part of the island I chose. I was also allowed the privelege of visiting the neighboring islands with the King and Chiefs, and of remaining on them as long as I wished. I fine, I had the liberty of leaving them in whatever vessel should arrive, and would take me off. Some years elapsed, prior to the arrival of a vessel, when fortunately I was succored, and taken on board the ship clay, of Salem, where I remained until her arrival at Manilla, when I obtained my discharge, and shipped on board the Quill, of Salem, on another expedition to the Fejees, having assisted in procuring a cargo for the brig, on her departure I shipped in the Glide as linguist and part trading master."

In this capacity, endeared to all, Mr. Carey remained until the loss of the ship. Upon the arrival of the Glide at Manilla (some months prior to her loss,) Mr. Carey who had received a handsome sum for his services during 9 or 10 months, and eager to return to his long absent friends, had made arrangements for that purpose, and eventually succeeded in removing himself and baggage on board a ship then about sailing for the United States; but from some unknown cause he was induced to reship in the Glide, and was unfortunately again wrecked. The Glide was lost about the 20th of March 1831. Shortly after her loss Mr. Carey in company with others of the ship's crew, repaired in one of the boats to the windward island of "Bon". Towards the latter part of May, following, that part of the ship's company resident at the Leeward Islands, was relieved by the arrival of the schooner "Harriet", of—(inelligable) and soon after proceeded to the Windward, where fortunately the barque "Peru" of Salem had arrived, and had already secured the remaining part of the ship's crew, together with that of the brig "Niagra", also lost. It was at this time I again saw Mr. Carey, but to my knowledge he was not connected with the barque: and in this situation I left him, the schooner proceeding for Wallis Island, and consequently I can advance no more information in regard to him.

[*For C.P.I. Ed. Note see VATOA 1.*]

VATOA 8

New Bedford Mercury
Mar. 5, 1841: 34, 1, 1
MNBedf

Capt. Howland also confirms the report of the loss of the ship Shylock, Taber, of Sippican, as having been received at the Bay of Islands just before his departure. The Shylock was wrecked on Turtle Island, one of the Fejee group. He did not learn any particulars of the fate of the crew or the disposition of the wreck.

C.P.I. Ed. Note: The text of this report is one item in a news column headed "NEWS COLUMN," the rest of which is irrelevant.

[*For additional C.P.I. Ed. Note see VATOA 1.*]

VATOA 9

New Bedford Register
Mar. 24, 1841: 3, 3, 2
MNBedf

THE SHYLOCK

A letter from Capt. Taber, late of the ship Shylock, dated Bay of Islands, Oct. 17, 1840, giving an account of the loss of that vessel, states that she struck on an unknown reef, situated to the South and East of the Fejee Islands, on the night of the 20th of June, while going at the rate of 7 knots, before the wind. He had shaped his course that night, with the intention of passing 30 miles to the Eastward of an island called Turtle Island, which is not laid down as a reef Island on the chart. No land was seen, though the night was far from being dark. Three of the crew, viz: Seth Alden, Hiram Crowell, of Fairhaven, and a Cape de Verd native were drowned, and the rest escaped from the wreck with scarcely a rag of clothing. The ship went to pieces in two hours after she struck. The first landing effected was at one of the Friendly Isles, a distance of 200 miles from the reef, the passage to which was performed in the boats, without a particle of food. Capt. Taber adds that the Shylock is the third ship known to have been lost on the same reef.

[*For C.P.I. Ed. Note see VATOA 1.*]

VATOA 10

New Bedford Mercury
Jun. 4, 1841: 34, 1, 2
MNBedf

[Similar reports in *Boston Courier,* June 1, 1841 (MB) and *Boston Daily Evening Transcript,* June 5, 1841 (MB; MBAt). Report in *Weekly Courier,* Boston, June 3, 1841 (MBAt) has '. . . unwilling to repair to the Fijii Islands . . .' and '. . . succeeded in reaching the Fijii Islands, . . .' in place of 'Turtle Island' in both instances. Otherwise the report is similar.]

We are indebted to Mr. Hatch for the following particulars not before reported, relating to the loss of this whale-ship, as furnished by her late commander, Capt. Charles M. Taber, who arrived at Boston last week in the ship Herald, Capt. Reynolds, from the Bay of Islands. The Shylock was in the vicinity of the Fejee Islands, on the 20th of June, 1840, about 20 miles S.E. from Turtle Island, under full sail at the rate of about 8 miles an hour, with a fresh wind from S.W., weather thick and hazy, when at about 10 o'clock P.M. Capt. Taber was called upon deck by the cry of 'breakers' and almost immediately the ship struck on a detached ledge of rocks not laid down in any chart. Two of the boats were hastily manned by sixteen of the crew, together with Capt. Taber and the mate, fortunately securing a compass, but without water or provisions, and leaving as it was subsequently ascertained, seven persons, comprising the remainder of the crew, upon the wreck. Capt. Taber was unwilling to repair to Turtle Island on account of the hostile disposition of the natives, and accordingly the boats made for one of the Friendly Islands, distant about 200 miles; which they reached after three nights and two days, nearly exhausted with fatigue and suffering; having been in the meantime without provisions or refreshment of any kind. Their reception by the natives was friendly and kind in the extreme,—in requital as they afterwards learned for the benevolent offices which had recently been rendered by missionaries at the island,—and during their stay upon the island the hospitality of the natives towards them seemed unbounded. Of those of the crew left upon the wreck, as Capt. Taber subsequently ascertained, three of the number were drowned while assisting in completing a raft, upon which the others succeeded in reaching Turtle Island, where they remained until providential opportunity afforded to them the means of taking passage thence on shipboard. Of those who were in company with Capt. T. it is believed that all are now in safety. After encountering many hardships, Capt. Taber at length worked his way to the Bay of Islands whence he took passage to Boston, and arrived here on Saturday.

C.P.I. Ed. Note: The text of this report is one item in a news column headed "NEWS COLUMN," the rest of which is irrelevant.

Friendly (Tonga) Islands, consisting of 100 islands and islets, lying between lat. 18° 21° S., lon. 173° and 175° W. H.O. Chart No.2016. (*H.O. Pub.* No. 166, vol. II, 4th ed. 1933, p.192.)

[*For additional C.P.I. Ed. Note see VATOA 1.*]

VAVAU 1

Daily Columbian Centinel, Boston, Mass.
Oct. 21, 1835: No. 1428, 2, 7
MHi

WHALE SHIPS

An explosion took place, on board a ship, (probably the Superior) belonging to N. London, commanded by a person the name of Fitch, (who was brother to the 2nd mate of the ship, Phenix, of New London) while off Vavaoo, in March by some person setting fire to some cartridges, which killed the Captain, one of the mate, a boats-steerer, and some others of the crew.

C.P.I. Ed. Note: The text of this report is one item in a newspaper column headed "WHALE SHIPS."

Vavaoo is probably another spelling for Vavau Island of the Friendly, or the Tonga Group.

Vavaoo Island is Lat. 18°37′ S., Lon. 174° 01′ W. *(H.O. Pub.* No. 166, Vol. II, 4th Ed. 1933, p. 238.)

VAVAU 2

Salem Gazette
Nov. 3, 1835: 13, 3, 1
MHi

Whalers: The ship, on board of which an explosion took place off Vavoo, was the Superior, of New London. Captain Fitch, an excellent man, was killed, as was his third mate, and a boat steerer. Capt. F. was preparing his muskets to land, when a keg of powder accidently exploded.

C.P.I. Ed. Note: The text of this report is one item in a newspaper column, the rest of which is irrelevant. Vavaoo is probably another spelling for Vavau Island.

[For additional C.P.I. Ed. Note see VAVAU 1.]

VAVAU 3

Salem Mercury
June 14, 1837: 6, 3, 2
MSaE

WHALERS

Off Marquesas, in Oct. ship Barclay, Nan 450 bbls. The B. had been into the Bay, and landed a boat's crew, including the captain, when the natives made Capt Barney prisoner—the crew having regained the ship by swimming. The mate slipped the chain, and was proceeding to sea, but on learning that the natives were preparing to burn Capt. B. succeeded in effecting his ransom at about $500 in goods, &c.

Arr at Newburyport, 9th, ship Newburyport, Starbuck, Bay of Islands, New Zealand, 101.2700 bbls sp oil—absent 33 1-2 months. Reports Feb 17, Wm. Hamilton, of New Bedford, out 31 mos 3800; Wiscasset, of Wiscasset, out 33 mos 2300. At Bay of Islands, in Feb. Navy, Neil.of Newburyport, full, for home in few days; Sam'l Robertson, New Bedford, do. do.; Clarkson, Nantucket, 2600; Mt Vernon, do 1950.—Capt Plasket, of the Clarkson, spoke on Jan. 31, last. lat 29 S.lon 177 30 W. ship Mary, Coffin, Nan. 900 bbls sp oil. Capt. C. informed that in Jan. a day or two after leaving Vavaoo, he passed a great number of spars—the weather being bad at the time could not save many, but picked up a ship's maintopmast with the cap of the lower mast attached to it, and a cask of oil. He likewise saw a number of shooks. The cap and mast judging from the size, belonged to a large ship, and looked like American work. Jan. 9, lat 17 to 19, lon 170 50 W saw and boarded the wreck of barque Anastasia, of Sudney, water logged, and not a spar attached to her; was able to get but a few things out of her, such as sail, some cordage, and a few small articles from the cabin. From appearances it would seem that the barques company had staid by the wreck several days at least after the disaster, as a number of ropes were seen leading about in different directions, probably for the sufferers to support themselves by. There was a dripping stone upon the taffrail, which had had fire in it, and a slate hung on the stump of the mizen mast, on which was written as follows— "Dismasted the last of Dec. in a hurricane—crew gone on a raft, steering SW—God have mercy on us poor souls, without water. J.Chapman, master." Capt Coffin spoke the ship Braganza, Baker, 2,050 bbls sp oil, not far from where the wreck was seen. Capt B. informed that during the preceding gale he had stood in his cabin gangway and seen all his boats blown and washed off the cranes, together with his spare boats—he only saved the wrecks of three of them in a very shattered state. He also lost his ship's head and had his spars more or less damaged.

Arr at Stonington, 31st, schr Eveline, Falkland Islands, 56, with seal skins and elephant oil.

C.P.I. Ed. Note: The text of this report is one item in a newspaper column, the rest of which is irrelevant.

[*C.P.I. worker copied only parts of this report. Text is taken from original newspaper.*]

VAVAU 4

The Atlas, Boston, Mass.
Sept. 13, 1837: 6, 2, 4
MHi

[Identical report in *New Bedford Mercury,* Sept. 15, 1837
(MNBedf). Reports in *Columbian Centinel,* Boston, Sept. 13,
1837 (M) and Sept. 14, 1837 (MBAt) have 'Cleveland' but are
otherwise identical. Report in *Evening Gazette,* New Bedford,
Sept. 10, 1837 (MNBedf) omits last sentence but is otherwise
identical.]

REPORTED LOSS OF SHIP INDEPENDENCE

Capt. Downs of the Clifford Wayne at Fairhaven, spoke, on the
31st ult. ship Leonidas, Cleaveland, from Pacific Ocean for Bristol, and was informed by Capt. C. that the ship Independence,
Fisher, of this port, while laying at anchor in Vavaoo, Friendly
Islands, in a severe hurricane dragged her anchors, and struck
on a coral reef, notwithstanding her masts had been cut away to
prevent it; a change of wind took the ship off, when jury masts
were rigged, and she sailed for Sydney to repair, but subsequently returned to Vavaoo, where she was probably abandoned, being too much injured in her bottom to perform the
passage.—The last previous accounts from the Independence reported her near New Zealand, 20th February, with 1050 bbls.
oil.

C.P.I. Ed. Note: The text of this report is one item in a newspaper column headed "REPORTED LOSS OF SHIP INDEPEND-
ENCE," at Friendly Islands, the rest of which is irrelevant.

Friendly is identified as Tonga Island.

Friendly Islands lies between lat. 18° 01′ to 21° 28′ S. and 173° 54′ to 175° 33′ W.

(H.O. Chart No. 2016, H.O. Pub. Chart No.166, Vol. II, 4th ed. 1933, p. 192.)

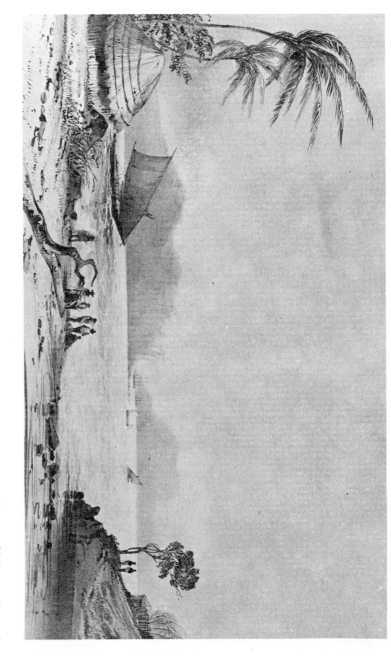

Bay at Vavau, Tonga. From Dumont D'Urville, *Voyage au Pole Sud*, 2nd expedition, 1837-1840, plate 75.

VAVAU 5

New York Observer
Apr. 5, 1845: 23, 2, 5
MBC

JUSTICE AMONG THE ISLANDERS

Vavao, one of the Friendly Islands, a sailor from the bark Autumn, deserted from his vessel, and was arrested by the chief and another native, to be conveyed back to the ship, and while they were in the act of doing so, he stabbed the chief, who died almost immediately. The following is the verdict of the council, Capt. Wady of the Autumn, acting as judge:

The Natives Verdict.—We are of opinion that the chief was acting according to our laws in bringing the deserter back to his ship. We say that a man at Pallo was convicted of murder and hung, and the Island being all of one groupe, we must use our laws accordingly. Therefore, we find him guilty of murder, and we sentence him to be hung by the neck on Tuesday next, 5th November, at 12 o'clock meridian, and may god have mercy on his soul.

C.P.I. Ed. Note: The text of this report is one item in a news column headed "JUSTICE AMONG THE ISLANDERS," the rest of which is irrelevant.

[*For additional C.P.I. Ed. Note see VAVAU 1.*]

VAVAU 6

Boston Daily Advertiser
Apr. 10, 1850: 75, 2, 6
M

WHALERS

Arrived at New Bedford, April 8, ship Mary Corey, South Pacific 480 bbls sp. 700 do wh oil 1600 lbs bone. Reports sld from Vavaoo June 27, Geo. Champlin, Swain, Newport, 20 sp.

C.P.I. Ed. Note: The text of the above report is a copy of an item in a newspaper column headed "WHALERS," . . .

[*For additional C.P.I. Ed. Note see VAVAU 1.*]

VAVAU 7

Weekly Aita California, San Francisco, Cal.
Mar. 1, 1851: 3, 3, 4
MH

Loss of the Whale Ship Mexican

The Ophalia, from the South Sea Islands at Sydney, Nov. 20th, brings the intelligence of the loss of the above vessel. She was wrecked on a reef bearing south from Vavau, distant 25 miles, on the 27th of September, at 11P.M. No lives were lost, and 600 barrels of sperm, and 150 barrels of whale oil were saved. The vessel is totally lost. Capt. Cudworth and four seamen are passengers per Ophalia. The reef was not laid down on any chart on board the ship.

C.P.I. Ed. Note: The text of this report is one item in a news column, the rest of which is irrelevant.

The Vavau Group, a part of the Tonga Islands, consists of the large island of Vavau and numerous smaller islands extending north-northeast and opposite direction for 18 miles with a breadth of 9 miles. *(H.O. Pub.* No. 166, Vol. II, 4th ed. 1933, p. 234.)

Vavau Island is 18° 37′ S., 174° 01′ W., and is nearly 9.5 miles long with an extreme breadth of 6.8 miles. *(Ibid.* p. 238)

VAVAU 8

Boston Daily Journal
Apr. 9, 1851: 19, 4, 3
MH

Whale ship Mexican, (of New Bedford) Cudworth was wrecked on a reef bearing S. from Vauvan, distant 25 miles, on the 27th of Sept., at 11 P.M.   No lives were lost, and 600 bbls.sp. and 150 bbls. wh. oil were saved.   The vessel is totally lost.   The reef was not laid down on any chart on board the ship.

C.P.I. Ed. Note: The text of this report is one item in a news column headed "DISASTERS," the rest of which is irrelevant.
Vauvan in text is probably Vavau Island.

[*For additional C.P.I. Ed. Note see VAVAU 1.*]

VAVAU 9

Boston Daily Atlas
Apr. 9, 1851: 19, 2, 7
MBr

Whale ship Mexican (reported yesterday by Telegraph) was wrecked on a reef bearing S. from Vauvau, distant 25 miles, on the 27th of September at 11 P.M. No lives were lost, and 600 bbls sp. and 150 bbls wh oil were saved. The vessel is totally lost. Captain Cudworth and four seamen had arrived at San Francisco. The reef was not laid down on any chart on board the ship. Last time heard from June 3, 1850: was then at Guam, with 600 sp and 150 wh on board, and bound to Japan.

C.P.I. Ed. Note: The text of this report is one item in a news column headed "DISASTERS," the rest of which is irrelevant.

[*For additional C.P.I. Ed. Note see VAVAU 1.*]

VAVAU 10

The Republican Standard, New Bedford, Mass.
Apr. 17, 1851: 2, 3, 4
MNBedf

Whale ship Mexican, Cudworth, of New Bedford, was lost on a reef not laid down in the chart, 25 miles S. of Vauvoo, Sept. 27, 11 P.M. crew saved, as also 600 bbls sp. 150 do wh oil. Capt. Cudworth and four men proceeded to San Francisco in the Ophelia.

C.P.I. Ed. Note: The text of the report is one item in a news column headed "MARINE NEWS," the rest of which is irrelevant.
Vauvoo in text is probably another spelling of Vavau.

[*For additional C.P.I. Ed. Note see VAVAU 7.*]

VAVAU 11

Salem Gazette
May 23, 1851: 5, 3, 2
MSaE

[Report in *The Essex County Mercury and Danvers Courier (W)*, Salem, May 28, 1851 (MSaE) omits 'crew saved; cargo of 280 bbls sp oil, landed at Vauvau' and has 'Opalta' and 'Vuva Fejee . . .' but is otherwise similar.]

> Viwa, Fejee Islands,
> Oct. 31, 1850.

On the 27th of Sept last, the ship "Mexican", of New Bedford was wrecked at Vauvau, crew saved; cargo of 280 bbls sp oil landed at Vauvau, vessel total loss. The sch "Opalia", of and for Sydney, touched at Fejee with part of the oil, on her way to Sydney—the remainder would be shipped in a vessel sent from Sydney, to take in the oil, rigging &., saved from the wreck.

C.P.I. Ed. Note: The text of this report is one item in a news column headed "MARINE JOURNAL," the rest of which is irrelevant.

[*For additional C.P.I. Ed. Note see VAVAU 1.*]

VAVAU 12

Boston Daily Advertiser
Sept. 15, 1854: 84, 2, 7
M

DISASTERS

Whale ship Sally Anne,(of New Bedford) Hathaway, was totally lost at Vavao, one of the Friendly Islands, on the 2nd of April last, having been carried upon a reef, by a current, not described on the chart. The wreck was sold for a trifling sum. She had on board at the time about 80 bbls.of wh. oil. Capt. Hathaway, the first and second officers, and two men took passage for Horn Island, and arrived there on the 18th of April. The crew were taken off by an English brig which was wrecking the vessel. The 1st and 2nd officers subsequently went on board of ship. Champton, Pease, of Edgartown, bound to Ochotsk sea. The Sally Anne was owned by Messrs. David R. Green & Co. and others, of New Bedford, and was insured at the Commercial Mutual Marine Insurance office for $7625, and at the Union Mutual Marine for $1600 in New Bedford and in Boston offices for $11,000—

The Sally Anne was upward of 50 years old, and was formally owned by David Hinckley Esq. of this city.

C.P.I. Ed. Note: The text of this report is one item in a column headed "DISASTERS," the rest of which is irrelevant.

[*For additional C.P.I. Ed. Note see VAVAU 1.*]

VAVAU 13

Boston Post
Sept. 15, 1854: 45, 2, 5
M

[Similar report in *The Republican Standard,* New Bedford, Sept. 21, 1854 (MNBedf). Report in *The Daily Evening Standard,* New Bedford, Sept. 14, 1854 (MNBedf) is similar except for last sentence which reads '. . . David R. Greene & Co., and others, of this city, and was insured at the Commercial Mutual Marine for $4,600, in this city; and in Boston offices for $11,000.]

DISASTERS &C.

A letter received from Captain Jobez Hathaway of ship Sally Anne of New Bedford, dated at Sydney, May 24th reports the loss of that vessel at Vavao, one of the Friendly Islands on the 2d of April last. The Sally Anne was bound in to recruit, and was taken by a current not described in the chart, and carried upon a reef where she was wrecked. The wreck was sold to Capt. Lyons, but brought only a trifling sum—the vessel proving nearly a total loss. She had on board at the time 80 bbls. of wh. oil. Capt. Hathaway, the 1st and 2d officers subsequently went on board and two men took passage for Horne Islands and arrived there on the 18th of April. The crew were taken off by an English brig which was wrecking the vessel. The 1st and 2d officers subsequently went on board of ship Champion, Pease of Edgartown bound to the Ockotsk Sea. The Sally Anne was owned by Messrs. David R. Greene & Co., and others, and was insured in New Bedford at the Commercial Mutual Marine Insurance office for $7625 and at the Union Mutual Marine $1600, and in Boston offices for $11,000.

C.P.I. Ed. Note: The text of this report is an item in a newspaper column headed "Disasters," . . . the rest of which is irrelevant.

[*For additional C.P.I. Ed. Note see VAVAU 1.*]

VAVAU 14

The Daily Mercury, New Bedford, Mass.
Sept. 15, 1854: 24, 2, 1.
MNBedf

LOSS OF SHIP SALLY ANNE, OF THIS PORT
The whaleship Sally Anne, Capt. Hathaway, which sailed hence July 9, 1853, was lost on the Friendly Islands on the 2d of April last. The particulars of her loss are stated in the following letter, addressed to her owners, which we are permitted to publish:—

Sydney,N.S.W.,May 24,1854.

Messrs. David R. Greene, & Co., New Bedford,

Gentlemen—I am under the painful necessity of informing you of the loss of your ship "Sally Anne", on the morning of the 2d of April last, just before daybreak, on a reef off the Island of "Vavow", (Friendly Islands). By my observations the afternoon previous, the East part of the Island of Vavow bore North 25 degrees,W steering N.N.W., one point variation, East distance 65 miles; fine clear weather through the night, the ship going three and four miles per hour. At 5 o'clock the mate informed me that he saw the land; I went on deck and saw a small low land island, and gave orders to luff the ship to the wind; in a minute or two afterwards felt the ship touch lightly. In a few minutes more she struck quite hard, and the next struck heavy, unshipped rudder and became unmanageable, striking heavy all the time; saw breakers ahead, and no possibility of saving the ship. I ordered the boats to be lowered away, and to lay off from the ship; to cut away the masts to ease her. That being done, commenced getting the most valuable things on deck, the ship filling with water fast. As the tide rose she beat over the outer reef, and went on to the inner, one where she lay more easy; succeeded in landing some water and provisions and other small things; at 12 o'clock the water nearly up to the lower deck; at night left the ship, she laying on the bottom, and went on to the small island for the night. In the morning myself and 2d officer left the island in two boats for the harbor, to see what arrangement I could make about the ship; not knowing a passage there was for boats, did not get there until after sunset.

Soon after we left, the natives got here in large numbers and stole everything they could lay hands on. About 12 o'clock the King's son and an English Missionary came, and partly put a stop to their thieving.

Upon my arrival at the habor, I found the English brig Ocean, loading for Melbourne. Capt. Lyons had gone to the wreck, but returned soon after I got on board. I gave notice that the ship and all on board, would be sold the following morning at 9 o'clock at the King's son's house, for whom it may concern. She was purchased by Capt. Lyons and delivered to him. When I got back to the ship, she was full of water to the upper deck. I took passage in the Brig for myself, mate (Tristram Mayhew) 2nd mate, (Thomas Gifford), and two men and left there the 8th for Horn Island, to complete her cargo, and on arrival there the 18th found the Champion of Edgartown, recruiting with 150 bbls, whale oil, and the mate, 2d mate and two men went on board of her bound to Ochotsk Sea.

Capt. Lyons stopped at Vavow and engaged some of the crew to help wreck the ship, and the brig is to return, and take them away. We left Horn Island on the 25th, when Capt.Sullivan of the James Arnold came on board. She has 400 bbls. sperm, and 80 bbls. whale on board bound to Japan; he reported ten days previous, Sea Gull, 40 bbls. on board.

My intention was to lay off and on at Vavow, for recruits, found a strong westerly current at the Island; had perceived none before, and expected to have been 10 miles to the eastward in the morning; it is not laid down correctly on the chart. The ship went ashore about two miles to the north, of where that Nantucket Ship was lost about one year since, (supposed Paragon).

I think I shall take passage on the ship Kashay, Capt. Stoddard via China, as he had been kind enough to offer me a passage. We had such a long passage we were compelled to touch at Sidney with the brig. The Sally Ann had 80 bbls. whale oil on board; had seen sperm whales but twice on the voyage, but no chance to get any. I believe I have given you all the particulars of this unfortunate affair and remain

Yours etc.,
Jabez S. Hathaway.

The Sally Anne is insured in this city at the Union Mutual Marine Insurance office for $1688; Commercial Mutual Marine $7625; and at two offices in Boston for $11,000.

[*For C.P.I. Ed. Note see VAVAU 1.*]

VAVAU 15

Newburyport Herald
Sept. 19, 1864: 59, 4, 3
MNe

Ship Sally Ann, of New Bedford, was lost at Vavoo, one of the Society Islands, 2d April. She had 80 bbls. of whale oil. She was insured at the Commercial Mutual Marine Ins. office for $7625, and the Union Mutual Marine for $1000, in New Bedford, and in Boston offices for $11,000.

C.P.I. Ed. Note: The text of this report is one item in a news column headed "SHIPPING JOURNAL," the rest of which is irrelevant. The correct name of this ship mentioned in report as the *Sally Ann* is given as the *Sally Anne (Ship Registers of New Bedford,* Mass., Vol. I, 1940 ed., p. 285.)

[*For additional C.P.I. Ed. Note see VAVAU 1.*]

VAVAU 16

Boston Daily Advertiser
July 27, 1857: 90, 1, 5
M

WHALERS

Ar. at New Bedford 25th, ship Kensington, Clark, Pacific Ocean, Vavoo, Friendly Islands. April '57 with 1200 bbls. sp. 50 do wh. oil and 500 lbs. bone.   In lat. 30N. lon. 60W. saw an immense school of sperm whales bound W—took one which made 50 bbls.

C.P.I. Ed. Note: The text of this report is an item in a newspaper column headed "WHALERS," . . .

[*For additional C.P.I. Ed. Note see VAVAU 1.*]

VITI LEVU 1

Independent, New York, N.Y.
July 10, 1851: 111, 115, 6
MBC

[Report printed above as SAMOA 9 has 'Pettegrew' for "Pettigan' and "Vitileque' for 'Viti Levu'.]

FROM THE FEEJEE ISLANDS

The sloop-of-war, Falmouth, Commander Pettigan, arrived in the harbor of San Francisco on the 29th May, after a seven months cruise among the Feejee and Marquesas Islands. The papers say, "Capt. Pettigan found it necessary to make an example of a native chief, on the island of Vitilevu, who had murdered an American, and a formal court-martial was held on board the Falmouth for that purpose, while she lay in the Rewa Roads. The testimony against the accused was positive, and he was condemned to death and executed."

C.P.I. Ed. Note: The text of this report is an item in a newspaper column headed "FROM THE FEEGEE ISLANDS," . . . the rest of which is irrelevant. Vitilevu mentioned in the text is identified as Viti Levu Bay. [*This is incorrect. Viti Levu is the largest island of the Fiji Group.*] Rewa Roads mentioned in text is identified as Port Nukulau. Port Nukulau, at the extreme southeast port of Lauthala Harbor, is a good harbor for shipping produce from Rewa River, leading from Rewa Roads between Nukulau and Mokaluva Islands.

Port Nukulau is in lat. 18°10'S., lon. 178°31'E., H.O. Chart No. 2863. *(H.O. Pub.* No. 166, vol. II, 4th ed. 1933, p. 316.)

VOSTOCK 1

Independent Chronicle and Boston Patriot
July 23, 1829: 66, 2, 6
MNBedf

[Identical report in an unnamed Salem newspaper, July 24, 1829 (MHi), *Salem Gazette*, July 24, 1829 (MSaE), *Salem Courier*, (Weekly) July 29, 1829 (MSaE) and *Boston Courier*, Sept. 21, 1829 (MB). Report in *Boston Patriot & Mercantile Advertiser*, July 22, 1829 (MHi) has "Nantucket, July 13—' but is otherwise identical.]

Nantucket, July 18—Capt. Coffin, of the Reaper, recently arrived, discovered, in lat 9 55 S. lon. 152, 40, an island not laid down on any chart he has seen, and which he named after his ship. It was low, covered with wood, uninhabited, apparently about 12 miles in circumference, and surrounded with a coral reef.

C.P.I. Ed. Note: The text of this report is a true copy of article. There is no designation of longitude shown, whether E., or W. Island described, may possibly be Vostok Island which is 10° 06′ S., 152° 23′ W., H. O. Chart No. 1980 *(H.O. Pub.* No. 166, Vol. II, 4th ed. 1933, p. 479.)

[*P.I.Y.B., p. 74 gives Reaper as an alternative name for Vostock.*]

VOSTOCK 2

Salem Observer
July 25, 1829: 7, 3, 5
MSaE

Capt. Coffin, arr at Nantucket, discovered in lat 9 55, S. long 152 40, an island not laid down on any chart he has seen, and which he named after his ship. It was low, covered with wood, uninhabited, apparently about 12 miles in circumference, and surrounded by a coral reef.

C.P.I. Ed. Note: The text of this report is a true copy of article. There is no designation of longitude shown, whether E., or W.

[*For additional C.P.I. Ed. Note see VOSTOCK 1.*]

VOSTOCK 3

Boston Courier
Apr. 24, 1837: 12, 2, 6
MBAt

Extract from log book of whale ship Peruvian, ar. at St. John N. B. April 13, 1835: This day saw land to leeward, bore up for it, and sent boat off, but there was so much surf could not land. It was a small island, covered with trees, with a white sand beach all round, about a quarter of a mile long. There being no such island laid down in our chart, we considered it first discovered by us, and gave it the name of "Leavitt's Island" being in lat 10. 4 S., lon. 152. 25. W.

C.P.I. Ed. Note: The text of this report is one item in a news column, the rest of which is irrelevant.

Leavitt's Island, mentioned in text, may possibly be "Vostok Island (10° 06′ S., 152° 23′ W., H.O. Chart No. 1980) (British) was discovered in 1820, . . ."

(H.O. Pub. No. 166, Vol. II, 4th ed. 1933, p. 479.)

Report . . . [*VOSTOCK 4*] pertaining to same island, previously forwarded, gives year of discovery as 1837 (?), and latitude as 10° S.

VOSTOCK 4

New Bedford Daily Mercury
May 2, 1837: 7, 2, 3-6

[Identical report in *New Bedford Mercury*, May 5, 1837 (MNBedf). Report in *Salem Gazette*, May 5, 1837 (MSaE) gives longitude as '102 25 W' but is otherwise identical.]

A NEW ISLAND

Extract from the Log Book of the Whale Ship Peruvian, Capt. J. Wood, of this town, arrived at St. Johns, N .B. April 13, 1837:—

"This day saw land to leeward, bore up for it, and sent a boat off, but there being so much surf could not land. It was a small island, covered with trees, with a white sand beach all around, about a quarter of a mile long. There being no such island laid down in our charts, we considered it first discovered by us and gave it the name of "Leavitt's Island", being in lat 10 S, lon. 152/25 W."

[*For C.P.I. Ed. Note see VOSTOCK 1.*]

VOSTOCK 5

Morning Register, New Bedford, Mass.
Mar. 21, 1845: 7, 2, 4
MNBedf

A New Island

We learn from the Nantucket Telegraph that the first officer of ship Obed Mitchell at that port, writes that on the 1st of April last, saw Flint Island, and the next day saw a small round island, moderately high and well wooded.—Not finding it laid down in any books or charts, Capt. Coffin gave it the name of Carr's Island (after the name of the boat steerer who discovered it.) This is directly in the course of our whalers, being in latitude 10 degrees 3 minutes South, bearing from Flint Island North, 16 degrees West; distant from Flint Island, 89 miles. It being very squally at the time, Capt. Coffin did not attempt to land.

C.P.I. Ed. Note: Flint Island is 11° 26′ S., 151° 48′ W., H.O. Chart No. 1980 *(H.O. Pub.* No. 166, Vol. II, 4th ed. 1933, p.478.)

[*The island sighted may be Vostock.*]

WAKE 1

Boston Courier
Dec. 19, 1826: 3, 2, 2
MB

Edgartown, Dec. 14, Arr. ship Almira, Osborne, from Pacific ocean with 2300 bbls sperm oil. Ships spoken by the Almira, on the coast of Japan, in April, May and June 1826. At Wakes Island, April 24, Mercury, Austen, New Bedford, 350 bbls oil; Persia, Barnard, do. 250 bbls; Mayflower, Harris, Plymouth, 950 bbls. May 25th lat. 32 N. lon. 164 E. North America, Ramsdall, Nantucket, 1450 bbls. June 1, lat. 31, 44 N. lon. 169 E. Com. Perry, Smith, N. London, 500 bbls. June 19, lat. 34, 27, lon. 178 W. Planter, Bunker, Nantucket, 250 bbls. June 30, lat. 33, 10 N. lon. 174 W. Winslow, Chase N. Bedford 500 bbls. Left at the Sandwich Islands Aug. 6, ship Parthian, Rogers, from Canton; brigs Tamakama, Meek, do; Chinchilla, Meek, N. York; and 2 or 3 English ships. Left on N. W. Coast, ships Sultana and Volunteer; brigs Griffin, Convoy, and Tallyho.

C.P.I. Ed. Note: The text of the above report is taken from a column headed "MARINE JOURNAL," the rest of which is irrelevant.

Wake Island (southeast end, 19° 16′ N., 166° 37′ E., H.O. Chart 162), . . . *(H.O. Pub.* No. 165, Vol. I, 4th ed. 1938, p. 318.)

WAKE 2

New York Semi-Weekly Times
July 31, 1866: 12, 1, 5
MBr

MISCELLANEOUS

By the way of San Francisco, news is received of the loss of the bark La Belle, on the 4th of March, near the Ladrone Islands, which most of the passengers and crew succeeded in reaching in safety. The Captain with seven men who took the small boat, had not been heard from and a schooner had been sent in search of them. Mme Anna Bishop and party were among the passengers.

C.P.I. Ed. Note: The text of this report is one item in a newspaper column headed "MISCELLANEOUS," the rest of which is irrelevant.

Ladrone Islands mentioned in text may possibly be the Marianas Islands.

"The Archipelago of the Marianas of Ladrone Islands is composed of a chain of volcanic islands, which extend in a North and South direction for a space of 420 miles, between lat. 13°, 12′ and 20°, 32′, N.—

(Findlays *Directory of the North Pacific Ocean,* Third Ed. 1886, p. 1037.)

WAKE 3

Boston Daily Advertiser
July 31, 1866: 107, 1, 2
MB

[Report in *New England Farmer,* Boston, Aug. 4, 1866 (MH) omits last two sentences but otherwise is similar. Report in *New York Observer,* Aug. 2, 1866 (MBC) begins 'From San Francisco we have an account of the loss, on the 4th March, . . .' but thereafter is similar.]

WRECK OF THE BARQUE LA BELLE

The ship Silas Greenman from Hong Kong, at San Francisco, brings an account of the loss, on the 4th of March, of the barque La Belle, on the uninhabited reef called Wake Island, where the passengers and crew remained three weeks, but finding no water started in the ship's long boat for the Ladrone Islands, in charge of the first mate. The Captain and eight persons taking the gig. The former was saved but the latter has not been heard from.

Madam Anna Bishop and party were among the passengers. A schooner has been sent in search of the missing boat and to bring away $94,000 in treasure which was saved and buried on the island. The cargo was valued at $300,000.

C.P.I. Ed. Note: The text of this report is an item in a newspaper column headed "WRECK OF THE BARQUE LA BELLE," the rest of which is irrelevant.

[*For additional C.P.I. Ed. Note see WAKE 1.*]

WAKE 4

The Daily Herald, Newburyport, Mass.
Aug. 1, 1866: 35, 2, 6
MNe

Wreck of the Barque La Belle

The ship Silas Greeman from Hong Kong, at San Francisco, brings an account of the loss, on the 4th of March, of the barque La Belle on the uninhabited reef called Wake Island where the passengers and crew remained three weeks, but finding no water started in the ship's long boat for the Ladrone Island, in charge of the first mate. The captain and eight persons taking the gig.

The former was saved but the latter have not been heard from.—Madame Anna Bishop and party were among the missing boat and to bring away $94,000 in treasure, which was saved and buied on the island. The cargo was valued at $300,000.

Letters from Eugene M. Roll and Madame Anne Bishop confirm the statement that the passengers and crew of the barque La Belle were all saved except seven men who accompanied the Captain and his gig. Much praise is awarded to the Governor of Marana Islands for his efforts to relieve the ship wrecked people.

C.P.I. Ed. Note: The text of this report is one item in a column of news headed "Shipping Journal," the rest of which is irrelevant.

[For additional C.P.I. Ed. Note see WAKE 1.]

WAKE 5

Boston Daily Advertiser
Aug. 1, 1866: 108, 4, 3
MBr

Brem barque Libelle, Tobias, which cleared at San Francisco, Jan. 23 for Hong Kong via Honolulu, (with the following cargo, viz 1 case cigars 4098 qt. sacks flour, 30 cases hardware, 150 pkgs old iron, 1000 flasks quicksilver, 1 case seeds, 2050 sacks wheat and 10 kegs wine-value $51,555.27—and $93,943,08 in treasure) was totally wrecked on an uninhabited reef called Wake Island, March 4. The passengers and crew remained on the reef three weeks, when, finding no water, they started in the long boat and gigs for the Ladrone Islands. The long boat arrived, but the gig with the captain and eight men had not been heard from. A schooner had been sent in search of the missing boat and to bring away the treasure, which had been burried on the Island.

C.P.I. Ed. Note: The text of this report is one item in a news column headed "DISASTERS," the rest of which is irrelevant. Wakes Island is a dangerous low island of triangular form, with a reef around it, lying in lat. 19°10′54″N., long. 166°31′30″E., (*Directory of the North Pacific Ocean.* Findlay, Third ed. 1886, pp. 1035-1036.)

"It is thus very probable the *Halcyon Island,* said by Kotzebue to have been discovered by an American captain in lat. 19 23 N., long. 165 33 E., is the same Wakes Island, because Captain Wilkes passed by its assigned position without seeing it. Krusenstern calls Wakes Island by the name of Halcyon, on this supposition. (*Ibid:* p. 1036)

[For additional C.P.I. Ed. Note see WAKE 1.]

WAKE 6

Hawaiian Gazette, Honolulu
Aug. 18, 1866: 2, 1, 5
MH

Loss of the "Libelle" with Madame Anna Bishop and troupe and board. The Alta quotes the following particulars of the disaster from the China Mail, of May 31st, together with letters from Madame Bishop and Eugene M. Van Reed:

The loss of the Bremen bark Libelle, from San Francisco to Hong Kong, which sailed in January last, is reported by a gentleman who arrived in this colony yesterday, in the Finculo, Mr. Van Reed, of Kanagawa. For many reasons it is impossible to describe all the painful details of such occurrences as are here narrated, but the sufferings of the crew and passengers may be partly imagined, when the circumstances in which they were placed are understood. Mr. Van Reed's account is as follows;

The Bremen bark Libelle, under the command of Captain Tobias, on the passage from San Francisco to Hong Kong, with a valuable cargo valued at our $300,000, was cast away on the night of March 4th, on an uninhabited and dangerous reef, called Wake Island. The passengers and crew remained on board during the night, the sea breaking fearfully over the wreck all the while and landed with difficulty through the breakers the following day.

After an ineffectual search for water for three weeks, and much privation, it became imperative to take to the boats and endeavour to reach the nearest habitable island, friendly disposed to defenceless shipwrecked people.

Several days were spent in finding a suitable and safe point for departure, the breakers encircling the island, which appeared to be some twenty miles in circumference. Taking such provisions and water as were saved from the wreck, the passengers were transferred to the ship's longboat in charge of the Chief Mate, the Captain preferring his gig; and on the 27th of March both boats sailed for the Ladrone or Mariana Islands.

Twenty-two persons, with provisions, in an open boat but twenty-two feet in length, to undertake a voyage of 1,400 miles, subject to equinoctial storms, calms, and a tropical sun, with short rations, and an ocean studded with hidden rocks and coral reefs, gave but poor hope of arriving at a port with life.

The dangers which were imminent from the frequent squalls, cross seas, and shipping seas encountered, were the greatest trials, and in thirteen days, the boat being 6 degrees of longitude in error, arrived off the town of Guam, all in a pitiable and forlorn condition. The Captain with eight persons, in a boat twenty feet long, leaving at the same time, has not been heard from, and unless picked up by some chance vessel, must have been swamped, as a heavy cross sea was met after leaving the Island. This, it is said, was the third vessel the Captain has been so unfortunate as to lose within the past few years.

Among the passengers were Mad. Anna Bishop, Miss Phelan, Mr. M. Schultz and Mr. Charles Lascelles, of the English opera troupe, and Mr. Eugene van Reed of Kanagawa, almost all nations being represented.

Too much praise cannot be awarded to His Excellency Francisco Moscoso y Lara, Governor of the Mariana Islands, for his prompt and humane efforts to relieve the distress of the shipwrecked, who had lost their all and were in want of everything. A schooner also has been charted and sent to search for the missing boat among the islands to the northward, and to return to Wake Island and remove the large amount of treasure which had been saved and buried there.

Mr. Van Reed, holding an official position, together with a Japanese, were alone allowed to leave Guam, prior to the return of the vessel from the scene of the wreck, and has arrived here in the Finculo, which had put in on her way from Australia.

The Treasure

There was despatched for Hong Kong, by Macondray & Co., January 24th, all the treasure, valued at $93,000, which was saved and buried by the Captain on the island. The boat arrived at Guam on the 10th of April.

> Letter From A Passenger.
> Hong Kong, May 13, 1866.

Editors Alta: You find me here, having arrived but yesterday from my long and dangerous trip from San Francisco. The Libelle, in which I took passage at Honolulu, together with Madame Anna Bishop and party, ran ashore and was totally wrecked on Wake Island, an uninhabited coral reef, two thousand miles west of Honolulu, where after great danger, we landed through the breakers to find no water, yet our troubles were not over, for we were forced to take to our boats, and in an open boat sail fourteen hundred miles through the equinoctial gales, for Guam. The captain and eight men in the gig have not been heard from. We were twenty-two persons in a boat twenty-two feet in length. In a helpless position we arrived in 13 days at Guam, our condition pitiful.

I arrived with Kisabow yesterday, and shall be in Japan, I hope, within a month.

You will find a lengthened account in the China Press of this date, which I forward to the Alta.

> Eugene M. Van Reed.

We are informed by Messrs. Macondary & Co. that their letters do not contain a list of the saved, but one of them says: "Madame Anna Bishop and three friends were in the boat with

Mr. Van Reed". The inference is that all the passengers were in the boat which was saved. The captain preferred the gig, and took with him, as we infer from the letters of Mr. Van Reed, only the eight sailors alluded to.

Letter from Madame Bishop.

Mr. Gray, No. 613 Clay Street, has received the following from Madame Bishop, the best evidence of her safety:

> Guam. Mariana Islands.
> May 7, 1886.

You will be shocked to learn we have been wrecked on Wake Island on the 5th of March, and lost all.

We were three weeks on an uninhabitable island. No water and had to wait three days before we could get any from the ship. We had no clothing but what we stood in up to arriving at this island. The Governor and inhabitants have been most kind, and furnished us with a few materials to make up a little clothing. They have no store here. We came, twenty-two of us, in an open boat, fourteen hundred miles. How we wished it was to San Francisco! A perfect miracle our safe passage to this place. The captain of the Libelle left at the same time we did from Wake Island in a small boat, with four of his men and three Chinese, but up to this time we have not heard of them. We are here a month today. The Governor has sent a schooner to Wake Island for the specie saved from the wreck and we have to wait its return to take it to Manila, where we hope to commence operations. Mr. Van Reed and the Japanese are allowed to go with this to Hong Kong.

You cannot imagine how we suffered all one night, from 9 o'clock P.M. till 8 A.M. thinking every moment would be our last but the Almighty was watchful over us poor sinners!

Mr. Schultz, Mr. Lascelles and Maria are with us.

> Truly yours,
> Anna Bishop Schultz.

C.P.I. Ed. Note: The text of this report is one item in a news column headed "LATER FROM CHINA," the rest of which is irrelevant.

[For additional C.P.I. Ed. Notes see WAKE 1 & 5.]

WAKE 7

Boston Daily Advertiser
Aug. 23, 1866: 108, 2, 2
MB

MADAM ANNA BISHOP AS ROBINSON CRUSOE

The Bremen barque Libelle from San Francisco for Hong Kong was totally lost on the night of March 4, on Wake Island. Among her passengers was Madame Anna Bishop, and the following letter from her to a gentleman of San Francisco, Cal., describes the catastrophe:—

Guam, Mariana Islands, May 7, 1866. "You will be shocked to learn we have been wrecked on Wake Island on the 5th of March, and lost all. We were three weeks on the uninhabited Island, no water and had to wait three days before we could get any from the ship. We had no clothing but what we stood in up to arriving on this island. The Governor and inhabitants have been most kind, and furnished us with a few materials to make up a little clothing. They have no stores here. We came, twenty-one of us, in an open boat fourteen hundred miles. How we wished it was to San Francisco. A perfect miracle our safe passage to this place. The captain of the Libelle left at the same time we did from Wake Island, in a small boat, with four of his men, and three Chinese; but up to this time we have not heard of them. We are here a month today. The Governor has sent a schooner to Wake Island for the specie saved from the wreck and we have to wait its return to take us to Manila, where we hope to commence operations. Mr. Van Reed and the Japanese are allowed to go to Hong Kong. You cannot imagine how we suffered all one night, from nine P.M. till eight A.M. thinking every moment would be our last;

but the Almighty was watchful over us poor sinners.   "Mr. Schultz, Mr. Lascelles and Maria are with us.

"Truly yours, Anna Bishop Schultz"

C.P.I. Ed. Note: The text of the above report is a copy of an article in a newspaper column headed "MADAM ANNA BISHOP, AS ROBINSON CRUSOE."

[*For additional C.P.I. Ed. Note see WAKE 1.*]

WAKE 8

The Friend, Honolulu
Sept. 1, 1866: 23, 86, 1
MSaP

WRECK OF THE "LIBELLE"

This vessel was supposed to have been lost, but recent intelligence makes known her fate. It was our privilege to have seen much of two of the passengers, during their visit at Honolulu, viz., Messrs. Van Reed and Kisaboro. A notice of this Japanese traveller will be found in our issue for March last. Among the passengers were Madame Bishop and Mr. C. Lascelles, distinguished singers, whose performances in Honolulu were so noted. Mr. Van Reed furnishes for the *China Mail* the following:

The Bremen bark *Libelle,* under the command of Captain Tobias, on the passage from San Francisco to Hongkong, with a valuable cargo valued at over $300,000, was cast away on the night of March 4th, on an uninhabited and dangerous reef, called Wake Island. The passengers and crew remained on board during the night, the sea breaking fearfully over the wreck all the while, and landed with difficulty through the breakers the following day.

After an ineffectual search for *water* for three weeks, and much privation, it became imperative to take to the boats and endeavor to reach the nearest habitable island, friendly disposed to defenceless ship wrecked people.

Several days were spent in finding a suitable and safe point for departure, the breakers encircling the islands which appeared to be some twenty miles in circumference. Taking such provisions and water as were saved from the wreck, the passengers were transferred to the ship's longboat, in charge of the

First Mate, the Captain preferring his gig; and on the 27th of March both boats sailed for the Ladrone or Mariana Islands. Twenty-two persons, with provisions, in an open boat but *twenty-two* feet in length, to undertake a voyage of 1,400 miles, subject to equinoctial storms, calms and a tropic sun, with short rations, and an ocean studded with hidden rocks and coral reefs, gave but poor hope of arriving at a port with life.

The dangers which were imminent from the frequent squals, cross seas, and shipping seas encountered, were the greatest trials, and in thirteen days, the boat being 6 degrees of longitude in error, arrived off the town of Guam, all in a pitiable and forlorn condition. The Captain with eight persons, in a boat twenty feet in length, leaving at the same time, has not been heard from, and unless picked up by some chance vessel, must have been swamped as a heavy cross sea was met shortly after leaving the Island.

This, it is said, was the third vessel the Captain was so unfortunate as to lose within the past few years.

Among the passengers were Madame Anona Bishop, Miss Phelan, Mr. M. Schultz and Mr. Charles Lascelles, of the English opera troupe; and Mr. Eugene M. Van Reed, of Kanagawa, almost all nations being represented.

Too much praise cannot be awarded to His Excellency Francisco Moscoso y Lara, Governor of the Mariana Islands, for his prompt and humane efforts to relieve the distress of the shipwrecked, who had lost their all and were in want of everything. A schooner also has been chartered and sent to search for the missing boat among the islands of the northward, and to return to Wake Island and remove the large amount of treasure which has been saved and buried there.

DOUBTFUL ISLANDS AND REEFS.—An old and experienced shipmaster has handed us two items, regarding Wake Island, the scene of the disaster to the *Libelle,* and the reef noticed in our last upon which a vessel was lost, and the crew reached Tahiti.

Wake or Halcyon Islands is fifteen miles in circumference, and has a lagoon inside. The island is surrounded by rocks, and the beach is covered with short brush wood. Its position is in lat. 19° 11′ N., 166°31′ E. Vessels leaving, or passing, Honolulu should get into a lat. 18 30′ N., which parallel will carry them through the Ladrones, clear of all danger up to 130° E., then steer for the Bashees. Vessels taking this course have the full strength of the northeast trades at all seasons.

[*For C.P.I. Ed. Note see WAKE* 5.]

WAKE 9

Evening Standard, New Bedford, Mass.
Oct. 15, 1866: 17, 3, 2
MNBedf

An old and experienced ship-master has furnished the Pacific Commercial Advertiser with the following items in regard to the reef upon which the ship Libelle was lost.

"Wake or Halcyon Island is fifteen miles in circumference, and has a lagoon inside. The island is surrounded by rocks, and the beach is covered with short brush wood. Its position is in lat. 19 deg 11 Min N, 166 deg. 31 Min E. Vessels leaving or passing Honolulu should get into lat 18 30 N, which parallel will carry them through the Ladrones, clear of all danger, up to 130 deg E, then steer for the Bashees. Vessels taking this course have the full strength of the north-east trades at all seasons.

C.P.I. Ed. Note: The text of this report is one item in a news column headed "MARINE INTELLIGENCE," the rest of which is irrelevant.

[*For additional C.P.I. Ed. Note see WAKE 5.*]

WAKE 10

The Pacific Commercial Advertiser, Honolulu
Apr. 27, 1867: 11, 2, 3
MH

[Similar report in *The Friend,* Honolulu, May 1, 1857 (MH)]

CRUISE OF THE CAROLINE MILLS

The American schooner Caroline Mills, Capt. Nicholas, returned to port on the 22d inst., having left there on a wrecking voyage to the westward about three months ago. She was provided with all the appurtenances for recovering wrecked property, and her Captain and crew were thoroughly experienced in those enterprises, and equipped with proper instruments for navigation. A complete modern diving apparatus was on board—commonly known as a "submarine armor", with two men to operate it, one to don the "armor" and the other to attend to the signals of his confederate while exploring the bottom of the ocean. The first island visited by the schooner, and the principal object of the expedition, was Wake or Halcyon Island, one of the Palmyra group, lying in latitude 19° 11 N. and longitude 166° 31′ E. Here they obtained some flasks of quicksilver from the wreck of the bark Libelle, which left here last year, having as passengers, Madam Anne Bishop and others.

C.P.I. Ed. Note: The above text is an excerpt taken from a longer article for a separate report on island mentioned. ". . .Wake Island is a possession of the United States and is under the jurisdiction of the Secretary of the Navy for administrative purposes." *(H.O. Pub.* No. 165, Vol. I, 4th ed. 1938, p. 518.)

[*For additional C.P.I. Ed. Note see WAKE 1.*]

WAKE 11

Boston Daily Advertiser
June 7, 1867: 109, 1, 4
MB

[Report in *Boston Daily Evening Transcript,* June 7, 1867 (MBAt) has 'Sibellas Island' while that in *Daily Evening Traveller,* Boston, June 6, 1867 (MB) has 'Sibella Island'. Both omit 'to San Francisco' but are otherwise similar.]

AN OLD WRECK DISCOVERED

The schooner Caroline Mills has returned to San Francisco from an unsuccessful wrecking expedition to the barque La Belle lost on Wake Island in March 1866.

The Caroline Mills also visited Sibello Island, and discovered the ship Canton, which left Sitka in 1816, and was never afterwards heard from. Portions of the wreck are in a perfect state or preservation. A piece of armor and a shield, with coat-of-arms of the East India Company and of England, fastened thereon, were found on the wreck and brought back.

C.P.I. Ed. Note: The text of the above report is a copy of an item in a newspaper column headed "AN OLD WRECK DISCOVERED," the rest of which is irrelevant.

The text of report in *Boston Daily Evening Transcript* is similar to others gathered from various sources which taken collectively tend to prove, despite variations in position given that Canton Island is where wreck occurred.

Canton Island is in Lat. 2° 49' lon. 171° 45'W. H.O. Chart No. 1211 *(H.O. Pub.* No. 166, vol. II, 4th ed., 1933. p. 471.)

in the Central Pacific

[*This is extremely doubtful, as the* Canton *which was wrecked on Canton Island was lost in 1854 (see CANTON 1).*]

[*For additional C.P.I. Ed. Note see WAKE 1.*]

WAKE 12

The Friend, Honolulu
Apr. 1, 1871: 29, 30, 3
MSaP

LOSS OF THE BARK "DASHING WAVE."
FEARFUL SUFFERINGS OF THE CREW

We have to record one of the most miraculous escapes from death at sea in many forms that have ever been made public. The bark Dashing Wave, a successful China tea clipper, is down as missing in the Sydney Morning Herald. Captain Vandervord was the master of the vessel, and from him we learn the following particulars:—He left Foochow on July 29 bound for Sydney; and on the night of August 31, the weather being thick and squalls coming down at intervals, Captain Vandervord took in the maintop-gallantsail at 10 P.M., and went below to lie on the sofa in the cabin; at half-past 10 he went on deck again and was just in time to see a small island right ahead; he shouted to the man at the wheel to put the helm down, and the vessel had nearly come round when her keel touched on the reef which surrounds the island. Half an hour after taking the bottom the copper came over the weather-side in sheets, and the foremast sunk 18 inches; the mainmast was cut away, but the ship began to break up fast. The island proved to be Wake Island, small and uninhabited, surrounded by a reef, rendering it impossible to land if there is any wind blowing at all. Captain Vandervord says it is 10 miles out of the position given in the chart, 10° 30′ N., 167° E. The crew took to the long boat, and Captain Vandervord secured a chart and nautical instruments, but strange to say no compass was saved; a case of colonial wine, a bag and a half of bread and two buckets were put in the boat, but no water; and for 31 days the thirteen men were in the open boat

without seeing land or a ship, or receiving any assistance whatever. They left the wreck at 10 the morning after, and with
sail made of blankets sewn together, and fixed to an oar, began
their weary journey in search of some inhabited land. Their
sufferings may be imagined. For the first five days they had not
a drop of water, and the captain served out one bottle of Ca-
warra daily between the thirteen; that saved their lives; after
that time they had rain and caught water, but except at the time
it was actually raining a half pint of water each only a day was
served out and a handful of bread. To the credit of the men
and their commander there was no insubordination, no attempt
to obtain more than their share of the scanty provisions and precious water; silently but resigned they passed day after day, the
sun pouring down on their unsheltered heads. Every day Captain Vandervord got the boat's position by means of his instruments, but when the weather was dull of course they went in all
directions for want of a compass, and especially on cloudy
nights; it was the master's intention to make for the Kingsmill
group, but the current was against them, and then a course was
steered for Ascension Island, and had any of the party been able
to row they might have reached it, but weak as they were, all
they could do was to keep their boat before the wind with the
blanket sail. After 30 days of suffering, their mouths parched,
tongues swollen, wet with grateful showers, scorched by a tropical sun they sighted Strong's (Ualan) Island, the easternmost of
the Caroline group. Here the castaways saw a canoe outside taking produce from one part of the island to another, and had they
been able to get some provisions Captain Vandervord would
have kept on, and tried to make on of the islands of the Marshall
or Gilbert groups adjacent. The boat refused to trade with
them, and they went inside and were received by the King with
the uttermost hospitality; he took the captain and mate to live
with him, and assigned quarters to the men in the town. After
some days Captain Vandervord and part of the crew took the

boat and tried to reach Kingsmill, and were fitted out by the King with sails, mast, and provisions of every kind, but met with a gale and had to return to Strong's Island. Altogether 39 days were spent on the island, when the Oriti put in short of provisions, and they came on in that vessel and arrived on Thursday at midnight. Captain Vandervord desires to acknowledge the kindness of Captain Beatson to himself and his unfortunate crew.

Fiji Times, January 7.

[*For C.P.I. Ed. Note see WAKE 1.*]

WASHINGTON 1

The Friend, Honolulu
Oct. 19, 1861: 18, 72, 1
MSaP

[Report in *The Pacific Commercial Advertiser,* Honolulu, Oct. 24, 1861 (MB) omits third sentence but is otherwise identical. The report acknowledges *The Friend* as source.]

Singular Marine Phenomena

The Rev. Mr. Bicknell, who has just returned from a visit to Washington Island, situated about seventy-five miles to the westward of Fanning's Island, reports as follows: that there is a lake of fresh water in the center of this island. It is coralline in formation, and is five or six miles in diameter. The land is low and covered with cocoanut and pandanus trees. In some places the land is a mile in width. The lake, of course, is large. He tasted the water and found it fresh. We have lately heard of another similar phenomenon on the coast of California or Mexico. It would be interesting to learn full particulars respecting these islands.

Washington Island was originally uninhabited, but Messrs. English & Co., have procured about seventy natives from Humphrey's Island, one of the Hervey group, and are now manufacturing cocoanut oil, under the superintendence of Mr. Bicknell. The same firm is now at work upon Fanning's Island, with about one hundred and thirty natives.

C.P.I. Ed. Note: Humphrey's Island, mentioned in text, may possibly be "Manahiki (Humphrey) Island (10° 23′ S., 161° 01′

W., H.O. Chart No. 1980), 190 miles eastward of Penrhyn Island, was discovered in 1822." *(H.O. Pub.* No. 166, Vol. II, 4th ed. 1933, p. 483.)

Washington Island (4° 43' N., 160° 25' W., H.O. Chart No. 1839), also called New York Island, lying 75 miles northwestward of Fanning Island, was discovered in 1798." *(H.O. Pub.* No. 166, Vol. II, 4th ed. 1933, p. 498.)

WILLIS 1

Boston Daily Advertiser
Nov. 28, 1853: 82, 2, 7
M

NOTICE TO MARINERS

Willis Islands, Torres Straits—Sir: I beg to apprise you of the discovery of the Willis Islands, near the Southern entrance of Torres Straits. Capt. Parsons, who discovered them, gives the following positions.—

Westernmost Island lat. 15° 44′ S. lon. 143° 43′ E.

The Easternmost is abt. 8 miles, a little North of East of it. F. Beaufort, Hydrographer. Capt. G.A. Halsted. R.N.

Secretary Lloyds.

C.P.I. Ed. Note: The text of the above report is a copy of an item in a newspaper column headed "NOTICE TO MARINERS," that mentions no ship, only newly discovered islands, which lie in Torres Straits, between the northwest coast of Australia and the island of New Guinea. Available reference material does not contain any hydrographic notes to help us identify the above.

[*The report may refer to the Willis Group, 15° 20′ S., 150° E. although the difference in longitude is difficult to explain.*]

WINSLOW REEF 1

The Daily Mercury, New Bedford, Mass.
Mar. 10, 1853: 23, 2, 2
MNBedf

[Identical report in *New Bedford Mercury,* Mar. 11, 1853 (MNBedf). Similar report in *Whalemen's Shipping List,* New Bedford, Mar. 15, 1853 (MDarHi). Report in *Boston Daily Journal,* Mar. 11, 1853 (MB) is similar to first two paragraphs. Report in *The Friend,* Honolulu, Sept. 1, 1853 (MSaP) is similar except for introductory sentence which reads:
'Mr. Editor.— From the Nantucket Inquirer.
On the late voyage of the ship "Phoenix" of Nantucket in the Pacific Ocean under my command, I made several important discoveries which I consider of sufficient interest to the commercial world to make public:—
In July, 1851. . .']

DISCOVERIES IN THE PACIFIC

Capt. Perry Winslow, of the ship Phoenix of Nantucket, has communicated to the Inquirer, as follows: In July 1851, I made a dangerous reef in lat. 140 S., long. 174 50 W., extending from N. W. to S. E. about one mile, and nearly 3-4 of a mile broad, on which I got soundings from the boat of 4 fathoms, where I also discovered two pointed rocks just below the surface; we remained with two boats anchored on the reef, about three hours, and caught a large number of codfish. This reef is not laid down on any chart that I know of.

The position of Rapid Reef S. W. of the Fegee's, laid down on the chart, is in lat. 21 36 S., lon. 175 10 E., which is erroneous; the true position is lat. 21 36 S lon. 174 50 E., and is a very dangerous reef being in the track of ships from King's Mill group to New Zealand.

The following information I obtained from Capt. Bulger, an experienced ship-master at Bay of Islands, New Zealand, which may be useful to be known:

At the Island of Apee (New Hebrides) on the S.W. side, there are yams to be procured in abundance from the month of February to the latter part of August. Also at Bank's Southern Island, on the west side. If you should go so far to the Westward as the Louisades there is plenty of yams to be had at Cape Dennis, on the north side of the group. At Achilles Island, in 8 S. 178 E., there are plenty of pigs to be had for boat axes. Yams at the above named Islands. Iron hoop is the trade. There are also plenty of yams to be had at the Northern Bank's Island, also bananas, taro, breadfruit, and other fruits in plenty. I have always made it a rule in trading with the above Islands, to make the officers in charge of the boats buy the yams first, and fruit afterward, because if the natives are traded with for fruit they will not bring the yams for sale.

Nantucket, March 5, 1853

Perry Winslow.

C.P.I. Ed. Note: The above text is a complete copy of a newspaper article. . . .

"Winslow Reef, about 120 miles north-northwestward of McKean Island, was discovered in 1851 from the ship *Phoenix*. Capt. Winslow says "it extends 1 mile northwest and southeast, and is 1,500 yards wide, with two pointed rocks awash, 1° 40′ S., 174° 50′ W.

"In 1922 the steamer *Hauraki* passed over the charted position of Winslow Reef and saw no signs of any shoal water. The weather was fine at the time and there was a moderate swell.

"The master of the British steamer *Nassa* reports that on the af-

ternoon of May 10, 1928, his vessel passed over the Charted position of Winslow Reef and saw no sign of the reef or of shoal
water. The weather at the time was fine and clear with moderate easterly swell.

"The American steamer *Golden Cross* reported (1932) having passed over the charted position of Winslow Reef and saw
no sign of shoal water.

"Reef—The second officer of the British Auxiliary
schooner *Doris Crane* reports his vessel passed about 3 miles
northward of a sand bank or coral reef, about 1 mile long east
and west, in approximately 0° 55′ S., 174° 51′ W. The reef was
clearly visible from the masthead and appeared to be just awash,
while broken water was visible from the deck. The weather was
clear and calm. This reef is located about 45 miles northward
of the charted position of Winslow Reef.

"It is therefore considered that the existence of Winslow
Reef in its charted position is doubtful and it is possible that the
reef is identical with that reported by the Doris Crane." *(H.O.
Pub.* No. 166, Vol. II, 4th ed., 1933, pp. 472, 475.)

"Conway Shoal (Rapids Reef), discovered in 1838, has been
many times reported as a new discovery, and has also been called
Mercator Shoal, having been seen in the ship of that name.
The assigned positions do not vary too much to prevent this
identification. It lies in lat. 21° 44′ 48″ S., long. 174° 37′ 45″
East." (Findlay, *Directory of the South Pacific Ocean,* Fifth
Edition, 1884, p. 552.)

Conway Reef is 21° 45′ S., 174° 37′ E. H.O. Chart 1996.
(H.O. Pub. No. 166, Vol. II, 4th ed., 1933, p. 50.)

Apee is probably another spelling for Epi Island in the
New Hebrides.

Epi Island, center, 16° 44′ S., 168° 17′ E., H.O. Chart 2891
(H.O. Pub. No. 165, Vol. I, 4th ed., 1938, p. 207.)

Banks Islands (13° 15′—14° 30′ S., 167° 15′—168° 05′ E.,
H. O. Chart 2877), . . . comprise the islands of Gaua, Merig,

Morlay, Vanua Lava, Mota, Ureparapara, Rowa, Valua, and Vatganai. Gaua and Vanua Lava Islands are the largest of the group,. . .Merig, Rowa, and Vatganai are merely small islets. *(H.O. Pub.* No. 165, Vol. I, 4th ed., 1938, p. 257.)

Cape Dennis is probably another spelling for Cape Denis. "Cape Denis in lat. 8° 24', long. 151° 06', is the N.E. Point of Trobriand Islands." (Findlay, *Directory of the South Pacific Ocean,* Fifth Edition, 1884, p. 939.)

No mention of Achilles Island is found in available reference material.

Nuku Fetau (De Peyster) Atoll is 8° 00' S., 178° 29' E., H.O. Chart No. 1802. *(H.O. Pub.* No. 166, Vol. II, 4th ed., 1933, p. 438.)

WRECK REEF 1

Columbian Centinel, Boston, Mass.
July 28, 1804: 41, 3, 1
MH; MHi

MEMORANDA

We have been favored with the "Sydney Gazette, and New South Wales Advertiser," published in the British Territory of New South Wales.— It contains no other news, than the loss of His Britannic Majesty's armed vessel Porpoise, of 10 guns, and the Cato, merchant vessel, on a newly discovered reef, in about lat. 23°, 27′ S. and long. 155° 43′ E., and 166 miles, N. 55 E. from Sandy Cape, on the coast of New South Wales.

C.P.I. Ed. Note: The text of this report is one item in a newspaper column headed "MEMORANDA." Complete text is used. . . .

Wreck Reef, on which the *Porpoise* and *Cato* were lost, with Capt. Flinders on board, on the night of August 15, 1803, is the central part of a chain of reefs, extending 18½ miles E. by N. and W. by S. . . . Wreck Reef has a sand bank on it; one third of a mile in circumference, and 4 ft. above high water, in lat. 22° 11′ 20″ S. lon 155° 19′ E. . . . (Findlay, *Directory of the South Pacific Ocean*, 5th ed., 1884. p. 956.)

WRECK REEF 2

Salem Register
Sept. 6, 1804: 5, 3, 2 & 3
MSaE

From the Providence Gazette
By Samuel Snow, Esq. who arrived last week at Boston, from Canton, in the ship Patterson, Capt. Aborn, of this port, we are favoured with a file of papers printed at Sydney, (New Holland) from which we extract the following account, and a description of Wreck Reef, upon which two British armed ships were lost, for the information of our nautical readers. "The Porpoise, with the honourable East India Company's extra ship Bridgewater, and the ship Cato in company, on August 17, 1803, at 2 o'clock in the afternoon fell in with a sand bank in about 23.7 South lat. 255 26 E lon, and 157 miles N. 51 E. from Sandy Cape. on the coast of New South Wales. This bank being 2 degrees to the Eastward of the situation where the Eliza, whaler, found the reefs lying off the coast to terminate, it was thought to be such a detached bank as some others seen by Lieut. Ball and Mr. Bampton, which lie much further over towards the north end of New Caledona, and no expectation of meeting with any more was entertained, especially as the Investigator has before steered for Torris' Straits, from reef several degrees further to the W. without interuption. At 8 o'clock the Porpoise sounded with 35 fathoms, but found no bottom—at half past 9 breakers were seen ahead, and the Porpoise's helm was put down, in order to tack from them, but the foresail being furled up, to keep the outer ships in sight, she was then under three double reefed topsails, and only came up head to the wind; in paying off again, she struck upon the coral reef which occaisioned the breakers. The longitude corrected is 155. 36 E. a dry land bank was seen

near the wreck sufficient to receive every person and all the provisions that might be saved. "Wreck-Reef extends about E. N.
E. and W. S. W. about 24 miles. The bank on which his Majesty's ships Porpoise and Catos respective crews landed is situated
in lat. 22.11; 46 S. and long. 155.35.30 E of Greenwich; by the
mean of sixty sets of distances, this bank is near the middle of
the reef".

C.P.I. Ed. Note: The text of this report is one item in a news
column headed "NAUTICAL," the rest of which is irrelevant.

[*For additional C.P.I. Ed. Note see WRECK REEF 1.*]

WRECK REEF 3

Columbian Centinel, Boston, Mass.
Oct. 27, 1804: 42, 2, 5
MHi

MISCELLANEOUS

Wreck Reef, so called from the unfortunate circumstance of the loss of the (Eng.) ships Cato and Porpoise, lies in lat. 22, 11 S. long. 155, 36E from Greenwich. Cato's Bank. lies in lat. 23, 28, S. long. 155, 49,E. from Greenwich. Their situation has been ascertained from the means of sixty sets of observatory, &c.

C.P.I. Ed. Note: The text of this report is an item in a newspaper column headed "MISCELLANEOUS." . . .

[*For additional C.P.I. Ed. Note see WRECK REEF 1.*]

WRECK REEF 4

Boston Daily Advertiser
Apr. 24, 1857: 89, 1, 3
M

WHALERS

Whaleship Lion, of Providence, before reported wrecked on Wreck Reef, off the coast of New Holland, had been sold as she lay ashore together with 500 bbls. sp. oil. Capt. Hardwick was at Aukland, New Zealand, Jan. 27. and would return to the United States by the first opportunity.

C.P.I. Ed. Note: The text of this report is one item in a newspaper column headed "WHALERS."

[*For additional C.P.I. Ed. Note see WRECK REEF 1.*]

WRECK REEF 5

Boston Post
Apr. 24, 1857: 50, 2, 8
M

WHALERS

Whaleship Lion of Providence, (before reported lost), was wrecked on Wreck Reef, off the coast of New Holland on the 30th of November last. Crew saved, and arrived Sydney, N S W. The vessel as she lay ashore together with—bbls Sp. Oil. had been sold. Capt. Hardwick was at Auckland, New Zealand Jan. 27, and would return to the United States, at the first opportunity.

C.P.I. Ed. Note: The text of this report is an item in a newspaper column headed "WHALERS," the rest of which is irrelevant.

[*For additional C.P.I. Ed. Note see WRECK REEF 1.*]

ZEPHYR SHOAL 1

Daily Evening Standard, New Bedford, Mass.
Nov. 2, 1855: 6, 3, 1
MNBedf

[Similar report in *The Daily Mercury,* New Bedford, Nov. 3, 1855 (MNBedf).]

MARINE INTELLIGENCE

The American bark Fanny Major, at Sydney from San Francisco, reports:—

July 25, lat 15 45 S, lon 176 54 E, passed over a coral reef not laid down in the chart, and upon sounding found ten fathoms of water; the reef extended east and west a mile and a half, and about half a mile north and south.

C.P.I. Ed. Note: The text of above report is taken from a column of similar material headed "MARINE INTELLIGENCE," the rest of which is irrelevant.

The reef mentioned in report is probably identical with that located by the *Penguin* and *Manapouri.* The E. lon. possibly should be W.

"The British surveying vessel *Penguin* (1895) searched for Zephyr Shoal; a bank was found in approximately 15° 55′ S., 176° 46½′ W.

"The British naval vessel *Penguin* anchored on this bank in a depth of 21 fathoms (38.4 m), and obtained a least depth of 11 fathoms (20.1 m) 1,000 yards eastward of the above position, the extent of the bank being 1,500 yards east and west. It is possible that less water may exist. In the course of this search the

Zephyr position 16° 00′ S., 177° 06′ W. was crossed and sounded over without shoal water being found. "The steamer *Manapouri,* in January 1901 saw bottom and obtained soundings of 13 fathoms (23.8 m), over a distance of about 11 miles in approximately 15° 55′ S., 176° 50′ W. . ." *(H.O. Pub. No. 166, Vol. II, 4th ed. 1933, p. 421.)*

[*An alternative identification, which would accept the designation 'E' as correct would be with Balmoral Reef, in approximately 15° 42′S., 175° 54′E.*]

APPENDIX

LIBRARY SOURCES

National Union Catalog Symbol	Library
M	Massachusetts State Library, Boston
MAmHi	Amesbury Historical Society
MB	Boston Public Library
MBAt	Boston Athenaeum
MBC	Congregational Library, Boston
MBevHi	Beverly Historical Society
MBr	Brookline Public Library
MChels	Chelsea Public Library
MCo	Concord Public Library
MDarHi	Old Dartmouth Historical Society, New Bedford
MH	Widener Library, Harvard University
MHi	Massachusetts Historical Society, Boston
MHingM	Hingham Marine Museum
MLy	Lynn Public Library
MMe	Medford Public Library
MNan	Nantucket Athenaeum
MNanW	Nantucket Whaling Museum
MNBedf	New Bedford Free Public Library
MNe	Newburyport Public Library
MNeHi	Newburyport Historical Society
MQ	Thomas Crane Public Library of Quincy
MS	Springfield Public Library
MSaE	Essex Institute, Salem
MSaP	Peabody Museum of Salem
MWA	American Antiquarian Society, Worcester

INDEX TO VOLUME SEVEN

Names in CAPITALS are of vessels, with type or rig specified where possible. All other listings are of persons or ports. This index is for the seventh volume only. A complete index, spanning all volumes of *American Activities in the Central Pacific, 1790-1870,* may be found in Volume 8.

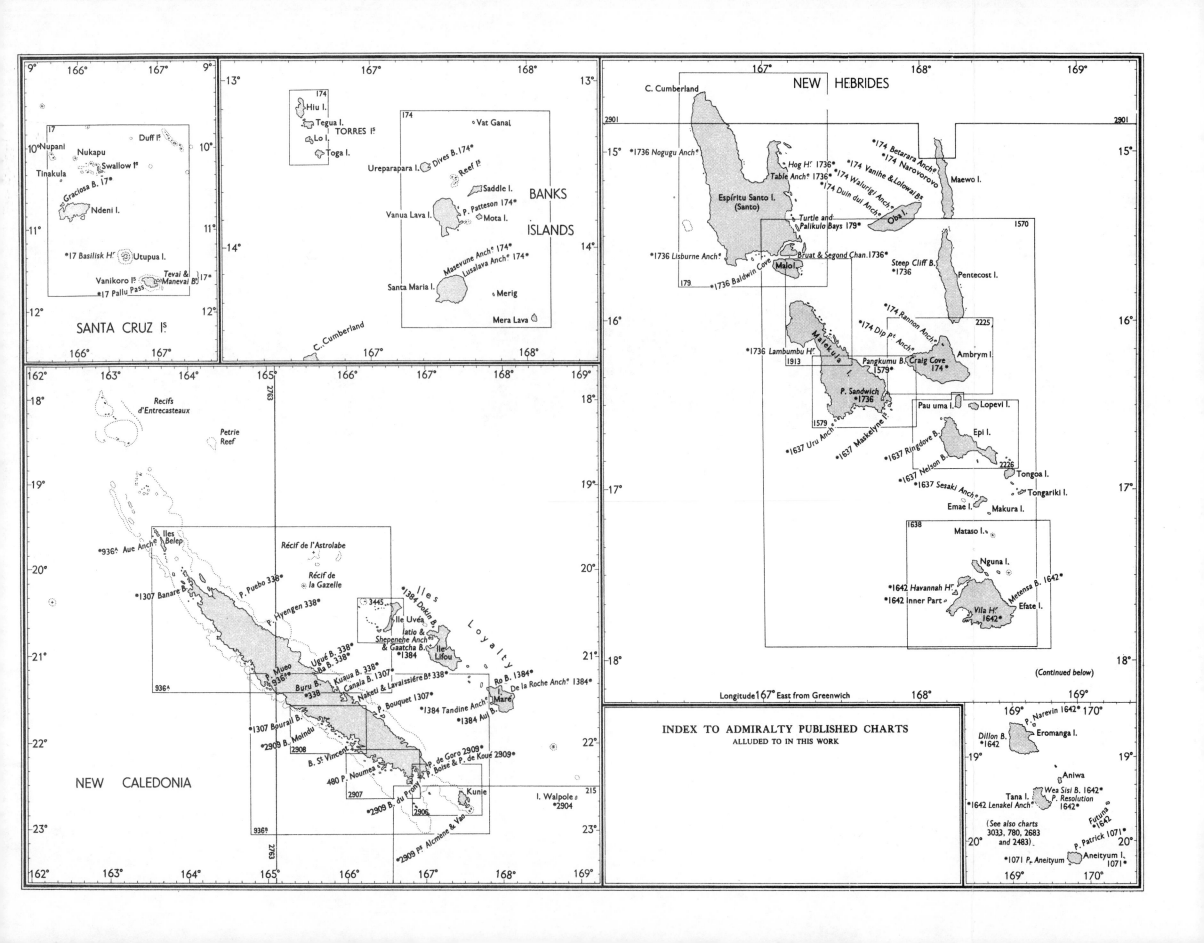

SANTA CRUZ I⁵

9° · 166° · 167° · 9°

10° Nupani
Nukapu
Swallow I⁵
Tinakula
Graciosa B. 17⁵
Ndeni I.

Duff I⁵

17 Basilisk H⁵ · Utupua I.

Vanikoro I⁵ · Tevai & Manevai B⁵ 17
17 Pallu Pass.

12° · 166° · 167° · 12°

13° · 167° · 168° · 13°

174 Hiu I.
Tegua I.
Lo I. · TORRES I⁵
Toga I.

174 · Vat Ganai

Ureparapara I. · Dives B. 174·
Reef I⁵
Saddle I.
Vanua Lava I. · P. Patteson 174·
Mota I.

BANKS ISLANDS

Masevune Anch· 174· · Lusalava Anch· 174·
Santa Maria I.
Merig

Mera Lava

C. Cumberland

NEW HEBRIDES

C. Cumberland

2901

·1736 Nogugu Anch·

Hog H⁵ 1736·
Table Anch· 1736·
Espíritu Santo I. (Santo)

174 Betarara Anch·
·174 Yanihe & ·174 Naravoravo
·174 Walurigi Anch·
·174 Duin dui Anch·

Maewo I.

Oba I.

Turtle and Palikulo Bays 179·
·1736 Lisburne Anch·
Bruat & Segond Chan.1736·
179 · 1736 Baldwin Cove
Malo I.

1570

Steep Cliff B⁵
·1736

Pentecost I.

·174 Rannon Anch·

2225

·1736 Lambumbu H⁵
1913
Malekula
·174 Dip P⁵ Anch·
Pangkumu B⁵ Craig Cove
1579 174
Ambrym I.

P. Sandwich
·1736
1579
Pau uma I. · Lopevi I.

·1637 Uru Anch· · ·1637 Maskelyne I⁵
·1637 Ringdove B⁵
·1637 Nelson B⁵
Epi I.

·1637 Sesaki Anch·
2226 Tongoa I.
Tongariki I.
Emae I. · Makura I.

1638
Mataso I.
Nguna I.
·1642 Havannah H⁵
·1642 Inner Part
Vila H⁵ 1642·
Metensa B. 1642·
Efate I.

(Continued below)

Longitude 167° East from Greenwich · 168° · 169°

NEW CALEDONIA

162° · 163° · 164° · 165°

Recifs d'Entrecasteaux

Petrie Reef

Iles Belep
·936^ Aue Anch·

Récif de l'Astrolabe

1307 Banare B⁵
P. Puebo 338·
Récif de la Gazelle

P. Hyengen 338·
·1384 Dokin B⁵
Iles Loyalty
3445
Ile Uvéa
Iatio & Shepenehe Anch· & Gaatcha B⁵ ·1384
Ile Lifou

Ugué B. 338· Ba B. 338·
P. Mueo 936^
Buru B⁵ ·338
Kuaua B. 338·
Canala B. 1307
Naketi & Lavaissiére B⁵ 338·
P. Bouquet 1307
·1384 Tandine Anch·
·1384 Aui B⁵
Ro B. 1384·
De la Roche Anch· 1384·
Maré

936^

·1307 Bourail B⁵
·2909 B. Molindu
2908
B. St Vincent
480 P. Noumea
2907
2909 B. du Prony
2906
Kunie
·2909 P⁵ Alcmene & Vao

P. de Goro 2909·
P⁵ Boise & P. de Koué 2909·
215
I. Walpole
·2904

2763

936^

162° · 163° · 164° · 165°

INDEX TO ADMIRALTY PUBLISHED CHARTS
ALLUDED TO IN THIS WORK

169° · P. Narevin 1642· 170°
Dillon B⁵ · Eromanga I.
·1642

Aniwa
Tana I. · Wea Sisi B. 1642·
P. Resolution
·1642 Lenakel Anch· 1642·
Futuna 1642

(See also charts 3033, 780, 2683 and 2483).

P. Patrick 1071·

·1071 P⁵ Aneityum · Aneityum I. 1071·

169° · 170°

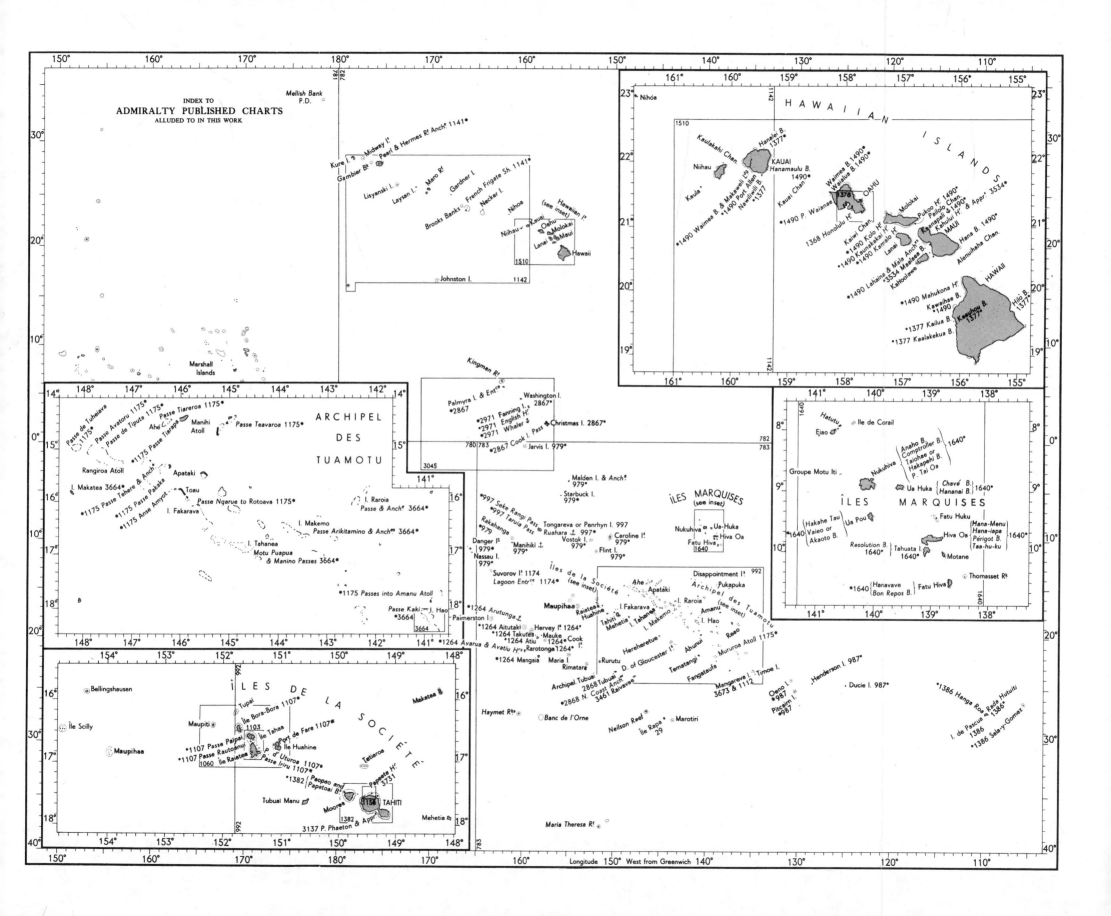

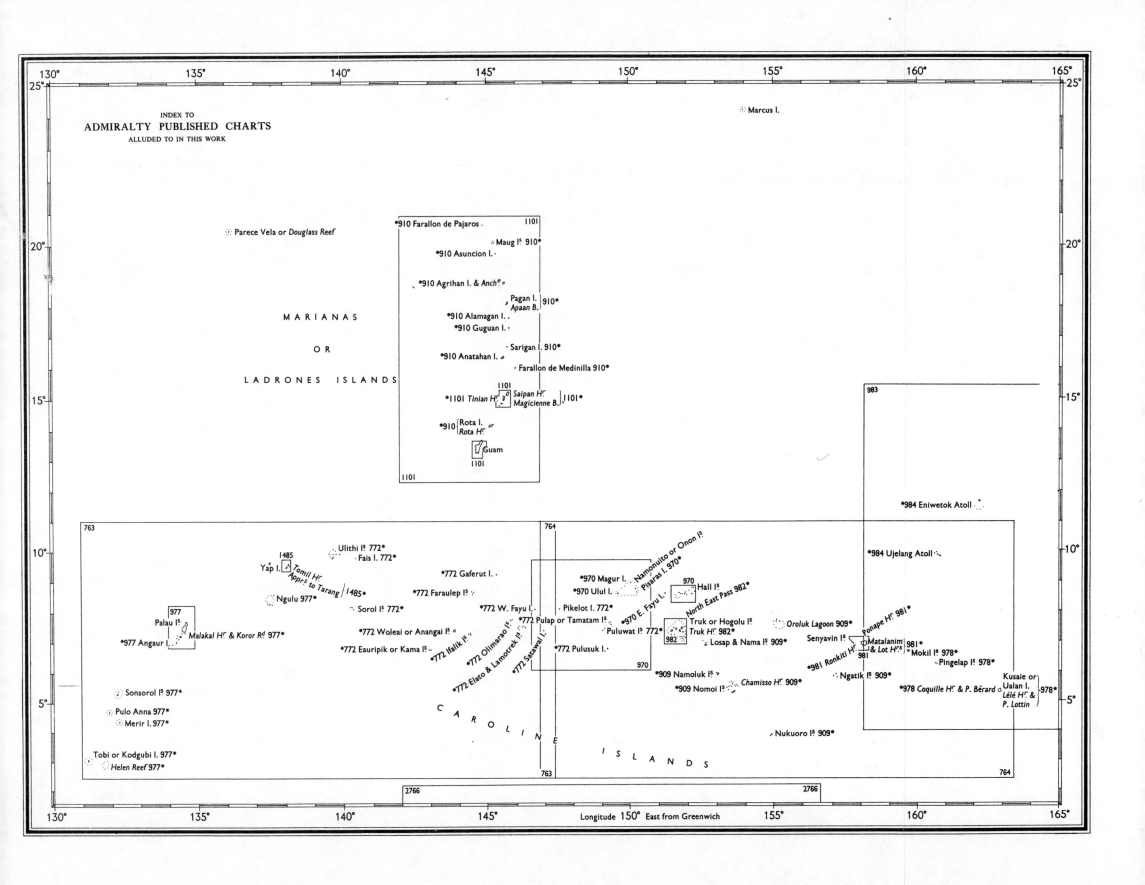

INDEX TO
ADMIRALTY PUBLISHED CHARTS
ALLUDED TO IN THIS WORK

Marcus I.

Parece Vela or *Douglass Reef*

•910 Farallon de Pajaros .   1101

Maug Is 910•

•910 Asuncion I. .

•910 Agrihan I. & Anchᵉ .

Pagan I. 910•
Apaan B.

M A R I A N A S

•910 Alamagan I. . .

•910 Guguan I.

O R

Sarigan I. 910•

•910 Anatahan I. .

. Farallon de Medinilla 910•

L A D R O N E S   I S L A N D S

1101
•1101 *Tinian* Hᵣ   Saipan Hᵣ 1101•
Magicienne B.

983

Rota I.
•910 {Rota Hᵣ

Guam

1101

•984 Eniwetok Atoll

763   764

•984 Ujelang Atoll

Ulithi Is 772•
Fais I. 772•

1485
Yap I. Tomil Hᵣ
Apprˢ to Tarang } 1485•

•772 Gaferut I. .

•970 Magur I.   Namonuito or Onon Iˢ

•970 Ulul I.   Pisaras I. 970•

770
Hall Iˢ

Ngulu 977•

•772 Faraulep Iˢ

North East Pass 982•

Sorol Iˢ 772•

Pikelot I. 772•

•772 W. Fayu I. .   •970 E. Fayu I.

970
Truk or Hogolu Iˢ
Truk Hᵣ 982•

Oroluk Lagoon 909•   Ponape Hᵣ 981•

977
Palau Iˢ

•772 Woleai or Anangai Iˢ

•772 Pulap or Tamatam Iˢ   982   Losap & Nama Iˢ 909•

Puluwat Iˢ 772•   Senyavin Iˢ   Matalanim 981•
& Lot Hˢ   981

•981 Ronkiti Hᵣ

•977 Angaur I.   Malakal Hᵣ & Koror Rᵈ 977•

•772 Eauripik or Kama Iˢ   •772 Ifalik Iˢ   •772 Olimarao Iˢ

•772 Pulusuk I.   •Mokil Iˢ 978•

Pingelap Iˢ 978•

•772 Elato & Lamotrek Iˢ   •772 Satawal Iˢ

970   •909 Namoluk Iˢ .   Ngatik Iˢ 909•

Kusaie or
Ualan I.   978•

Sonsorol Iˢ 977•   •909 Nomoi Iˢ   Chamisso Hᵣ 909•   •978 Coquille Hᵣ & P. Bérard   Lélé Hᵣ &
P. Lottin

Pulo Anna 977•

C A R O L I N E

Merir I. 977•

Tobi or Kodgubi I. 977•   . Nukuoro Iˢ 909•

Helen Reef 977•   I S L A N D S

763   764

2766   2766

Longitude 150° East from Greenwich

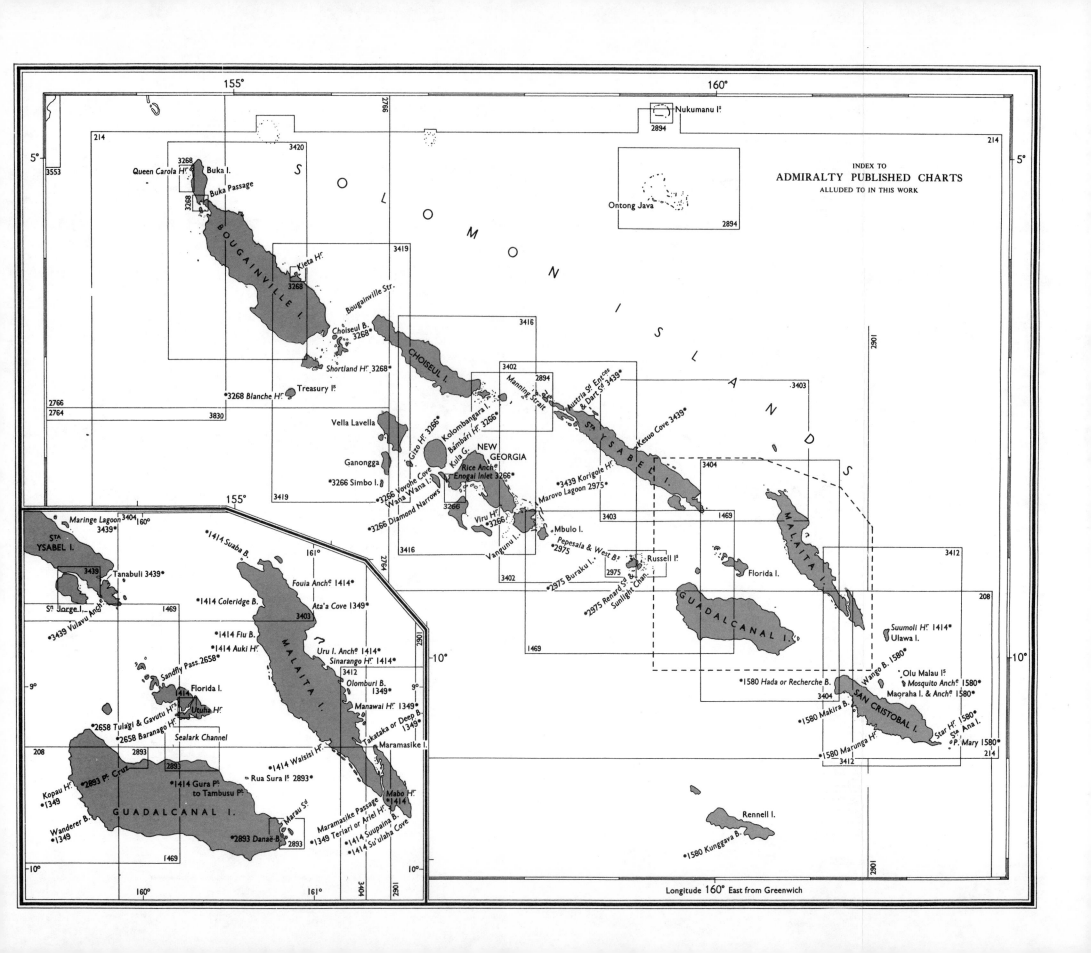

INDEX TO
ADMIRALTY PUBLISHED CHARTS
ALLUDED TO IN THIS WORK

Ontong Java

Nukumanu Iˢ
2894

2894

S
O
L
O
M
O
N
I
S
L
A
N
D
S

5°   5°
214   214
3553
3420
3268 Queen Carola Hᵣ Buka Iˢ
3268 Buka Passage
BOUGAINVILLE I.
3268 Kieta Hᵣ
Bougainville Str.
3419
Choiseul B. 3268
CHOISEUL I.
3266 Shortland Hᵣ 3268
3268 Blanche Hᵣ Treasury Iˢ
2766
2764
3830

3416
3402 Manning Strait 2894
Austria Sᵗ Entᶜᵉˢ & Darᵗ Sᵈ 3439
Kesuo Cove 3439
Sᵀᴬ YSABEL I.

Vella Lavella
Gizo Hᵣ 3266 Kolombangara I.
Bámbári Hᵣ 3266
Kula G.
Ganongga
NEW
GEORGIA
Rice Anchᵉ
3266 Vovohe Cove Enogai Inlet 3266
3266 Simbo I. Wana Wana I.
3266 Diamond Narrows
3266
Viru Hᵣ
3266
3439 Korigole Hᵣ
Marovo Lagoon 2975
3439

3403
3404
MALAITA I.
3403
1469

Mbulo I.
Pepesala & West Bˢ
2975
2975 Buraku I.
Vangunu I.
3402
Russell Iˢ
2975 Renard Sᵈ &
Sunlight Chanˡ
2975

3416
1469
Florida I.
GUADALCANAL I.
1469

Sᵀᴬ YSABEL I.
Maringe Lagoon 3404 160°
3439
3439 Tanabuli 3439
Sᵗ Jorge I.
3439 Vulavu Anchᵉ
1469
1414 Suaba B.
161°
1414 Coleridge B.
Fouia Anchᵉ 1414
Ata'a Cove 1349
3403
MALAITA I.
1414 Fiu B.
1414 Auki Hᵣ
Sandfly Pass. 2658
Uru I. Anchᵉ 1414
Sinarango Hᵣ 1414
2764
2901
10°

Florida I.
1414
Olomburi B.
1349
3412
9°
Manawai Hᵣ 1349
2658 Tula'gi & Gavutu Hʳˢ
Utuha Hᵣ
Takataka or Deep B.
1349
2658 Baranago Hᵣ
Sealark Channel
Maramasike I.
208
2893
2893
1414 Walsisi Hᵣ
2893 Pᵗ Cruz
Rua Sura Iˢ 2893
Kopau Hᵣ 2893 Gura Pᵗ
1349 to Tambusu Pᵗ
Mabo Hᵣ
1414
GUADALCANAL I.
Marau Sᵈ
Maramasike Passage
Wanderer B. 2893 Danaé B. 2893 1349 Teriari or Ariel Hᵣ
1349 1414 Suupaina B.
1414 Su'ulaha Cove
1469
3404
2901
160° 161°
10°

Suumoli Hᵣ 1414
Ulawa I.
208
Wango B. 1580
Olu Malau Iˢ
Mosquito Anchᵉ 1580
Maoraha I. & Anchᵉ 1580
1580 Hada or Recherche B.
3404
SAN CRISTOBAL I.
1580 Makira B.
Star Hᵣ 1580
Sᵗᵃ Ana I.
P. Mary 1580
1580 Marunga Hᵣ
3412
214
3412

Rennell I.
1580 Kunggava B.

9°
10°   10°

Longitude 160° East from Greenwich

155°   160°

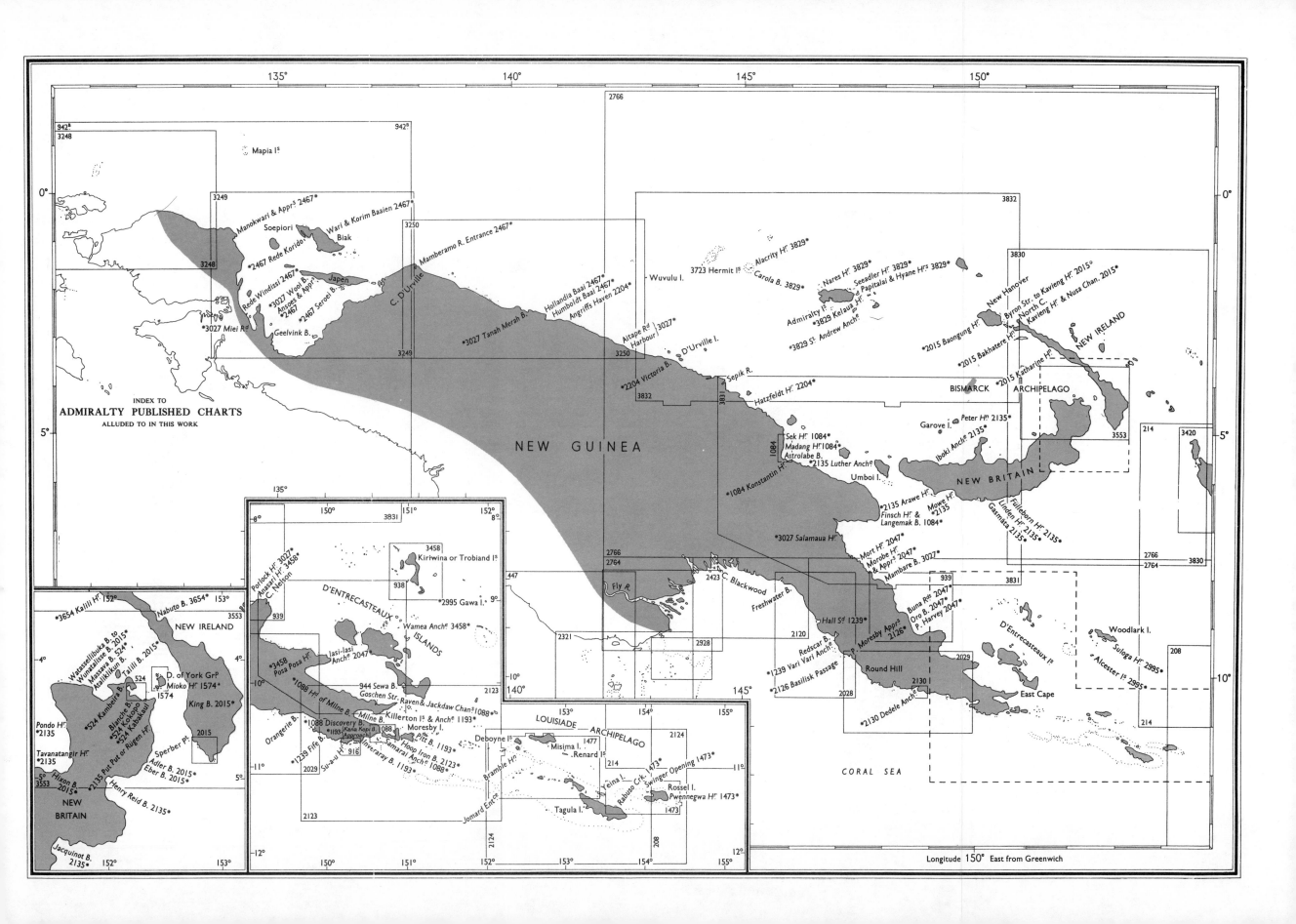

INDEX TO
ADMIRALTY PUBLISHED CHARTS
ALLUDED TO IN THIS WORK

NEW GUINEA

BISMARCK

ARCHIPELAGO

NEW IRELAND

NEW BRITAIN

CORAL SEA

D'ENTRECASTEAUX

ISLANDS

LOUISIADE ARCHIPELAGO

Longitude 150° East from Greenwich

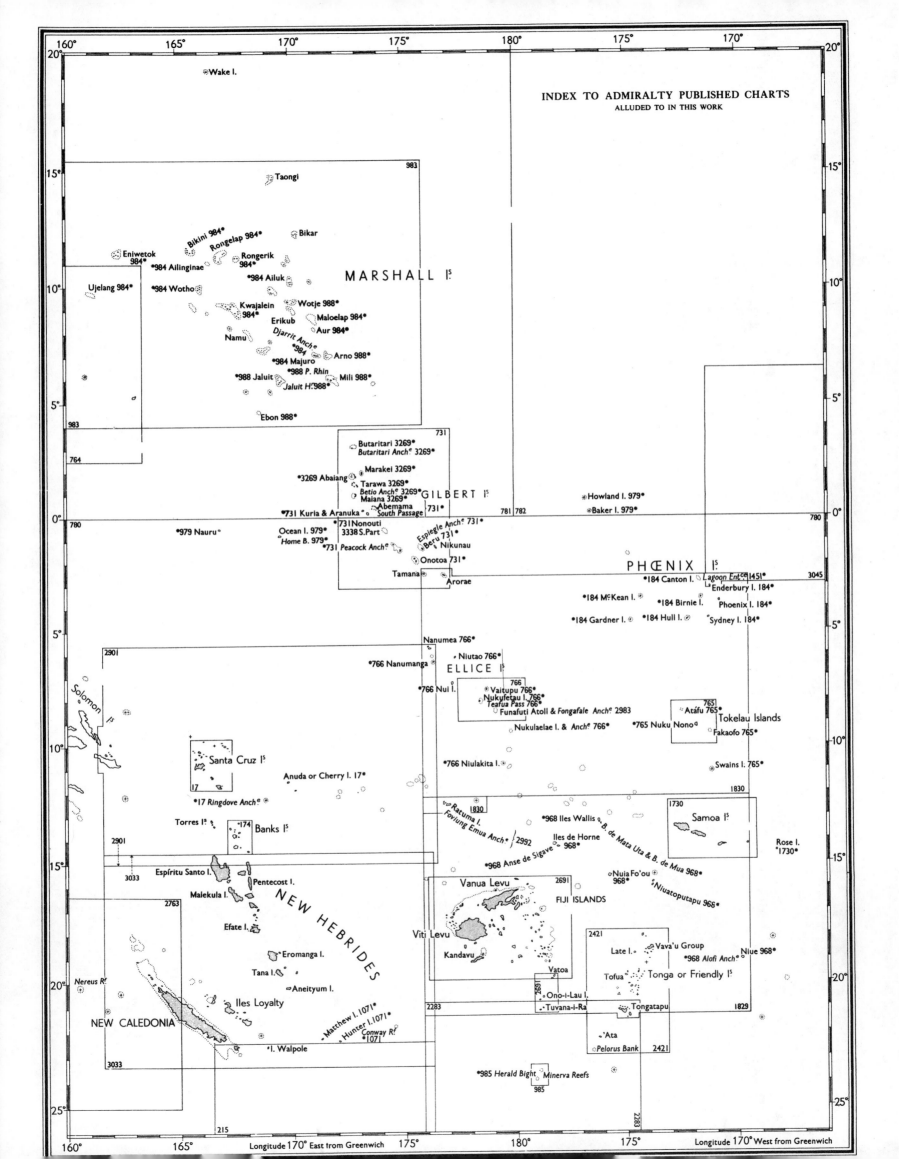

INDEX TO ADMIRALTY PUBLISHED CHARTS
ALLUDED TO IN THIS WORK

⊙ Wake I.

983

⊙ Taongi

Bikini 984•
Rongelap 984•   ⊙ Bikar

⊙ Eniwetok
984
                    Rongerik
•984 Ailinginae   984•

Ujelang 984•   •984 Wotho   ⊙ Ailuk

MARSHALL Iˢ

•984 Ailuk

Kwajalein   Wotje 988•
984•   Maloelap 984•
Erikub   Aur 984•
Djarrit Anchᵉ
Namu   •984   Arno 988•
    •984 Majuro
•988 Jaluit •988 P. Rhin   Mili 988•
        Jaluit Hᵇ 988•

Ebon 988•

983

764

Butaritari 3269•
Butaritari Anchᵉ 3269•
731
Marakei 3269•
•3269 Abaiang   Tarawa 3269•
Betio Anchᵉ 3269•
Maiana 3269•
Abemama   731•   GILBERT Iˢ
•731 Kuria & Aranuka   South Passage

Howland I. 979• ⊛
Baker I. 979• ⊛

781 782   780

•979 Nauru ⊙   Ocean I. 979•   731 Nonouti
            Home B. 979•   3338 S.Part
            •731 Peacock Anchᵉ   Espiegle Anchᵉ 731•
                        Beru 731• Nikunau
                    Onotoa 731•
            Tamana   PHŒNIX Iˢ
                    Arorae   •184 Canton I. Lagoon Entᶜᵉ 1451•
                                Enderbury I. 184•
                                            3045
            •184 MᶜKean I.   •184 Birnie I.   Phoenix I. 184•
            •184 Gardner I. ⊛   •184 Hull I.   Sydney I. 184•

780

Nanumea 766•

2901

•766 Nanumanga   • Niutao 766•

ELLICE Iˢ

•766 Nui I.   766
            Vaitupu 766•
            Nukufetau I. 766•   765
            Teafua Pass 766•   Atáfu 765•   Tokelau Islands
            Funafuti Atoll & Fongafale Anchᵉ 2983
            Nukulaelae I. & Anchᵉ 766•   •765 Nuku Nono
                                Fakaofo 765•

•766 Niulakita I.

                        Swains I. 765•

Santa Cruz Iˢ

Anuda or Cherry I. 17•   1830

•17 Ringdove Anchᵉ

Torres Iˢ   •174   Banks Iˢ   Ratuma I.   1830
                        Foviung Emua Anchᵉ 2992   •968 Iles Wallis B. de Mata Uta &
2901   Iles de Horne   Samoa Iˢ
3033   968•   Rose I.
Espíritu Santo I.   •1730•
Pentecost I.   •968 Anse de Sigave   B. de Mua 968•
Malekula I.   Nuia Foʻou
NEW HEBRIDES   Vanua Levu   2691   968•   Niuatoputapu 968•
2763   FIJI ISLANDS

Efate I.   Viti Levu   2421
Eromanga I.   Late I.   Vavaʻu Group   Niue 968•
Tana I.   Kandavu   •968 Alofi Anchᵉ
Aneityum I.   Vatoa   Tofua   Tonga or Friendly Iˢ

Nereus Rᶠ   2691   Ono-i-Lau I.
            Iles Loyalty   •985 Tuvana-i-Ra   Tongatapu
NEW CALEDONIA   Matthew I. 1071•   2283   1829
                Hunter I. 1071•
                Conway Rᶠ   •Ata
            •I. Walpole   1071•   Pelorus Bank   2421

                    •985 Herald Bight Minerva Reefs
                                    985

3033   215

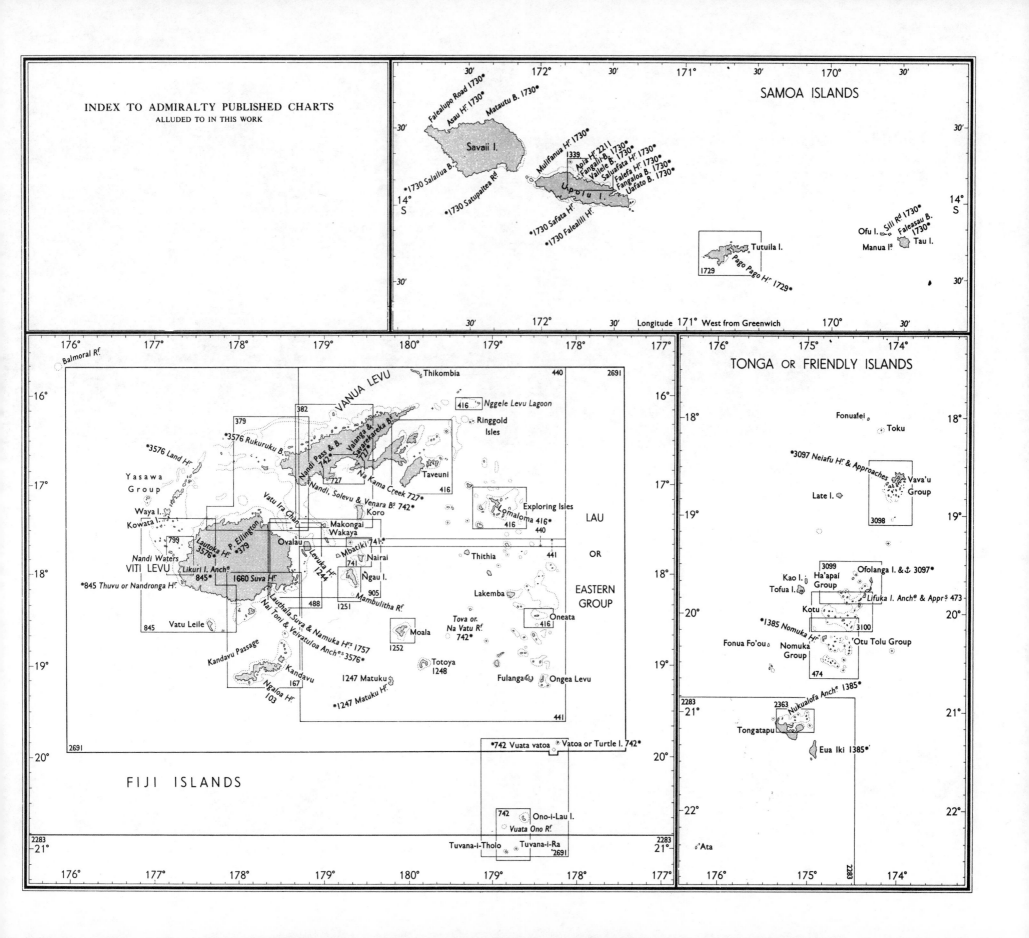

INDEX TO ADMIRALTY PUBLISHED CHARTS
ALLUDED TO IN THIS WORK

SAMOA ISLANDS

Falealupo Road 1730•
Asau Hr. 1730•
Matautu B. 1730•
Savaii I.
•1730 Salailua B.
•1730 Satupaitea Rd
Mulifanua Hr 1730•
1339
Apia Hr. 2211
Fangalii B. 1730•
Vailele B. 1730•
Saluafata Hr. 1730•
Falefa Hr. 1730•
Fangaloa B. 1730•
Uafato B. 1730•
Upolu I.
•1730 Safata Hr.
•1730 Falealili

Ofu I. Sili Rd 1730•
Faleasau B. 1730•
Manua Is Tau I.
14°
S
Tutuila I.
1729 Pago Pago Hr. 1729•

30'
172°
30'
171°
30'
170°
30'
Longitude 171° West from Greenwich
170°
30'

FIJI ISLANDS

Balmoral Rf.
2691 440 2691
Thikombia
VANUA LEVU
Nggele Levu Lagoon 416
382
379
Ringgold Isles
•3576 Rukuruku B.
•3576 Land Hr.
Vaianga & Savaresareka B.
Nandi Pass & B. 742•
777
Taveuni
Yasawa Group
Nandi, Solevu & Venara Bs 742•
727 Na Kama Creek 727•
416
Koro
Waya I.
Vatu Ira Chan.
Makongai
Wakaya
Exploring Isles
Lomaloma 416•
416
LAU
Kowata I.
799
Lautoka Hr. 3576• P. Ellington •379
Ovalau 741•
Mbatiki
Levuka Hr. 1244
Nairai 741
Thithia 441
OR
Nandi Waters
VITI LEVU
"Likuri I. Anche 845•
1660 Suva Hr.
Ngau I.
905 Mambulitha Rf.
Lakemba
EASTERN GROUP
•845 Thuvu or Nandronga Hr.
Lauthala Suva & Namuka Hrs 1757
Nai Toni & Velvatuloa Anch•s 3576•
488 1251
Tova or Na Vatu Rf. 742•
Oneata 416
845 Vatu Leile
Moala
1252
Totoya 1248
Fulanga Ongea Levu
Kandavu Passage
Kandavu
167
1247 Matuku
Ngaloa Hr. 103
•1247 Matuku Hr.
441
2691
•742 Vuata vatoa Vatoa or Turtle I. 742•
2283 742 Ono-i-Lau I.
Vuata Ono Rf.
Tuvana-i-Tholo Tuvana-i-Ra 2691

TONGA OR FRIENDLY ISLANDS

Fonualei
Toku
•3097 Neiafu Hr. & Approaches
Vava'u Group
Late I.
3098
Kao I. 3099 Ofolanga I. & ‡ 3097•
Ha'apai Group
Tofua I.
Lifuka I. Anche & Apprs 473
Kotu 3100
•1385 Nomuka Hr.
'Otu Tolu Group
Fonua Fo'ou Nomuka Group 474
Nukualofa Anche 1385•
2283 2363
Tongatapu
Eua Iki 1385•
'Ata

176° 177° 178° 179° 180° 179° 178° 177° 176° 175° 174°